Bibliografische Information der Deutschen Nationalbibliothek

Die Deutsche Nationalbibliothek verzeichnet diese Publikation in der
Deutschen Nationalbibliografie; detaillierte bibliografische Daten sind
im Internet über http://dnb.d-nb.de abrufbar.

ISBN 978-3-8325-3530-8

Logos Verlag Berlin GmbH
Comeniushof, Gubener Str. 47,
10243 Berlin
Tel.: +49 (0)30 42 85 10 90
Fax: +49 (0)30 42 85 10 92
INTERNET: http://www.logos-verlag.de

Adapting Hardware Systems by Means of Multi-Objective Evolution

Dissertation

A thesis submitted to the
Faculty of Computer Science, Electrical Engineering and Mathematics
of the
University of Paderborn
in partial fulfillment of the requirements for the
degree of *Dr. rer. nat.*

by

Paul Kaufmann

Paderborn, Germany
Date of submission: 21.05.2013

Supervisor:
 Prof. Dr. Marco Platzner

Reviewers:
 Prof. Dr. Marco Platzner
 Prof. Dr. Jim Tørresen
 Prof. Dr. Franz Rammig

Additional members of the oral examination committee:
 Prof. Dr. Christian Plessl
 Dr. Theodor Lettmann

Date of submission:
 21.05.2013

Date of public examination:
 08.07.2013

Acknowledgment

I would like to thank my advisor, Prof. Dr. Marco Platzner, for his guidance, support, and advice. I have greatly benefited from working with him and I am highly appreciative the opportunities I have had at his research group. I also would like to thank:

- Prof. Jim Torresen, for the fruitful collaboration, the opportunities to visit his research group, and for serving as a reviewer for my dissertation.

- Prof. Franz Rammig, for serving as a reviewer for my dissertation.

- Prof. Christian Plessl, for the many inspiring discussions and for serving as a reviewer for my dissertation.

- Dr. Theodor Lettmann for serving as a reviewer for my dissertation.

- Prof. Kyrre Glette, for the excellent joint work we have done together and for the continued collaboration.

- Prof. Bernhard Sick, for the support and patient introduction to the world of data mining.

- My colleagues Andreas Agne, Tobias Beisel, Alexander Boschmann, Klaus Danne, Stephanie Drzevitzky, Heiner Giefers, Mariusz Grad, Marcus Happe, Tobias Kenter, Enno Lübbers, Sebastian Meisner, Lars Schäfers, and Tobias Schumacher for discussions, and for valuable and constructive suggestions.

- My student assistants Tobias Knieper, Sven Kurras, Daniel Breitlauch, Bertrand Defo, and Jens Lischka, as well as the Bachelor, Master, and Diploma students I have supervised, for helping me implement and evaluate the manifold aspects of hardware evolution.

- The Deutsche Forschungsgemeinschaft (DFG), for funding the priority program "Organic Computing" (SPP1183) and the Allianz Industrieforschung, for funding projects on novel prostheses and prosthesis control (KF2071402-KM9, KF2071403-KM9, KF2071414-KM1).

Finally, I would like to thank my parents and my sisters Anna and Helene for their support, and my wife Monika, for her continuous care and encouragement.

Abstract

Reconfigurable circuits have opened up a fundamentally new way of creating adaptable electronic systems. Combined with artificial evolution, reconfigurable circuits allow an elegant adaptation approach to compensating for changes in the distribution of input data, computational resource errors, and variations in resource requirements. Referred to as "Evolvable Hardware" (EHW), this paradigm has yielded astonishing results for traditional engineering challenges and has discovered intriguing design principles which have not yet been seen in conventional engineering.

In this thesis, we present new and fundamental work on a holistic Evolvable Hardware approach, motivated by the insight that Evolvable Hardware needs to compensate for events with different change rates. Adaptation to gradual changes, such as variations in the distribution of the input data, can be handled by simulated evolution, but adaptation to radical changes, such as fluctuations in resource requirements, needs almost a complete re-evolution. To solve the challenge of different adaptation speeds, we propose a unified approach based on multi-objective evolution. In our method, we evolve and propagate candidate solutions that are diverse in objectives that may experience radical changes. In case of a radical event, a candidate solution that comes closest to meeting the new requirements will be instantiated. Afterwards, the evolutionary algorithm proceeds with the continuous optimization and evolution of diverse solutions.

In our work, we focus on the algorithmic challenges of multi-objective hardware evolution. Employing the Cartesian Genetic Programming (CGP) model for circuit encoding, we introduce a meaningful recombination operator. This recombination operator enables the use of Pareto based multi-objective evolutionary algorithms (MOEA) for hardware design. As scalability becomes challenging with multi-objective hardware design, we introduce techniques such as objective scaling and global- and local-search periodization to achieve a better computation time. Additionally, we enhance the evolution of structured functions by the automatic acquisition and reuse of subfunctions and investigate age- and cone-based subfunction acquisition.

We demonstrate our methods on hardware classifier adaptation, compensation for the impact of architecture reconfiguration on classification accuracy, and the optimization of processor execution time and energy consumption.

Zusammenfassung

Rekonfigurierbare Logikbausteine eröffnen neue Perspektiven für autonome Systeme. Kombiniert mit den Methoden der künstlichen Intelligenz, können rekonfigurierbare Logikbausteine auf elegante Weise dazu benutzt werden, Veränderungen in der Verteilung der Eingabedaten und der Anforderung an die Systemressourcen sowie Fehler in der Hardware zu kompensieren. Bekannt unter dem Begriff *Evolvable Hardware*, hat dieses Prinzip auf eindrucksvolle Weise das Entdecken neuer Entwurfsprinzipien und neuartiger sowie leistungsfähiger Lösungen für bestehende Ingenieursaufgaben aufgezeigt. In dieser Arbeit präsentieren wir einen ganzheitlichen Ansatz für Evolvable Hardware. Unsere Motivation gründet in der Einsicht, dass es mehrere Zeitebenen geben kann in denen sich ein autonomes System anpassen soll. Während kontinuierliche Veränderungen mit niedrigen Veränderungsraten–wie sie häufig in der Natur vorkommen–durch kontinuierliche Optimierung kompensiert werden können, bedürfen rasche Veränderungen im Voraus berechneter Lösungen, wie etwa Veränderungen in den Systemressourcen. Um die Herausforderung der verschiedenen Veränderungs- und Adaptationsraten aufzulösen, setzen wir auf einen einheitlichen Mechanismus basierend auf multikriterieller Optimierung. Der multikriterielle Optimierer verbessert kontinuierlich die bestehende Lösung und kompensiert damit Variationen mit niedriger Veränderungsrate. Gleichzeitig evolviert der Algorithmus für Zielfunktionen, die raschen Veränderungen ausgesetzt sind, verschiedenartige Lösungen. Somit kann im Falle einer schnellen Änderung, z. B. der benutzbaren Rechenressourcen, eine geeignetere und bisher inaktive Lösung die aktive Lösung ersetzen. Anschließend fährt der Algorithmus mit der kontinuierlichen Verbesserung und Optimierung fort.

In unserer Arbeit konzentrieren wir uns hauptsächlich auf die algorithmischen Aspekte der Evolution von rekonfigurierbaren Schaltungen. Dazu erweitern wir das populäre Modell für digitale Schaltungen, die Kartesische Genetische Programmierung, um einen strukturbasierten Rekombinationsoperator. Dies erlaubt uns den Einsatz globaler Optimierer und damit auch der modernen Pareto-basierten evolutionären Algorithmen für den Schaltungsentwurf. Zur Kompensation der dabei auftretenden langsameren Konvergenz führen wir die Skalierung von Optimierungskriterien und ein Periodisierungsschema ein, das die Konvergenzperformance lokaler Optimierer mit den Eigenschaften globaler Optimierer verbindet. Weiterhin beschleunigen wir den Schaltungsentwurf durch die automatische Identifikation und Wiederverwendung von Substrukturen. Dabei untersuchen wir struktur- und zeitbehaftete Identifikationsmechanismen.

Die Performance unserer Verfahren und Methoden verifizieren wir zum einen im Bereich der Mustererkennung. Hier evolvieren wir Hardwareklassifizierer und vergleichen ihre Erkennungsraten mit einer repräsentativen Auswahl an leistungsfähigen Mustererkennungsalgorithmen. Mit der Auswertung gesammelter statistischer Daten können wir weiterhin die Erkennungsraten während der Rekonfiguration eines Hardwareklassifizierers verbessern. Zum anderen benutzen wir unsere Methoden, um die Ausführungszeiten und den Energieverbrauch eines Prozessors zu minimieren, indem wir die Adressumsetzungsfunktion eines Prozessorcaches evolvieren.

Contents

List of Figures

List of Tables

Chapter 1

Introduction

Reconfigurable hardware combined with nature inspired optimization gave birth to a new kind of adaptable and autonomous systems two decades ago. The key principle of the new paradigm, called Evolvable Hardware (EHW), is the adaptation to environmental changes, hardware defects, and resource requirement variations by the method of evolutionary optimization. The ability to execute the adaptation algorithms unattended, emphasizes the self-contained and autonomous nature of these systems.

The elegance of EHW lies in its simplicity. Conventionally autonomous, adaptable, and fault-tolerant hardware systems typically rely on *a priori* designed solutions and redundant elements. EHW, on the other hand, optimizes its solution continuously and is able to react to situations that have not been considered at design time. No special measures need to be taken to provide adaptability.

Introduced in 1993 by Higuchi et al. [163] and de Garis [93], the impact of Evolvable Hardware has been two-fold. The principle of EHW has been used to create circuits with astonishing properties [353], comprising innovative design principles [357], and which are competitive with the best human designed solutions [73]. On the other hand, Evolvable Hardware stands for a paradigm shift in engineering, replacing functional guarantees and determinism by gradual functional quality and life long adaptation.

1.1 The Evolvable Hardware Principle

The application areas of computing machines have become incredibly diverse since their introduction in the last century. In almost all areas of automation, computing machines are helping us to control all kinds of mechanical, electrical, hydraulic, and other systems. There are, however, areas computing machines struggle with. These are the areas with incomplete goal defini-

1

tions, fuzzy constraints, ill-defined and inconsistent environments, dynamic processes, and other uncertainties. The complexity of capturing and formalizing the complete and precise mechanisms of such environments may render a simple and well-defined task infeasible for a computing machine.

Biological systems had successfully conquered Earth's physical and chemical world for millions of years, creating exceptionally complex and complicated individuals. Lots of engineering impulses come from mimicking the principles observed from Nature. The inspiration from biological evolution of how to evolve efficient and robust systems in dynamic and fuzzy environments is helping engineers extend the coverage of today's computing machines. Additionally, computing machines themselves create, by pervading our world in large numbers and using sometimes almost unlimited communication capacities, new ecosystems with similar aspects to their biological counterparts.

Darwin observed a positive correlation between successful adaptation to changes and reproduction in his work on the general principles of biological diversity [88]. Adopted as "evolutionary computation" in the optimization algorithms discipline, Nature's iterative generate-and-test approach can be canonically applied to the evolution of non-biological systems. Figure 1.1 illustrates the mechanism with the example of a hardware image compressor. The goal of the presented application is to minimize the energy required to transmit an on-board recorded image of, e.g., a Mars vehicle over a radio link by continuously optimizing the image compressor to varying lighting conditions. The evolutionary optimization starts with a set of randomly initialized candidate solutions in Figure 1.1 (a). A candidate solution is a "construction plan" for an image compressor. In the next step, a candidate solution is used to configure a hardware device implementing the actual compressor and evaluate the compression rate on a image, recently recorded by the on-board camera (Figure 1.1 (b)). The compression rate is evaluated for all candidate solutions, as presented in Figure 1.1 (c). The best individual is selected in step (d) for reproduction. New candidate solutions are evolved by mutating the previously selected parent individuals (Figure 1.1 (e)). The evolutionary cycle finishes here and the next iteration starts with a new fitness evaluation. The best individual found so far is selected to define the system's behavior.

The example of Figure 1.1 briefly presents the general principle of evolutionary algorithms and also their special case—the continuous optimization of reconfigurable hardware. The continuous optimization model allows a system to start reacting instantly to changes in the distribution of its input data. Hardware defects in the reconfigurable fabric can also be addressed by the very same measure. Additionally, letting the evolution consider auxiliary goal functions such as the circuit size allows steering the evolution towards solutions with desired properties.

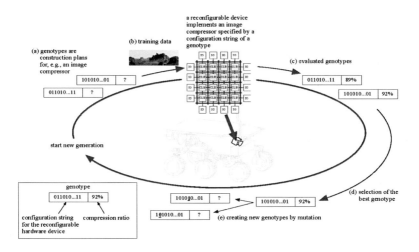

Figure 1.1: The Evolvable Hardware principle explained using the evolutionary loop applied to an image compressor.

There are only limited mathematical tools for a precise convergence analysis of randomized methods such as evolutionary algorithms. Environmental changes, as presented in the image compression example, may stimulate adaptation within a timescale of minutes. While it is often possible to build systems able to adapt to rather slow and gradual changes of the environment, adaptation to radical changes, such as variations of system resources, may be more challenging. For instance, the evolution of a new solution that would use one-half of the previously utilized resources may require a complete reevolution. To solve this challenge within a sufficiently short period of time, one can imagine executing multiple evolutionary algorithms evolving in parallel, covering potential radical adaptation situations. A more elegant approach is offered by multi-criteria evolutionary algorithms evolving a diverse set of candidate solutions embodying different trade-offs in, e.g., functional quality and area, in a single run. Adaptation to radical resource changes can now be done almost instantly, as shown in Figure 1.2. The very next time after the available resource size changes (Figure 1.2 (a)), the system replaces its behavior by a solution satisfying the new restrictions and demonstrating the highest functional quality (Figure 1.2 (b)). Then the evolution starts to improve the recently instantiated solution to benefit from unused resources (Figure 1.2 (c)).

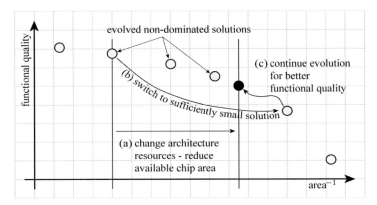

Figure 1.2: Adaptation to radical changes by means of Pareto based multi-criteria optimization. The optimization process maximizes the functional qualities and minimizes the resources used by candidate solutions. Candidate solutions are marked by a circle. When a radical change in, i.e., system resources occurs (step (a)), the method selects and activates a non-dominant solution that respects the new limitation in step (b). Later, evolution tries to improve the selected solution so as to employ the remaining resources in step (c).

1.2 Challenges of Evolvable Hardware

The very heart of Evolvable Hardware from the algorithmic perspective is its evolutionary circuit design and optimization. Its algorithmic and representational aspects can be characterized along three dimensions: the way an EHW circuit is expressed within a formal model, the granularity of the building blocks used to express the circuit, and the kind of knowledge utilized in the optimization. Figure 1.3 illustrates the model space for digital EHW. There, a circuit can be described structurally, e.g., by its schematic and the data flow. It also can be expressed behaviorally, capturing its function by a program. The functional blocks used in the description may cover simple Boolean gates and wires, and also complete IP cores and routing architectures. The design knowledge may come from the application domain, from the specifics of the application itself, or be of a more general nature. Balancing algorithmic and representational elements, the following aspects need consideration:

- EHW candidate solutions are described within a representation model. The representation model abstraction level is the first trade-off to specify. A higher level, while being more complex and expressive, allows

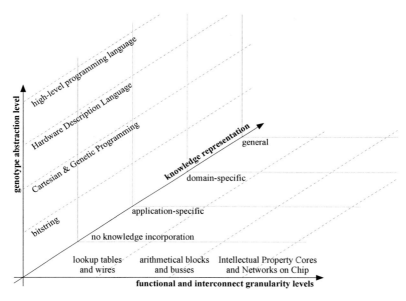

Figure 1.3: Functional, knowledge, and encoding space of Evolvable Hardware.

often for a relatively compact encoding of the solution. This may dramatically reduce the search time of the evolutionary algorithm. On the other hand, higher level representation models may imply a higher effort for mapping a solution to the reconfigurable device. Here, a balance of evolutionary convergence speed and mapping complexity has to be found, minimizing the overall effort.

- The functional granularity of the building blocks used by the representation model is the next trade-off to specify. Intuitively, one may describe this challenge as the selection of the most appropriate functional elements allowing for a simple and compact solution encoding. Thereby, the selection of building blocks may give an orientation for the structures employed by conventionally engineered solutions.

Complex building blocks facilitate compact solution encoding and often reduce the search effort. On the other hand, complex building blocks typically lose the capability of efficiently encoding fine granular structures. This hampers the discovery of solutions with a mixed kind of complexity, something which can be highly efficient. Lowering the complexity to the level of Boolean gates allows discovering any digital

5

function bounded by the size of the utilized reconfigurable device. This comes, however, at the cost of a large search space, rendering the evolution tremendously complex. The representation model abstraction level can be generalized even further, capturing transistor characteristics. As analog transistor properties are modeled approximately, this introduces non-determinism and implicit coding into the solution representation. Therefore, a solution evolved using a specific reconfigurable device may not generalize to another device.

With respect to the presented considerations, the goal of selecting an appropriate complexity level for the building blocks is to approach a compact and efficient solution encoding while avoiding unnecessary restrictions on the search space.

- Efficient mapping of a candidate solution to the reconfigurable hardware device is the third challenging issue. In the area of evolutionary computation, the mapping of a candidate solution to the execution platform is referred to as the *genotype to phenotype* mapping. Today's field-programmable gate array devices offer reconfigurability at the functional levels of the wire, the Boolean gate, and the arithmetic function. Native reconfigurability requires, however, the manufacturer's time- and resource-demanding tool sets. In case the device's native reconfigurability can not be used efficiently or the representation model and functional block granularity levels do not match the device's structures, a common approach is the implementation of an efficiently reconfigurable architecture on top of the reconfigurable device [127, 302]. Thereby, the goal is either to unify the evolution and reconfiguration abstraction levels or at least to match them as far as possible, so as to minimize the mapping effort.

- Introducing application- and representation-specific knowledge to evolutionary search helps reduce the search space. As evolutionary algorithms (EA) are algorithmically simple, the incorporation of additional methods is typically not much of a challenge. Specifically, in the area of digital circuit evolution, EAs offer manifold opportunities to improve scalability:

  - Application- and application domain-specific knowledge as well as digital logic design experience may help guide the evolution to more promising search areas. For instance, the representation model can be shaped in such a way that only specifically structured circuits can be expressed, whereas evolutionary operators can embed design rules to construct circuits with desired properties. An additional way to incorporate knowledge is to formalize "best practice" rules as metrics, preferring individuals matching certain design principles for reproduction.

- Meta techniques capture general design principles. For instance, the automatic acquisition and reuse of subfunctions introduces hierarchical design to circuit evolution, extending the set of functional blocks and increasing the complexity level of the functional blocks [199]. Storing intermediate partial solutions in non-coding genotype areas for later reuse is another technique for improving the convergence behavior [378].
- The choice of a suitable optimization approach is another pivotal point for fast convergence. Depending on the properties of the fitness space, either local or global or hybrid approaches may be highly beneficial. Global search implies information drift among individuals whereas local search traces disjoint paths through the solution space. Local search techniques can be very fast in evolving and optimizing digital circuits. To enable similar convergence speeds for global search multi-objective EAs, hybrid methods, combining the behavioral and functional properties of both local and global search algorithms, can be an elegant solution.

• An additional point when creating Evolvable Hardware systems is the correct matching of the reconfiguration time scales of the application as well as of the architecture and genotype. By architectural reconfiguration we mean, for instance, the change in available resources a solution may occupy. While genotype reconfiguration can be as time consuming as architectural reconfiguration, the goal is to keep the genotype reconfiguration as short as possible because it is executed every time a new solution is evaluated on the target hardware. The genotype reconfiguration rate is typically governed by the temporal behavior of the application. The application's rate of change dictates the required adaptation rate of the optimizer and, in consequence, puts bounds on the genotype reconfiguration time. Architectural reconfiguration, on the other hand, is, in our example, initiated by the system's control of the adaptation to resource changes.

These challenges consider mostly the algorithmic adaptation mechanism of Evolvable Hardware. From the hardware perspective, however, online reconfiguration is the major challenge. Guided by the temporal restrictions of an application, a system designer has to consider, for instance,

• the trade-offs between different reconfiguration kinds. Native full and partial reconfiguration of modern reconfigurable logic devices can take up to some milliseconds (cf. Section 3.2.1.3). Register-reconfigurable architectures implemented on top of reconfigurable devices may possess a much faster reconfiguration time while being less flexible and less resource efficient. Building an Evolvable Hardware system, one has to balance between reconfiguration flexibility and time complexity.

- whether the same chip area has to be used to execute the currently active solution and the fitness evaluation of candidate solutions. In this case, a system designer has to find an interleaved execution scheme respecting the temporal requirements of the application.

- sharing and balancing resources between multiple processes running on the same reconfigurable device. This can be useful to compensate for high change rates, as additional resources may improve the adaptation times.

While hardware reconfiguration is not covered in the present thesis, a holistic Evolvable Hardware approach needs to phase all presented aspects within a given time scale for an efficient and well-behaved solution.

1.3   Thesis Contributions

The present thesis presents research on a holistic Evolvable Hardware approach, proposing multi-objective evolution as the uniform adaptation method. Evolving and propagating a set of diverse solutions, multi-objective evolutionary algorithms can compensate for gradual changes by simulated evolution, and for radical changes by pre-evolved solutions. Our work is structured by the representational aspects, considering efficient digital circuit encoding, algorithmic methods improving the scalability of multi-objective circuit evolution, and a section on adaptable architectures , where we validate and compare our methods to state of the art solutions. We therefore contribute to the following areas:

- **Introducing Pareto based multi-objective evolution to Cartesian Genetic Programming: A meaningful crossover operator.** A Cartesian Genetic Program (CGP) in its original form is a representation model reflecting a two-dimensional functional block arrangement with a feed-forward interconnect. Formalized as a directed acyclic graph (DAG), CGP is well suited to encode solutions for the fine granular look up table-based field programmable gate arrays (FPGA), as well as to coarse granular data flow architectures. However, the implicit coding of the spatial block positions in CGP makes it difficult to create evolutionary operators acting on the inner structures of a candidate solution. As we rely on multi-objective evolutionary optimization that requires an information drift among the candidate solutions, we have first introduced a CGP crossover operator able to transfer meaningful partial solutions. With this, we are able to adopt modern Pareto based multi-objective optimizers for circuit evolution.

- **Efficient hierarchical circuit design: Cone- and age-based acquisition and reuse of subfunctions.** In conventional Boolean logic design, complex circuits typically have a hierarchical topology and are composed of repetitive substructures, such as half- and full-adders and multiplexers. These substructures often have a cone-like topology with many inputs and a few outputs. To enable CGP operators for hierarchical design, we have introduced automatic structural subfunction acquisition and reuse. Additionally, the concept of subfunction acquisition and reuse is a familiar principle of biological organs. Biological organs can encapsulate substructures which persist unchanged for a long period of time, thus contributing indirectly to an individual's success. We have mimicked this principle by composing subfunctions from nodes that have remained untouched by the mutation operator for some generations. With this cone- and age-based subfunction acquisition and reuse, we have significantly improved the scalability for structured and unstructured applications, such as arithmetical functions and pattern matching architectures.

- **Scalability for multi-objective circuit evolution: An efficient fitness aggregation scheme for Cartesian Genetic Programming.** Modern Pareto based multi-objective evolutionary algorithms (MOEA) show outstanding performance for a broad set of real world applications (cf. Section 2.2). Prominent Pareto based MOEAs such as the NSGAII and SPEA2 belong to the family of global optimizers. There are, however, application domains where global search algorithms fall significantly behind local optimizers, such as specifically configured Evolutionary Strategies. Evolution of CGP circuits is one of these application domains. To improve the scalability of Pareto based MOEAs, we have analyzed the relation of the objectives. It is typically challenging to precisely express the optimization goal dependencies for a digital circuit. Additionally, the correspondence may change with the location of the candidate solution within the design space. We have found an efficient linear combination of functional quality, circuit size, and propagation delay, and thus substantially improved the convergence speed of Pareto based MOEAs.

- **Scalability for multi-objective circuit evolution: Algorithm periodization and Pareto based Evolutionary Strategies.** For a systematic approach to improve the scalability of multi-objective evolution for application domains where local search-like algorithms excel, we have introduced an algorithm periodization scheme able to combine the behavioral and functional properties of different methods. To this end, we have proposed a rotational algorithm execution scheme. Each algorithm in the cycle can be executed either for zero, one, or multiple generations, depending on the repetition strategy that considers the history of the search. For instance, at the onset of a search, global search algorithms can be very fast and should be considered more frequently for execution, while in the final search phase, local search-like algorithms become more beneficial. For fast multi-objective circuit evolution we have formalized a *periodization scheme* for population based evolutionary algorithms and introduced a multi-objective Evolutionary Strategy (ES) based local search technique—the *hybrid ES* (hES). With these two measures, we have been able to significantly improve the scalability of the multi-objective evolution of CGP circuits.

- **Challenging conventional engineering: Evolvable Hardware for real world applications.** In our work we have verified the performance of our methods by comparing them to state of the art algorithms and using popular benchmarks as well as real world use cases. For a detailed analysis we have considered the following applications:

  - **Evolvable hardware classifiers.** We have developed a CGP based pattern matching architecture and compared it to a set of state of the art conventional algorithms as well as to the Functional Unit Row (FUR) EHW classifier of Glette and Torresen [127]. We are particularly interested in the classification of non-stationary data sets, as adaptable EHW architectures are inherently suited for this. In an additional experiment, we have demonstrated run-time adaptation capabilities for both EHW classifier architectures.

  - **Hardware adaptation to radical changes.** Related work on EHW adaptation typically considers two kinds of stimuli: defects in the reconfigurable fabric and adaptation to environmental changes. Extending these scenarios, we have studied Evolvable Hardware adaptation to run-time fluctuations in the resources. The ability to deal with fluctuating resources can be used to support the optimization process by, for instance, assigning more resources when the speed of adaptation is crucial. Additionally, energy considerations and resource sharing may make resource adaptable solutions very useful. For our investigation, we relied on the reconfigurable classification architecture of Glette and Torresen [127]. We have shown that the adaptation rate is related to the available amount of resources and quick adaptation is always possible, provided that a minimal amount of resources are present in the system.

  - **Processor evolution: An Evolvable Hardware cache.** While the primary application field of EHW is in autonomous adaptable embedded systems, in our last contribution we have applied the Evolvable Hardware principle to processor evolution. To this end, we have put the memory-to-cache address mapping functions of a modern, multi-level cache, under optimization, heading for minimal execution time. The outcome of the experiments is the insight that an evolved memory-to-cache mapping function built out of a few Boolean gates can significantly reduce the overall execution time and energy consumption of a processor.

Our contributions demonstrate that a holistic Evolvable Hardware approach can be realized, employing a unified adaptation method based on multi-objective evolutionary algorithms. This is an important insight, because adaptation in related research has typically been investigated regarding either changes in the environment, changes in the resource requirements, or degradation of the computational resources. To our best knowledge, no research except ours has proposed Evolvable Hardware adaptation to all cases at the same time.

The work presented in this thesis was conducted as part of the Priority Programme (SPP) 1183 "Organic Computing" of the German National Science Foundation (DFG) and as part of the "Adaptive Prosthesis Sockets" (KF2071402-KM9) and "Adaptive Knee and Foot Prosthesis Joints" (KF2071403-KM9) projects of the German Federal Ministry of Economics and Technology (BMWI). The results have been summarized in [15–17].

1.4 Thesis Organization

This thesis is structured as follows.

Chapter 2 introduces the fundamentals, history, and terminology of Evolutionary Computation. To prepare for our work on multi-objective optimizers, we also describe the SPEA2 and NSGAII algorithms in detail. Finally, performance analysis methods for single- and multi-objective algorithms are presented.

Chapter 3 begins with the basic idea and a historical overview of Evolvable Hardware. Before introducing prominent digital EHW examples, today's reconfigurable digital devices are illustrated. The chapter continues with analog Evolvable Hardware examples and concludes with an overview of Cartesian Genetic Programming—the circuit encoding scheme we are using in our thesis–and related representation models.

Chapter 4 describes our extensible MOVES toolbox, a framework for multi-objective evolution of embedded systems. We use these tools and instruments in the following chapters to evaluate our algorithms and approaches.

Chapter 5 starts with our work on structural and temporal evolutionary operators (cf. Section 5.1) as well as the automatic acquisition and reuse of meaningful subfunctions (cf. Section 5.2) for Cartesian Genetic Programming.

Chapter 6 continues outlining our work on improving CGP scalability, introducing fitness aggregation schemes (cf. Section 6.1) and the periodization of local and global search algorithms (cf. Section 6.2).

Chapter 7 evaluates our previously developed methods and compares them to conventional state of the art solutions. The first use case demonstrates an Evolvable Hardware signal classifier based on the Cartesian Genetic Programming. That classifier is compared to an Evolvable Hardware system tailored for signal classification and to state of the art pattern matching algorithms (cf. Section 7.1). In the next use case, we give an example of functional recovery after architectural reconfiguration: a signal classifier (cf. Section 7.2). Finally, Section 7.3 demonstrates Evolvable Hardware's creating adaptable caches, a challenge that have not been yet addressed in conventional engineering.

Chapter 8 concludes with an overview of our work and outlines some insights and potential future research directions.

Chapter 2

Evolutionary Algorithms

Within the family of heuristic optimizers, the "evolutionary computation" (EC) domain hosts methods inspired by biology's way of adapting and evolving systems. EC divides roughly into the areas of evolutionary optimization, design, learning, and theoretical foundations. Biological evolution, which is commonly referred to as "the survival of the fittest," was investigated by the English naturalist Charles Darwin 1859 in his book, *On the Origin of Species by Means of Natural Selection* [88]. More precisely, Darwin noted: "It is not the strongest of the species that survives, nor the most intelligent that survives. It is the one that is the most adaptable to change." Within EC, "evolutionary algorithms" (EA) refers to a group of methods first introduced in the middle of the 20th century, imitating biology's evolutionary process. While the methods were initially subdivided according to representation models and evolutionary-inspired operators, it is in the latter endeavor to unify EA's taxonomy with other search heuristics [279, 395, 397] from, e.g., operations research (OR) and artificial intelligence (AI). A simplified mechanism, which is common to EAs and to, e.g., hill climbing, Tabu search (TS) [132], and simulated annealing (SA) [60, 191, 246], is iterative generation and testing. This mechanism is presented in Algorithm 1. When applying generate-and-test to EAs, it becomes the scheme of perturbation-and-acceptation, where the first step comprises recombination and mutation, and the second step selection and reproduction [295]. EA's characteristic properties are its population based approach and information migration among the individuals.

Table 2.1 presents the basic terminology of EAs and Table 2.2, the biological development space. The terms are introduced best by describing an EA iteration according to Algorithm 1. An EA starts with a randomly initialized *population.* A population is a set of *candidate solutions* and each candidate solution is a container for a *genotype*. A genotype can be partitioned into multiple chromosomes. The genotype's unit elements are *genes*, which typically encode a single property of a solution. A gene can be, for example, a floating

---

Algorithm 1: `Generate-and-Test()`—EA's general perturbation-and-acceptation scheme.

Output: set of solutions Q

1 initialize(P) // initialize set of solutions
2 **while** *true* **do**
3     $Q \leftarrow$ perturb(P) // recombine and mutate
4   **if** Q *meets termination conditions* **then**
5   **return** Q
6     $P \leftarrow$ accept(P, Q) // select and reproduce

---

point number, a graph vertex, or a single bit. In this thesis, we refer to the logical structures encoded within a genotype as the *representation model*. A genotype can be considered a construction plan. Building the actual solution from the genotype is referred to as the *genotype-to-phenotype mapping*. Consequently, a phenotype is the expression of a genotype. In the next step of Algorithm 1, candidate solutions or individuals get recombined and mutated. *Recombination* is the sexual reproduction transferring information among individuals. Thereby, a new individual is created by blending genes from a set of parent individuals. Afterward, a *mutation* operator modifies some genes with a certain probability. The quality of the newly created individuals is computed in the *fitness evaluation* step. If the optimization goal is reached by some individuals, the EA terminates its execution. Otherwise a *selection* method, which can be deterministic or randomized, picks some individuals regarding their fitness or objective values for the next reproduction step.

Concrete EA variants will be presented in the next section. Before that, the following list presents some important key properties of evolutionary algorithms.

- **Evolutionary algorithms are exceptionally good at solving real world applications:** EA variants have been used to optimize the shapes of turbines [30, 114, 287] and cars [58], to understand protein folding [224], to analyze and predict financial markets [42–44, 115, 169, 226], to calculate the chemical kinetics of fuels [206], and to solve many other applications. From the user perspective, the attractiveness of EAs is based on the following properties:

  - **EAs are algorithmically simple:** As shown in Algorithm 1, EAs consist of a single loop containing a few operators. Thus, EAs are easy to understand, calibrate, extend, and tailor to an application. In its simplest form, only the fitness evaluation has to be specific to the application. A reference EA implementation can therefore be used out of the box. Additionally, a vast number

Table 2.1: Common evolutionary algorithms terminology.

candidate solution	element of the search space, genotype container
individual	a candidate solution
population	a set of candidate solutions
parent	candidate solution selected for reproduction
offspring individual, child	candidate solution, derived from at least one parent
phenotype	expression of the genotype, individual's observed properties (morphology, behavior, ...)
genotype	a set of genes, construction plan of a phenotype
representation model	genotype
chromosome	a subset of a genotype
gene	substructure of a genotype encoding a particular property
allele	gene's value
locus	allele's position within the genotype
crossover / recombination	exchange of genetic material, sexual reproduction
mutation	alteration of genetic material
selection	individual's reproduction, based on the objective function
objective function	metric for comparing individuals
objective space	objective function
fitness function / landscape	biology inspired notion of the objective function
fitness evaluation / assessment	computation of the objective function
decision space	typically, real valued objective function
decision variable	decision space dimension
elitism	passing best individuals to the next generation without any modification

Table 2.2: Biological development space.

phylogeny	development through inherited changes of the genotype, Mendel [245]
ontogeny / morphogenesis	individual's progress through cell growth and differentiation
epigenesis	individual's progress through interaction with the environment, learning, development of a immune system, inheritance of acquired characteristics

of EA software libraries exists for popular engineering systems, such as the Matlab Global Optimization Toolbox [241].

 — **EAs can deal with incomplete specifications:** EAs are sometimes considered as black box methods: they can operate without any information about what the goal function is modeling. Additionally, the goal function may only implicitly describe the overall optimization challenge.

The ability to optimize unknown and complex goal functions opens up an additional application case to EAs. When a new application is introduced with a parameter set that is too complicated to be solved by a human designer, an EA can be used to explore the topology of the solution space.

 — **EAs can be easily extended and customized:** Because of algorithmic simplicity, EAs are well suited for combination with other algorithms without an excessive implementation effort. Nested EAs and hybridizations of global and local search techniques are quite popular for larger and hard optimization functions. Knowledge about the optimized application can be incorporated into an EA's representation model and evolutionary operators to reduce the execution time. Optimization towards solutions with specific properties can also be done by shaping the representation model, embedding design methodologies, and prioritizing candidate solutions with the desired characteristic for reproduction.

• **EAs are well suited for multi-objective optimization:** The search spaces of applications often comprise multiple and sometimes contradictory trade-offs. As EAs are population based approaches, optimizing multiple objectives requires basically only a redefinition of the fitness function. With additional methods, such as Pareto based ranking and diversification algorithms, multi-criteria EAs are able to evolve close coverings within the trade-off space in a single run.

• **EAs are inherently parallel:** The computational costs of an EA are primarily defined by the complexity of the fitness evaluation. As fitness evaluations are typically independent, they can be efficiently parallelized. Thereby, the speed-up is often proportional to the population size. Especially the optimization of complex functions benefits dramatically from parallelization.

- **Real world EAs are often difficult to analyze:** The analysis of EAs by investigating the effects of the evolutionary operator and the relations of the search space neighborhood is typically complex. Particularly applications suffer from search space non-linearities and discontinuities. Complicated operators additionally hamper the analysis. Thus, vast part of the work on the convergence and computational effort of EAs concentrates on experimentally demonstrating the worst-, average-, and best-case rates. Theoretical results are available only for simple EA variants. For instance, Holland investigated the effects of evolutionary operators in [167] and introduced the Schema Theorem, which gives a lower bound on the generational propagation of some genotype patterns. The theorem, however, makes no statement on the convergence behavior. A more recent approach is convergence analysis by modeling search paths by Markov chains [106, 264, 288, 340, 395]. The analysis gets more precise, when allowing the mutation rate to decrease over generations [296]. Here, ideas inspired by simulated annealing (SA) convergence reasoning are reused [90, 91].

A formal convergence analysis is important for understanding the mechanism of an algorithm. For challenges, however, the estimation of the computational complexity is far more useful, as it allows deriving concrete execution times and computational requirements.

- **Evolutionary algorithms can handle incomplete and implicit goal functions:** For instance, the compression rate of an evolvable image encoder, as presented in Section 1.1, can be explicitly expressed by the ratio of the sizes of the input data and the output data. However, the fitness of an evolvable robot controller depends on non-deterministic environmental factors. A robot control function may perform differently when evaluated at different times and locations. A robot's evolved behavior also influences its environment which, in turn, may change its configuration and the way it interacts with the robot. While the handling of an implicit goal function may not be simple, defining the goal function without a complete knowledge of the optimized domain is one of the most important properties of EAs, allowing an approach to complex and dynamic optimization domains.

- **The genotype-to-phenotype mapping efficiency can be crucial for an EA's performance:** A common way to improve an EA's efficiency is the increase of the genotype's abstraction level and expressiveness. This allows reducing the search space more efficiently. On the other hand, mapping a genotype that is expressed in a complex encoding to a simpler phenotype level requires an elaborate transfer function. For instance, evolving circuits at the level of n-bit wide mathematical operators and mapping them to the level of the Boolean gates of a reconfigurable logic device needs the computationally complex step of logic synthesis (this procedure will be described in more detail in Section 3.2.1.3). Thus, the distance and disparity in the abstraction levels of the genotype and phenotype can necessitate a complex mapping function, contributing significantly to the temporal performance of an EA.

The remaining part of this section will present popular variants of single- and multi-objective EAs. Traditional single-objective EA families are evolutionary programming (cf. Section 2.1.1), evolutionary strategies (cf. Section 2.1.2), genetic algorithms (cf. Section 2.1.3), and genetic programming (cf. Section 2.1.4), listed chronologically in Figure 2.1. Extending the objective function to the concurrent evolution of multiple goals creates the family of multi-objective evolutionary algorithms, presented in Section 2.2. The families of parallel and hybrid EAs are presented in Section 2.3.1 and Section 2.3.2. An introduction to statistical methods for the comparison of heuristics concludes the chapter in Section 2.4.

2.1 Historical overview

Barricelli is considered to have published the earliest work on artificial evolution according to the principles observed by Darwin. Using a grid of numbers, he investigated two-dimensional patterns evolved by simple reproduction rules. Figure 2.1 gives a chronological classification of original work on evolutionary algorithms starting with the work of Barricelli [38] in 1954. Box investigated evolution inspired optimization for applications in [51]. He also proposed multi-objective evolutionary optimization and mentioned the disadvantage of subsuming multiple factors under a single valued goal function due to the different priorities of different components. We will focus our historical overview on the four EA variants most commonly used today: the evolutionary programming (EP) of Fogel et al. [121], the evolutionary strategies of Rechenberg et al. [282], the genetic algorithms (GA) of Holland [167], and Cramer's and Koza's Genetic Programming (GP) [198].

2.1.1 Evolutionary Programming

Evolutionary Programming (EP) was introduced by Fogel, Ownes, and Walsh [121] in 1966. EP is basically characterized by an application-specific representation model, reproduction only by mutations, and the use of a probabilistic selection scheme. In the initial paper, EP was used to optimize finite state

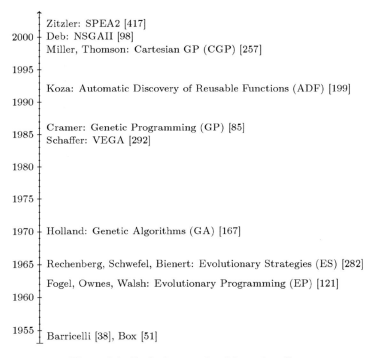

Figure 2.1: Evolutionary algorithms time line.

machines (FSM) to predict non-stationary time series. Following the general EA approach described by Algorithm 1, EP creates an offspring population by mutating all individuals from the parent population. Thereby, the operator might add and delete states, change the initial state and output symbols, and modify the transition function. Using tournament selection, the new population is made up from parent and offspring individuals. The (k, p) tournament selection scheme randomly picks k-subsets of individuals, sorts them from best fitness to worst, and selects the ith individual with probability $p(1 - p)^{i-1}$. In newer research, EP has become favored for real-valued optimization [327].

2.1.2 Evolutionary Strategies

A $(\mu \{{}^+_{\text{,}}\} \lambda)$ evolutionary strategy (ES) derives λ offspring from μ parents and selects the new population either from the offspring or the offspring and the parent individuals for the "," or the "+" variant, respectively. Introduced by Rechenberg, Schwefel, and Bienert [282], ES were designed to push the optimization onto the levels of phylogenetic evolution and epigenetic learning. Learning is implemented as a self-adaptive process of adjusting gene mutability factors.

An ES individual in the work of Rechenberg [282] comprises a set of real numbers representing the parameters of the engineered object. To each parameter some strategy variables are attached, controlling the step size of the mutation operator. While Rechenberg initially investigated a mutation-only ES [282], Schwefel [297] added recombination to the scheme later on. Similar to EP, ES does not restrict the genotype's encoding. One difference from EP is the deterministic selection scheme. ES takes the μ best individuals from either offspring, or offspring and parents, to the next generation without any randomization.

2.1.3   Genetic Algorithms

Genetic algorithms (GA) were introduced by Holland in 1975 [167]. A pivotal feature of Holland's canonical GA—which distinguishes it from EP and ES— is that the genotype encoding is application independent, consisting of a constant length bitstring. The genotype-to-phenotype mapping relies on a bitstring partitioning into bit sets. Each bit set corresponds to a phenotype property. With a generalized genotype, the evolutionary operators can also be defined independently of the application.

Holland's canonical GA was strongly inspired by the natural evolution cycle, comprising its major elements, such as a restricted alphabet genotype, pairwise parent selection, mating, and mutation. While for EP and ES, the mutation operator is considered to be the driving force of the evolution, GAs rely on the crossover operator. In Fig 2.2, a 2-point crossover is presented. A general n-point crossover for two genotypes is defined as the partitioning of the genotypes into $n + 1$ similarly sized sets and swapping every second set. A uniform crossover designates an $m - 1$ crossover for a genotype of length m. GA's standard bit-flip mutation operator inverts every bit of a genotype with some probability p. The biology inspired fitness proportionate selection, the so-called roulette wheel selection, interprets the individuals' fitnesses as intervals. The larger the interval, the more likely the individual is to be selected for reproduction.

Holland's book *Adaptation in Natural and Artificial Systems* explored in 1975 the question of why genetic algorithms work [167]. He formulated and proved the "Schema Theorem" for the canonical version of his GA, which traces the generational propagation of schemas (templates matching genotype substrings) under the mutation and crossover operators. As a consequence, Holland suggested the "building block hypothesis," which proposes that evo-

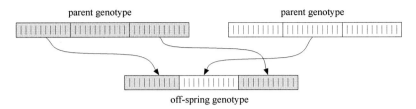

Figure 2.2: Genetic algorithm: A 2-point crossover.

lution should benefit from short, low order, better than average performing schemata (building blocks, genes), and that schemata arrangement within the genotype is of vital importance: related schemata should be placed near to each other. In later analysis, the explanation of GA's principle by the "building block hypothesis" has been criticized, as the hypothesis does not necessarily follow from the Schema Theorem [27, 142, 143, 387].

After the introduction of GAs in 1970, the algorithms have been extended to numerous new representation models, such as directed acyclic graphs [252], neural networks [203, 410], LISP expressions [95], trees [179], and real valued vectors [256]. Different kinds of selection strategies and mutation and crossover operators have been applied to improve their performance. The genetic algorithm itself has been extended to hybrid variants [283, 370] combining global, local and non-evolutionary approaches. An introduction to the area is given for example by Bäck et al. [36] and Eiben et al. [107].

2.1.4 Genetic Programming

Genetic programming (GP) demonstrates two key elements: the evolution of programs mapping some inputs to outputs and the automatic discovery of reusable subfunctions. Introduced by Cramer 1985 [85] and Koza 1992 [198, 199], GP's motivation can be stated as: "How can computers learn to solve problems without being explicitly programmed to do so" [59]. In its original form, GP evolved LISP programs expressed by a tree structure. GP utilizes the common evolutionary operators, such as selection, recombination, and mutation. The principle of the tree-type crossover is presented in Figure 2.3. With an unconstrained genotype length, the tree based crossover may induce uncontrolled genotype growth and the appearance of repetitive patterns, referred to as *bloat*.

The intriguing property of GP is its automatic definition and reuse of subfunctions (ADF), which introduces a divide and conquer-like concept to heuristic search. The dynamic extension of the functional block alphabet by new composite functions, which themselves are subject to evolutionary pressure, allows increasing the functionality and complexity level of the alphabet.

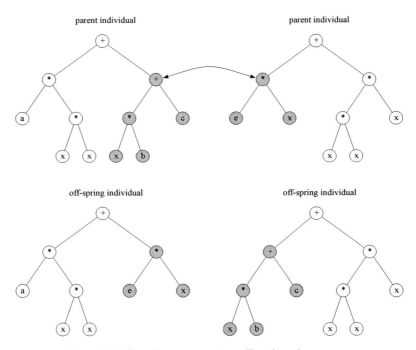

Figure 2.3: Genetic programming: Tree based crossover.

2.2 Multi-objective Evolutionary Algorithms

Engineering solutions for g applications often require the balancing of multiple trade-offs and the making of compromises. In this section we introduce the basic multi-objective optimization terminology, present two state of the art multi-objective EAs, and outline their computational complexity and methods for non-dominated set comparison.

2.2.1 Multi-objective Optimization Terminology

Before introducing the basic terminology for multi-objective optimization, we will clarify the basic notion of optimization. Let $\mathcal{X} \subseteq \mathbb{R}^n$, $n \in \mathbb{N}$, be the *decision space*. This could be, e.g., the parameter space of a gas turbine model. Let $\mathcal{Y} \subseteq \mathbb{R}^m$, $m \in \mathbb{N}$ be the *objective space*. This is the space in which the model's performance characteristics are expressed. The function $f : \mathcal{X} \to \mathcal{Y}$ is a metric assigning performance values to a potential solution, and is called the *objective function*. The goal of an *unconstrained optimization problem* is, without loss of generality, to minimize f for all $x \in \mathcal{X}$:

$$\min_{x \in \mathcal{X}} f(x).$$

A *constrained optimization problem* additionally introduces *equality constraints* $g_i : \mathcal{X} \to \mathbb{R}$, $i = 1, 2, \ldots, k$:

$$\forall i = 1, 2, \ldots, k : \ g_i(x) = 0,$$

and *inequality constraints* $h_j : \mathcal{X} \to \mathbb{R}$, $j = 1, 2, \ldots, l$:

$$\forall j = 1, 2, \ldots, l : \ h_j(x) \leq 0.$$

In the case of a multi-dimensional objective function $f(x) \in \mathcal{Y} \subseteq \mathbb{R}^{\geq 2}$, the optimization challenge is called *multi-objective*.

Extending an EA to the multi-objective approach needs, in its simplest version, only a redefinition of the objective function. As the EAs in the original definition were already designed to maintain a set of candidate solutions, introducing multi-objective optimization typically does not require any additional changes here. Related work on multi-objective optimization roughly splits into the scalarization approaches and Pareto approaches [96]. The first reduces the multi-valued objective function to the single objective case, often by rewriting it as a weighted linear combination. An important detail here is that the algorithm designer has to decide how to aggregate the objective function, which are the objectives interdependencies, and which weights to assign. In contrast to this, the Pareto approach frees the designer from introducing the mentioned expertise and from making assumptions about the search space, allowing for a more general objective function definition. In this thesis, we focus on the Pareto approaches, as they have proven to be very successful in optimizing complex functions.

To minimize f in a multi-dimensional objective space $\mathcal{Y}$, an order relation has to be defined. But how to re-define the notion of a "best" solution, when multiple and sometimes even conflicting goals have to be optimized at the same time? Francis Y. Edgeworth and Wilfredo Pareto gave an answer to this question. Edgeworth noted that for some objective functions P and π: "It is required to find a point (x, y) such that in whatever direction we take an infinitely small step, P and π do not increase together but that, while one increases, the other decreases" in [104] 1881. Similarly, Pareto indicated: "The optimum allocation of the resources of a society is not attained so long as it is possible to make at least one individual better off in his own estimation while keeping others as well off as before in their own estimation" in [267] 1906.

The formalization of the new concept of "best" can be done as follows: Let $x_1 \in \mathcal{X}$ and $x_2 \in \mathcal{X}$ be two objective vectors and $f = (f_1, f_2, \ldots, f_m)$ as previously defined. Then, x_1 *dominates* x_2, or $x_1 \prec x_2$, if:

$$x_1 \prec x_2 \quad \Leftrightarrow \quad \forall i : f_i(x_1) \leq f_i(x_2) \quad \wedge \quad \exists j : f_j(x_1) < f_j(x_2).$$

Additionally, *weak Pareto dominance*, or $x_1 \preceq x_2$, is defined as:

$$x_1 \preceq x_2 \quad \Leftrightarrow \quad \forall i : f_i(x_1) \leq f_i(x_2).$$

If $x_1 \preceq x_2$ and $x_2 \preceq x_1$, it follows that $f(x_1) \stackrel{!}{=} f(x_2)$. If neither condition holds, x_1 and x_2 are *incomparable* or *indifferent* (denoted $x_1 || x_2$).

The *Pareto set* $\mathcal{X}^*$ is defined as the subset of $\mathcal{X}$ containing all optimal solutions. "Optimal" means that for any $x^* \in \mathcal{X}^*$ there is no $x \in \mathcal{X}$ with $x \preceq x^*$. The *Pareto front* is defined by the images of $\mathcal{X}^*$ under f. The goal of a multi-objective algorithm is to calculate or approximate the Pareto set.

To prepare for the discussion of multi-objective algorithms, we need to introduce some further terminology. For a subset $P \subseteq \mathcal{X}$ that denotes a population of a multi-objective algorithm, the *dominance count* for $p \in P$, or $\mathrm{count}(p)$, is defined as:

$$\mathrm{count}(p) = |\{p' \in P | p \prec p'\}|,$$

the number of individuals in P dominated by p. *Dominance rank*, or $\mathrm{rank}(p)$, is defined by the number of individuals in P dominating p:

$$\mathrm{rank}(p) = |\{p' \in P | p' \prec p\}|.$$

P can be partitioned disjointly into subsets $\dot{\cup}_{i=1}^{q} P_i = P$, where all individuals from a certain P_i are mutually indifferent. Additionally, the P_i's are enumerated in such a way that for any individual from P_{i+1} there exists at least one individual in P_i dominating it. Thus, P_1 "dominates" P_2, $P_3, \ldots, P_q$; P_2 "dominates" P_3, $P_4, \ldots, P_q$, and so on. P_i is called a *non-dominated set* and the images of P_i under f a *non-dominated front*. The *dominance depth* of $p \in P_i \subseteq P$ is the index of its non-dominated set:

$$\mathrm{depth}(p \in P_i) = i.$$

The notion of ϵ-*dominance* denotes the factor $\epsilon \in \mathbb{R}$ in the objective space, by which one objective vector is at least better or worse than another. Given x_1, x_2 and f as previously defined, $f(x_1) \geq \vec{0}$, $f(x_2) \geq \vec{0}$, x_1 ϵ-dominates x_2, or $x_1 \preceq_\epsilon x_2$, if:

$$x_1 \preceq_\epsilon x_2 \quad \Leftrightarrow \quad \forall i : f_i(x_1) \leq \epsilon \cdot f_i(x_2).$$

The additive ϵ_+-*dominance* definition follows the definition of ϵ-dominance:

$$x_1 \preceq_{\epsilon_+} x_2 \quad \Leftrightarrow \quad \forall i : f_i(x_1) \leq \epsilon + f_i(x_2).$$

It is important to mention that there might be indefinitely many ϵ's for particular x_1 and x_2 satisfying the equations. We are interested in the smallest ϵ, as with its help a "quality" relation between two objective sets can be established. Assume that $P \subseteq \mathcal{X}$ and $P' \subseteq \mathcal{X}$ are two sets in the decision space. The greatest lower bound for ϵ's with $p \preceq_\epsilon p'$ for all $p \in P$, $p' \in P'$ defines the factor by which any element of P' is weakly dominated by at least one element of P. The function computing the according ϵ is called a *Quality Indicator* (QI) [419] and is formalized as:

$$I_\epsilon(P, P') = \inf_{\epsilon \in \mathbb{R}} \{ \forall p' \in P' \; \exists p \in P : p \preceq_\epsilon p' \}.$$

The definition of the additive I_{ϵ_+} QI follows the definition of the I_ϵ QI:

$$I_{\epsilon_+}(P, P') = \inf_{\epsilon \in \mathbb{R}} \{ \forall p' \in P' \; \exists p \in P : p \preceq_{\epsilon_+} p' \}.$$

With the help of a QI, the relation between two non-dominated sets can be mapped to a single real number symbolizing the factor or distance by which one non-dominated set outperforms the other. Additionally, the quality for a single non-dominated set can be computed by comparing it to a worst-case non-dominated set. Assuming $\mathcal{Y} = [0, 1]^m$, this would be the set holding the reference point $R = \vec{1}$. The according unary QI can now be formalized as:

$$I_\epsilon^1(P) = I_\epsilon(P, \{R\})$$

and

$$I_{\epsilon_+}^1(P) = I_{\epsilon_+}(P, \{R\}).$$

For a more detailed overview of the terminology, Zitzler et al. [419] and Knowles et al. [192] provide a thorough introductions.

The discipline of multi-objective optimization goes back to Cantor and Hausdorff (1895–1906), and Kuhn and Tucker (1951) [75]. Only in 1984 did Schaffer introduce the first implementation of a multi-objective algorithm, which is called VEGA [292]. VEGA is a non-Pareto approach differing from regular GA in the way the fitness function is defined. For k objectives, the fitness function partitions the population into k subpopulations, selecting candidate solutions for the next generation in the ith subpopulation with respect to the ith objective. The first generation of Pareto based algorithms was introduced in the 1990s. Some prominent examples are MOGA [122], NPGA [168], and NSGA [328]. Common to all these algorithms is the use of fitness sharing to ensure the evolution of a diverse Pareto set approximation. Fitness sharing can be roughly described as a function modifying the fitness of an individual according to its local population density [75]. Consequently, individuals in crowded regions are less likely to contribute to the next generation than individuals in sparsely populated regions. Modern MOEAs, such as NSGAII [98], SPEA [48], SPEA2 [417], PAES [193], PESAII [194], and μGA2 [277], extend the original ideas, employing more elaborate selection and diversity preserving techniques, and using elitism and archive populations. With the establishment of modern and successful generation of MOEAs, new challenges such as many-dimensional optimization [420] and efficient constraint handling [76] got into the focus of researchers. To prepare for discussing the multi-objective optimization of digital circuits, we will briefly report on the NSGAII and SPEA2 algorithms. These algorithms and their basic principles will be used in our thesis.

2.2.2 Non-Dominated Sorting Genetic Algorithm II

Presented by Deb et al. in [98], the non-dominated sorting genetic algorithm II (NSGAII) comprises two key methods: an efficient non-dominated set decomposition (non-dominating sorting) and a selection operator considering the fitness and spread of the candidate solutions. The general algorithm structure is presented in Figure 2.4. NSGAII iterates an archive population throughout the generations. In every generation, a working population is derived from the archive by means of regular GA operators. Afterwards, the archive and the working population are joined and a new archive is filled by selecting elements from the union by means of the non-dominated sorting and the density information.

The non-dominated set decomposition is detailed in Algorithm 2. It splits the input set P into disjoint non-dominated sets $\{\mathcal{F}_1, \mathcal{F}_2, \ldots, \mathcal{F}_l\} = \mathcal{F}$, $\dot{\cup}_{i=1}^{l} \mathcal{F}_i = P$, where any element of $\mathcal{F}_{i+1}$ is dominated by at least one element of $\mathcal{F}_i$. The algorithm has following parts: the computation of ranks and dominated sets, the assignment of dominance depths, and the segregation of non-dominated sets. The ranks and dominated sets are computed by the code from line 1 to 8. This is computationally the most complex part accounting for $O(mN^2)$ operations, where m is the number of objectives and N is the number of elements in the input set. Additionally, the first non-dominated set $\mathcal{F}_1$ is constructed during this phase. In the remaining part, the algorithm computes for an $\mathcal{F}_i$ its proximate $\mathcal{F}_{i+1}$ by looking at dominated sets of elements in $\mathcal{F}_i$. Those elements in $P \setminus \cup_{k=1}^{i} \mathcal{F}_k$ that are dominated only by elements of $\mathcal{F}_i$ define $\mathcal{F}_{i+1}$. Non-dominated set aggregation is done by the code from line 9 to 18 in Algorithm 2.

The second component of the NSGAII selection metric considers the local density information. The density of an element is computed with the help of the surrounding hypercube bounded by the element's neighbors. For corner Pareto elements that do not have bounding neighbors for at least one dimension, the surrounding hypercube becomes infinitely large. The density rank

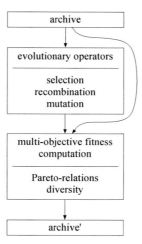

Figure 2.4: The general structure of second generation multi-objective algorithms (NSGAII, SPEA2).

$\mathrm{dr}(p)$ is then computed as the sum of the hypercube's side lengths. A small crowding rank indicates an element densely enclosed by neighbors while a large crowding rank indicates a sparsely populated neighborhood.

To fill a new archive population, NSGAII composes the selection metric as follows:

$$p \geq_n q \Leftrightarrow \begin{cases} \mathrm{depth}(p) < \mathrm{depth}(q) \\ \quad \mathrm{OR} \\ [\mathrm{depth}(p) = \mathrm{depth}(q)] \ \mathrm{AND} \ [\mathrm{dr}(p) > \mathrm{dr}(q)] \end{cases} \tag{2.1}$$

The union of the archive and the working population is sorted in descending order with respect to "$\geq_n$" and the new archive is filled with the first elements of the sorted union. The first condition of Equation 2.1 ensures that the new archive consists foremost of the non-dominated sets with lower depth indices $(\mathcal{F}_1, \mathcal{F}_2, \ldots)$. If the last added non-dominated set does not fit entirely into the archive, less-crowded elements of the set are added first. This is expressed by the last condition of Equation 2.1.

2.2.3 Strength Pareto Evolutionary Algorithm 2

Introduced by Zitzler in [417,418], the Strength Pareto Evolutionary Algorithm-2 (SPEA2) handles its archive and working population the same as NSGAII. Also similar is the idea of a two-component fitness function comprising a

---

Algorithm 2: `Non-Dominated set decomposition` [98].

Input: set of Pareto-points P

Output: $\mathcal{F} = \{\mathcal{F}_1, \mathcal{F}_2, \ldots, \mathcal{F}_l\}$ non-domination set decomposition of P

1 **for** $p \in P$ **do**
2   **for** $q \in P$ **do**
3   **if** $p \prec q$ **then**
4        $S_p \leftarrow S_p \cup \{q\}$ // S_p contains elements of P dominated by p
5   **if** $q \prec p$ **then**
6        $n_p \leftarrow n_p + 1$ // $n_p = \text{rank}(p)$, number of elements in P dominating p
7   **if** $n_p = 0$ **then**
8      $\mathcal{F}_1 \leftarrow \mathcal{F}_1 \cup \{p\}$ // detect non-dominated elements of P
9 $i \leftarrow 1$
10 **while** $\mathcal{F}_i \neq \emptyset$ **do**
11   $\mathcal{H} \leftarrow \emptyset$
12   **for** $p \in \mathcal{F}_i$ **do**
13   **for** $q \in S_p$ **do**
14       $n_q \leftarrow n_q - 1$
15   **if** $n_q = 0$ **then**
16         $\mathcal{H} \leftarrow \mathcal{H} \cup \{q\}$
17   $i \leftarrow i + 1$
18   $\mathcal{F}_i \leftarrow \mathcal{H}$
19 **return** $\mathcal{F} \leftarrow \{\mathcal{F}_1, \mathcal{F}_2, \ldots, \mathcal{F}_l\}$

Pareto- and crowding-based element. The SPEA2 density metric, however, is able to detect cluster hierarchies in the objective space, unlike the NSGAII local crowding metric. As SPEA2 differs from NSGAII only in the definition of fitness and in the way the archive is filled, we concentrate on these steps. The fitness of an element p from the union of the archive and the working population P is defined as

$$F(p) = \frac{1}{\sigma_p^k + 2} + \sum_{q \prec p, q \in P} \text{count}(q),$$

where σ_p^k denotes the Euclidean distance of p to its kth nearest neighbor. The second term sums the domination counts of all those elements that dominate p. If p is in the first non-dominated set, this term equal 0. The first term represents the density information. It takes values within $(0, 0.5]$ and becomes smaller when the distance to the kth nearest neighbor increases. k is set to the square root of $|P|$. The new archive is filled from the union of the old archive and the working population, sorted in increasing order with respect to F. In the first step, all individuals with a fitness below 1 (and therefore non-dominated) are inserted into the new archive. In the case the archive size allows of inserting more elements, they are taken from the union according to their sorting. However, when the archive's size has been exceeded, its elements are sorted in increasing order with respect to a new order relation "$\leq_n$," which is defined as

$$
p \leq_n q \Leftrightarrow
\begin{cases}
\sigma_p^i = \sigma_q^i & \forall i = 0, 1, \ldots, |archive| \\
\quad \text{OR} \\
[\sigma_p^j = \sigma_q^j] \ \text{AND} \ [\sigma_p^i < \sigma_q^i] & \forall j = 0, 1, \ldots, i-1; \\
& i \in \{0, 1, \ldots, |archive|\}
\end{cases}
\tag{2.2}
$$

The first condition of "$\leq_n$" indicates elements with identical objective space locations. The second condition expresses a situation where two elements have identical distances to the first, second,...,$i-1$th neighbor, but have different distances to the ith neighbor. In this case the element with the smallest distance to the ith neighbor consequently has a denser neighborhood and a smaller value in terms of the "$\leq_n$" relation than its opponent. After sorting the new archive, the first element is removed. Sorting and removing is repeated until the regular archive size is reached. This is a unique property of the SPEA2 cut-off operator as it assures an up to date sorting of the shrinking archive. The working population is subsequently filled from individuals of the new archive employing binary tournament selection and the previously defined fitness metric $F(p)$.

2.3 Variants of Specialized Evolutionary Algorithms

The major classification of EA families as presented in the previous sections would be incomplete without mentioning some relevant EA subfamilies. The first subfamily covers parallel EAs, which are essential when optimizing complex engineering tasks. The distribution of computationally demanding operations often reduces the execution time to acceptable levels. The second subfamily consists of EA hybrids. Specialized heuristics are combined here with EAs to, e.g., improve the convergence speed, enable multi-objective optimization, and introduce adaptivity to the search process.

2.3.1 Parallel Evolutionary Algorithms

Evaluating the fitness of individuals is typically independent and therefore distributable in a straightforward manner. There are two frequently applied concepts of parallel EAs. The first concept utilizes a global population and evaluates the individuals on multiple computing nodes. This is called the *master–slave* parallelization. In the second approach, multiple isolated EAs evolve their own populations, while recurrently exchanging solutions. To this end, the regular EA operators are extended by the *migrant selection* and *replacement* operators [80]. This so called *island* family of evolutionary algorithms comprises a vast variety of different algorithm flavors, differing in the time between migrations, what triggers the migration, and strategies of replacement as well as selection [145, 222, 389, 415].

An interesting island EA branch from the reconfigurable logic perspective are the cellular EAs. This approach does not utilize a global population. Instead, candidate solutions are organized in a spatial structure, defined by the candidate solution's local communication rules. A common way to define such a communication structure is by introducing *north*, *south*, *east*, and *west* communication links [23]. This spans a toroidal mesh. The evolutionary algorithm is then executed from the candidate solution's point of view, considering a population gathered from its neighbors. One of the characteristic elements of cellular EA's is the *isolation by distance*. This allows having implicitly defined sub-populations, operating as virtual islands.

The relevance of parallel and island EAs becomes visible with the numerous applications solved by these methods. Parallel and island EAs have been used to design rotor blades [221], evolve the aerodynamics of an airfoil [32, 180, 262], recognize objects [22], and find protein folding [229]. Additionally, aircraft [134, 274], nuclear plants [270], processors [330], mobile communications [341, 385] and floor-plans [54] have been optimized by parallel EAs.

2.3.2 Hybrid Evolutionary Algorithms

Evolutionary algorithms are very successful on a large set of complex applications. However, when leaving the domain of parameter-free black box-like methods, the performance can often be improved by employing knowledge about the optimized application [89]. This can be done by some specialized representation models, sophisticated genotype-to-phenotype mappings, and application tailored evolutionary operators. Another way to improve EAs is their combination with non-EA algorithms such as, e.g., simulated annealing [290]. This can be done either by merging the algorithms into a monolithic method or by defining a periodization scheme [13]. In a periodization scheme the algorithms remain largely unmodified and are executed rotationally according to some ordering. Hybrid EAs are used to schedule jobs [344], create information retrieval models [84, 342], model reservoir permeability [401], study inter-atomic potentials [55], simulate ecosystems [177], implement FPGA segmented channel routing [290], and optimize process structures [402].

2.4 Performance Analysis

A formal analysis of heuristics such as an EA often suffers from pessimistic assumptions and incomplete models. Especially in the area of evolutionary algorithms, only for some of the simplest EA variants do formal convergence criteria exist. In this context, computational complexity provides a more useful measurement to estimate their behavior. Computational complexity is typically represented by the worst, average, and best case, established over a set of experiments. In the area of EAs, computational effort (CE) [198] is a popular metric, giving an average lower bound of fitness evaluations to reach some optimization goal. CE will be presented in the following section. We additionally need a method to compare the evolved non-dominated sets. Section 2.4.2 shows two ways of doing this.

2.4.1 The Computational Effort

A popular approach to compare EAs is the *computational effort* metric, as defined by Koza in [198].

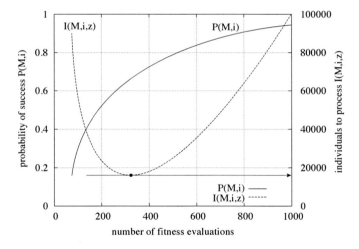

Figure 2.5: Computational effort: The idealized plot of the probability $P(M, i)$ to reach the optimization goal by the ith fitness evaluation. $I(M, i, z)$ shows the computational effort in fitness evaluations when successively restarting the search after reaching the ith fitness evaluation. At this, $I(M, i, z)$ fitness evaluations are needed to reach the goal with a probability z. The computational effort is defined as the I(M,i,z) minimum. It is reached in the example after 18,000 fitness evaluations.

It considers only the computational effort of the fitness evaluations, as they are assumed to be by far dominant compared to the computational effort of the EA algorithm itself and its operators. For each experiment with its executed number of fitness evaluations M per generation, a set of independent runs is conducted. In each run, the optimization goal might be reached by some generation i. The probability of reaching the optimization goal by generation i can then be expressed as follows:

$$P(M, i) = (\#\text{succeeded runs by generation } i)/(\#\text{runs}).$$

From this, $R(z)$ can be determined as the number of independent runs that have to be conducted to reach the optimization goal with a certain probability z:

$$R(z) = \lceil \log(1 - z)/\log(1 - P(M, i)) \rceil.$$

The estimated overall number of fitness evaluations required to reach the goal with probability z is then

$$I(M, i, z) = M \cdot (i + 1) \cdot R(z).$$

For each experiment with given M and z, the minimal value for $I(M, i, z)$ is referred to as the computational effort of the experiment. Figure 2.5 illustrates the typical behavior of $P(M, i)$ and $I(M, i, z)$. To conform with the related work and the work of Koza [198], we set z to 99% in this thesis.

2.4.2 Comparing Non-Dominated Sets

To analyze the performance of multi-objective optimizers, we need to compare the evolved non-dominated sets. There are two methods commonly used in related research: ranking by a quality indicator, and the analysis of the average non-dominated sets attained during multiple algorithm runs. Both methods are described by Knowles et al. [192] and are implemented in the PISA toolbox by Bleuler et al. [49].

The first method uses a unary QI to reduce a sequence of non-dominated sets evolved by a benchmark algorithm to a sequence of numbers. To compare the two sequences, we use the non-parametric Kruskal–Wallis test [83]. It differentiates between the null hypothesis H_0 = "The distribution functions of the sequences are identical" and the alternative hypothesis H_A = "At least one sequence tends to yield better observations than another sequence." In case the test rejects H_0, the table provides, for all sequence pairs, the *one tailed p-value* [83]. Table 2.3 presents an example: for an algorithm pair $(A_{\text{row}}, A_{\text{col}})$ a p-value less than or equal to α indicates a lower mean for A_{row}. Thus, one can conclude from Table 2.3 with $\alpha = 0.05$ that A_1 outperforms A_2 and A_3, and A_3 outperforms A_2.

An additional way of interpreting the results of multi-objective optimizers is to take a look at the Pareto points that are weakly dominated by solutions

Table 2.3: Example of the use of the Kruskal–Wallis test. The table entry is the one-tailed p-value for comparison of algorithm a_{row} with a_{col}.

	A_1	A_2	A_3
A_1	-	0.002	0.007
A_2	0.97	-	1.0
A_3	1.0	0.003	-

found in $x\%$ of multi-objective algorithm runs. The set of non-dominated points that have been reached in $x\%$ of the runs are referred to as the $x\%$-*attainment*. The attainment allows for a direct graphical interpretation as shown in Figure 2.6. In order to statistically compare the attainments, we

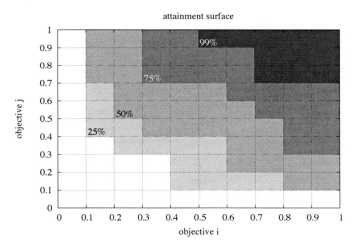

Figure 2.6: Non-Dominated sets reached in at least $x\%$ of multi-objective algorithm runs.

use the two-tailed Kolmogorov–Smirnov test [315]. It distinguishes between $H_0=$ "Sequences A and B follow the same distribution" and $H_A=$ "Sequences A and B follow different distributions." Table 2.4 contains exemplary results for three algorithms A_1, A_2 and A_3 evaluated by the Kolmogorov–Smirnov test. The results in Table 2.4 can be interpreted as: A_1 differs significantly from A_2 and A_3.

Table 2.4: Interpretation of the Kolmogorov–Smirnov test: A dot denotes an accepted H_0 hypothesis at given α. A star indicates significantly different non-dominated set distributions.

	A_1	A_2	A_3
A_1	-	*	*
A_2	*	-	.
A_3	*	.	-

2.5 Chapter Conclusion

In this chapter we described single- and multi-objective evolutionary algorithms, presented their terminology, and introduced statistical analysis tools for comparing algorithms. We also gave detailed implementations of some single- and multi-objective EAs relevant for our work. Having given this background, we will next introduce some novel hierarchical evolutionary operators (cf. Section 5) and efficient objective scaling (cf. Section 6.1) for digital circuits as well as a general scheme for evolutionary algorithm periodization for better scalability (cf. Section 6.2).

Chapter 3

Evolvable Hardware

The notion of Evolvable Hardware is composed of reconfigurable hardware, automatic circuit design, and continuous circuit optimization. The concept is intriguing as it allows for solutions beyond classical engineering, for insights into new circuit design rules, and for innovative, maintenance free embedded systems able to withstand defects and adapt to varying goals and resources.

EHW's idea of hardware adaptation became visible with the work of Higuchi et al. [163], published in 1993. The authors proved that genetic algorithms could succeed in evolving a 6-input multiplexer circuit for a reconfigurable logic device. While the function of a multiplexer is fixed, in later research, similar methodologies were used to evolve circuits adaptable to environmental changes [289]. Driven by technological and algorithmic progress, Evolvable Hardware's birth, though, was also influenced by fundamental questions of evolutionary biology. Inspired by the search for an understanding of emerging complex behavior from basic building blocks [174, 223, 249], de Garis combined the rising technology of reconfigurable hardware and biology-inspired optimization algorithms in his attempt to build a "A Darwin Machine": "a device which evolves its own architecture directly in hardware" 1993 [93, 163]. His idea of the "Cellular Automata Machine Brain" [94] was the evolution of replication rules for a massively parallel cellular automata implemented on a reconfigurable hardware device. The author expected his machine to discover complex design spaces, overcoming a human's limited creativity.

Since its introduction, Evolvable Hardware has proved its potential for innovative and astonishing designs, creating oscillators based on transistors' propagation delays [313, 353], more compact circuits than human built solutions [73, 124, 201], radiation- and temperature-hardened circuits [333, 335, 405], and multifunctional and polymorphic gates [304]. In the autonomous and self-adaptive domains, robot and cache controllers [189, 190, 351] [11], image compressors [343], laser calibration circuits [159], pattern matching systems [182] [9], and error recovery [155, 251, 352] have been within the focus of EHW. The many facets of EHW are accompanied by its paradigm simplicity: the continuous evolution of reconfigurable hardware.

This chapter has five parts. Section 3.1 gives a detailed view of electronic Evolvable Hardware. The second section starts with the introduction of digital reconfigurable hardware and presents original and prominent experiments in this area. Section 3.3 illustrates work on analog Evolvable Hardware showing two transistor- and a operational amplifier EHW architectures. Cartesian genetic programming (CGP) and its extensions are presented in Section 3.4. Finally, Section 3.5 summarizes the results and outlines the challenges of Evolvable Hardware.

3.1 The Basic Idea

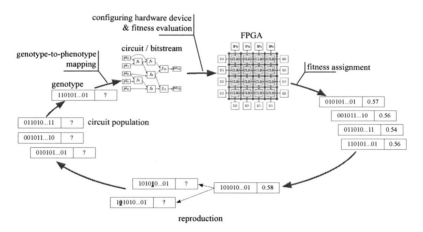

Figure 3.1: Evolving Hardware: Applying evolutionary algorithms to reconfigurable hardware.

Evolvable Hardware (EHW) is the continuous optimization of reconfigurable hardware. The classical notion of EHW relies on evolutionary algorithms [163] for adaptation. The evolutionary cycle, as illustrated in Figure 3.1, starts with a set of candidate solutions, encoding, e.g., a Boolean logic circuit. In the first step, according to Algorithm 1, the candidate solutions are used to generate offspring individuals. To this end, operators inspired by Nature, such as mutation operators and recombination operators, are employed. In the world of Boolean logic circuits, mutation can be interpreted as the modification of a connection or a function gene. Recombination is the making of an offspring individual by blending genetic material from parents. When recombining Boolean circuits, the offspring individual inherits its parents' structures, such as wires, gates, and complete subfunctions.

In the second step, the performance of the new population is evaluated. To this end, each candidate solution needs to be evaluated regarding some objective functions. From the biological perspective, this function is often referred to as the *fitness* and is therefore subject to maximization. In order to compute the fitness, the genotypes typically have to be transformed to the configuration language of the reconfigurable hardware device employed. This step might be easy, when the genotype's abstraction level matches the device's configuration structures. Otherwise, finding an efficient genotype-to-phenotype mapping and with it the right genotype abstraction level is of the utmost importance for the computational complexity of the optimization algorithm. In Figure 3.1, the Boolean logic circuit is mapped to an FPGA by undergoing logic synthesis. The fitness can also be evaluated by simulation. Additionally, the genotype-to-phenotype mapping complexity can be reduced by implementing reconfigurable architectures on top of FPGAs, matching genotype and reconfiguration abstraction levels more tightly. It is important to mention that the behavior of the individual's hardware implementation typically corresponds to the behavior encoded in the genotype, but does not have to. This can be due to an incomplete modeling of the reconfigurable device. Additionally, hardware defects might cause differences between the modeled and the actual hardware. The intriguing property of EHW is that such inconsistencies do not have to be treated in a special way. The nature of evolutionary algorithms allows us to handle properties of the optimized domain which are not modeled, or only loosely and implicitly given, as it typically focuses solely on the solution's behavior and not on its structure. Whenever the hardware instantiation might not exactly match the function described by the genotype, fitness evaluation has to be executed by the very same hardware that is going to execute the future solution, to ensure the validity of the fitness evaluation.

After the fitnesses have been evaluated in Figure 3.1, the evolutionary algorithm uses the performance numbers to establish a partial order relation in the next step. According to this relation and often combined with additional heuristics, individuals contributing to the next generation are selected. This finishes the evolutionary algorithm cycle and the next EA iteration can be started again.

The illustrated cycle of hardware evolution is a prerequisite for Evolvable Hardware. Generally, hardware that is designed by evolutionary optimization algorithms is referred to as *evolved hardware*. Extending evolved hardware by a continuous *modus operandi* and, as a consequence, by reconfigurable hardware, defines the area of *Evolvable Hardware*. With the additional temporal aspect, the scope of evolved hardware can be extended to adaptation tasks. The common EHW use cases are indicated by:

- **Input data distribution dependent functions:** When considering a class of algorithms that assumes that the input data obeys a specified distribution, later changes in the distribution of the data might have an impact on the algorithm's performance. Two different subclasses can be identified here: functions that can be solved perfectly given enough resources, and functions with no known perfect solutions. A hashing function belongs to the first subclass. It can be solved perfectly with the exact knowledge about the input data distribution and sufficient resources. However, precise input data distribution is not always known *a priori*. Additionally, a perfect hashing function may become very large and might be dismissed in favor of a compact version that has an acceptably small functional loss from the optimal case. A special case in this subclass consists of larger functions with behavior that is independent of the distribution of the input data. While probably having a general solution, compact and specialized implementations might restrict the considered input data to some subsets, and therefore become distribution dependent.

  A member of the second class is for instance the lossy image compression. Given a certain image quality loss factor, to the author's knowledge, there is no efficient method to compute the smallest lossy image representation possible. The goal of an optimization algorithm searching for an "optimal" image compressor is not to find "the best" but to find a "sufficiently good" solution.

  While probably identically formalized, the optimization goals for both subclasses can be interpreted differently. When given enough resources, the functions from the first subclass have optimal solutions. Hence, the objective function is bivalent, indicating whether an optimal or correct solution has been found or not. However, restricting the resources makes it difficult and probably impossible to reach the optimum. The optimization goal interpretation of the second subclass, the approximation to some sufficiency level, can in this situation also be applied to the first subclass.

  With input data distribution changes coming from the environment, the general motivation for EHW's continuous optimization is the immediate reaction to these events. The search for a perfect solution, if it exists, or a close approximation, is only secondary.

- **Deteriorating effects within the computational resources:** Faults in the computational resources may have many causes: the shrinking chip structure sizes can make the electronic components more sensitive to aging effects and disturbances from the environment. Radiation, extreme temperatures, and power supply fluctuations may cause temporal and permanent damages to a chip's elements and make the complete device non-functional. Some of the deteriorating effects can be elegantly compensated using the concept of Evolvable Hardware. When assuming a reconfigurable chip area implementing an evolved solution, degradations that induce an element's malfunctioning can cause inconsistencies between the actual hardware and its formalization. However, when having non-constructive evolutionary operators and a fitness definition based solely on the behavior of a candidate solution measured with the very same computational resources as those experiencing the deteriorating effects, implicitly given inaccuracies do not require the EA's taking any additional measures. Non-constructive EA operators do not have a concept about a correct and incorrect gene behavior. Instead, changing the way some elements of the reconfigurable device work, even if not desired, can be seen as a special kind of a mutation operator and has no impact on the general EA scheme.

• **Changing system requirements:** Sharing resources between multiple applications, energy considerations and other system demands might motivate a change in, e.g., the solution's resources. Optimizing a circuit regarding, e.g., its size and speed, requires a redefinition of the objective function and a multi-objective EA. Additionally, while changes in the environment typically happen gradually, allowing for adaptation by the means of evolutionary optimization, changes in system resources are single events in time with a potentially large impact on a circuit's configuration. When drastically reducing the maximal usable area or the maximal propagation delay, the evolutionary process may need a substantial amount of time before generating a new and valid solution. In this situation, the property of modern Pareto-based MOEAs to evolve and propagate a general covering of the objective space helps to overcome this issue. In case of an instantaneous requirement change, an individual respecting the resource constraints while showing the highest functional quality can replace the actual solution.

• **Incompletely specified systems:** This use case does not strictly rely on the continuous *modus operandi*. When using EHW for compensating errors in the computational resources, the genotype precisely describes the utilized hardware at system start. Differences between the hardware and its model may occur later on. EHW can also be applied to situations where the precise working of the hardware is unknown or its functioning is only approximately modeled. A prominent application domain are analog reconfigurable circuits. Modeled by idealized behavior, their actual parameters such as gain, slew rate, and frequency behavior may vary significantly. Even so, as evolutionary algorithms typically are not constructive, this application domain is well suited for EHW systems.

The presented use cases show an EHW classification by application scenarios. Torresen presented a fine-grained taxonomy considering algorithmic elements, technical and technological details, and the *modus operandi* in [363]. Gordon and Bentley [137] span the EHW space along three dimensions: the *level of abstraction*, which describes the genotype's building block granularity, the *bias implementation*, that specifies an EA's application-specific and systematic knowledge, and the *hardware evaluation process*, differentiating between hardware- and software-based fitness evaluations.

Figure 3.2 and Figure 3.3 present a chronological overview of the most visible and original EHW publications. The illustrations start with the work of Higuchi et al. [163] and de Garis [93] in 1993. The contributions marked in bold represent surveys covering a coherent topic or the general development of EHW. Initially, genetic algorithms and reconfigurable digital electronic devices encompassed the basic notion of EHW [93, 163, 363]. While still predominant, in recent years, new hardware domains and algorithms have been adopted by EHW. The common research directions of EHW are:

1. the creation of new EHW architectures with novel hardware building blocks and genotype encoding models,

2. the improvement of digital EHW's evolvability and scalability by

   - the analysis of new algorithms, evolutionary operators, and general techniques, and
   - the employment of hardware and application specific knowledge,

3. robustness enhancement of deteriorating and aging effects within reconfigurable fabrics, and

4. the investigation of new hardware domains for their suitability for the Evolvable Hardware paradigm.

The focus of our work lies on the first two mentioned topics.

3.2 Digital Logic Evolvable Hardware

To prepare for the discussion of Evolvable Hardware architectures, this section introduces reconfigurable devices for the digital logic domain.

3.2.1 Reconfigurable Logic Devices

Today's popular reconfigurable logic devices can be roughly divided into the families of simple programmable logic devices (SPLD), complex programmable logic devices (CPLD), and field programmable gate arrays (FPGA). These families are distinguished by properties such as the complexity of the

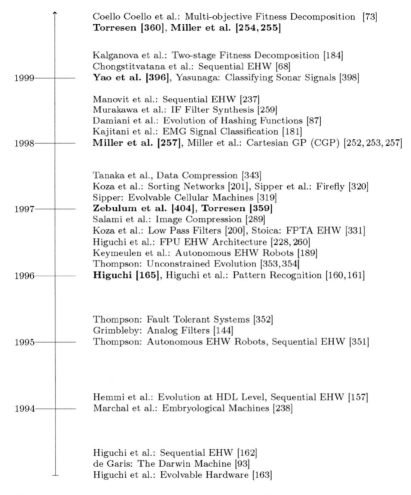

Coello Coello et al.: Multi-objective Fitness Decomposition [73]
Torresen [360], Miller et al. [254, 255]

Kalganova et al.: Two-stage Fitness Decomposition [184]
Chongstitvatana et al.: Sequential EHW [68]
Yao et al. [396], Yasunaga: Classifying Sonar Signals [398]

Manovit et al.: Sequential EHW [237]
Murakawa et al.: IF Filter Synthesis [259]
Damiani et al.: Evolution of Hashing Functions [87]
Kajitani et al.: EMG Signal Classification [181]
Miller et al. [257], Miller et al.: Cartesian GP (CGP) [252, 253, 257]

Tanaka et al., Data Compression [343]
Koza et al.: Sorting Networks [201], Sipper et al.: Firefly [320]
Sipper: Evolvable Cellular Machines [319]
Zebulum et al. [404], Torresen [359]
Salami et al.: Image Compression [289]
Koza et al.: Low Pass Filters [200], Stoica: FPTA EHW [331]
Higuchi et al.: FPU EHW Architecture [228, 260]
Keymeulen et al.: Autonomous EHW Robots [189]
Thompson: Unconstrained Evolution [353, 354]
Higuchi [165], Higuchi et al.: Pattern Recognition [160, 161]

Thompson: Fault Tolerant Systems [352]
Grimbleby: Analog Filters [144]
Thompson: Autonomous EHW Robots, Sequential EHW [351]

Hemmi et al.: Evolution at HDL Level, Sequential EHW [157]
Marchal et al.: Embryological Machines [238]

Higuchi et al.: Sequential EHW [162]
de Garis: The Darwin Machine [93]
Higuchi et al.: Evolvable Hardware [163]

1999
1998
1997
1996
1995
1994

Figure 3.2: Evolution of Evolvable Hardware: Some visible and original work on Evolvable Hardware considering applications, algorithmic innovations, failure tolerant systems, and architectures. Publications marked in bold provide surveys on EHW and its subfields.

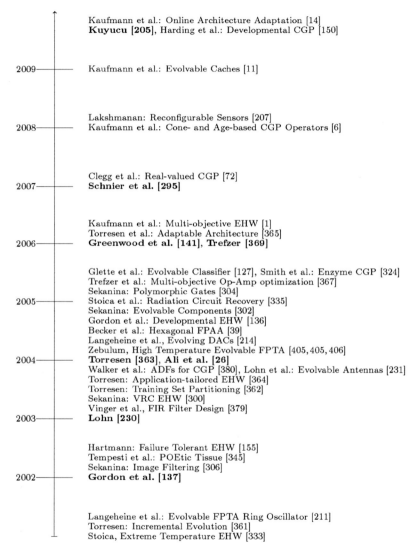

Figure 3.3: Evolution of Evolvable Hardware: Some visible and original work on Evolvable Hardware considering applications, algorithmic innovations, failure tolerant systems, and architectures. Publications marked in bold provide surveys on EHW and its subfields.

implementable circuits, the granularity of the functional blocks, input–output (IO) capabilities, memory sizes, and programmability. The application range spans from simple combinatorial circuits to multi-processor systems. This chapter starts with the motivation for PLD architectures from the perspective of digital logic design.

3.2.1.1 Simple Programmable Logic Devices

Any Boolean function has a unique representation by its *minterms*. To give an example and clarify the definitions, let us consider the function $f(a, b, c) = a(b + c)$. The corresponding truth table identifies M_5, M_6, and M_7 as the minterms of f:

a	b	c	$a(b+c)$	$minterm$	$notion$
0	0	0	0	$\bar{a}\bar{b}\bar{c}$	M_0
0	0	1	0	$\bar{a}\bar{b}c$	M_1
0	1	0	0	$\bar{a}b\bar{c}$	M_2
0	1	1	0	$\bar{a}bc$	M_3
1	0	0	0	$a\bar{b}\bar{c}$	M_4
1	0	1	1	$a\bar{b}c$	M_5
1	1	0	1	$ab\bar{c}$	M_6
1	1	1	1	abc	M_7

Alternatively, f can be rewritten as

$$
\begin{aligned}
f &= a(b + c) \\
&= ab + ac \\
&= ab(c + \bar{c}) + a(b + \bar{b})c \\
&= abc + ab\bar{c} + abc + a\bar{b}c \\
&= M_7 + M_6 + M_5.
\end{aligned}
$$

The presented general *sum-of-product* representation has a regular structure of n-ary conjunctions joined by a disjunction. The SPLD architecture is based on this structure, as shown in Figure 3.4. For any of the n inputs and their negations, a $2n$-input AND gate calculates a single minterm. A subsequent OR combines the outputs of multiple ANDs. To define the function of an SPLD, the interconnections on crossing points of the SPLD input lines and AND inputs, and the ANDs' output lines and OR inputs are programmable. Interconnection fuses can be set at least once after device manufacturing. Depending on the SPLD family, the device can also be manufactured with a specific or fixed programming for either the AND-planes or the OR-planes. For more complex and sequential circuits, ORs outputs can be fed back directly or through clocked registers to serve as inputs. Popular SPLDs, such as the 16V8, 20V8 and 22V10, are produced today by companies such as, e.g., Atmel and Lattice Semiconductor.

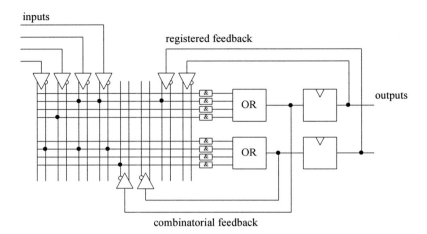

Figure 3.4: A simple programmable logic device consists of an AND-plane and an OR-plane evaluating a sum-of-product representation of a Boolean function. An SPLD is configured by setting the fuses on the wire interconnections. OR outputs can be fed back directly or with an interposed register to allow more complex and sequential functions.

3.2.1.2 Complex Programmable Logic Devices

Complex programmable logic devices (CPLD) extend the idea of SPLDs by introducing a more flexible programmable interconnect and larger and multiple logic block arrays. Additionally, memory elements allow for synchronous and state-full designs. Figure 3.5 presents the generalized structure of a CPLD. The central element is the programmable interconnect. It is enclosed by blocks containing multiple, SPLD-like structures called the *macro cells*. Macro cells connect to the chip's pins through buffering IO blocks. Today's popular CPLD manufacturers are, e.g., Altera with the MAX II and Xilinx with the Coolrunner II families.

3.2.1.3 Field Programmable Gate Arrays

First introduced by Xilinx Inc. 1985 [79], a *Field Programmable Gate Array* (FPGA) is an array of logic cells placed in an infrastructure of interconnections [291] (Figure 3.6). Together with the Input/Output blocks, the general FPGA structure remained the same while the complexity and versatility of the components increased over time. The following sections describe the primary components, architectural elements, and the design tool flow of an FPGA.

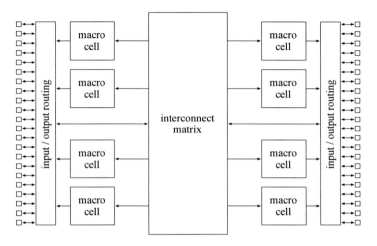

Figure 3.5: A complex programmable logic device consists of a programmable interconnect joining multiple macrocells. Each macrocell is composed of SPLD-like elements.

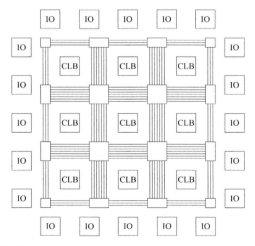

Figure 3.6: Field programmable gate arrays: Array of logic cells placed in an infrastructure of interconnections [291].

Configurable logic blocks (CLB) are the basic reconfigurable components of an FPGA, containing one or multiple universal logic cells. Logic
cells are implemented as *look up tables* (LUT). That is, with n inputs, a LUT
is a 2^n bit memory where every bit is separately addressable. Thus, any
Boolean function with n inputs can be realized by an n-input LUT. A LUT
can also be used as a memory element and as a shift register. Additionally,
LUTs can be cascaded to form deeper and wider memories, deeper shift registers, and wide multiplexers [393, 394]. The CLB structure of the popular
Virtex FPGA family from Xilinx divides into three levels: multiple LUTs
are joined in a *slice*, while two slices form a CLB (Figure 3.7). The general
structure of a Xilinx Virtex-5 FPGA slice is shown in Figure 3.8. It contains
four 6-input LUTs that can be configured to implement four pairs of 5-input
LUTs. In the latter case, a pair of adjunct LUTs share the same inputs. LUT
outputs can be routed to CLB outputs directly or through registers allowing for synchronous behavior. In addition to the slice structures shown in
Figure 3.8, LUTs may employ a specialized interconnect, called *carry chains*,
to implement wide arithmetic operators and logic gates. Carry chains allow
fast signal propagation between adjacent CLBs (cf. Figure 3.7). However,
as only vertically adjacent CLBs are connected by fast carry chain lines, this
also restricts the placing of circuits using these particular resources.

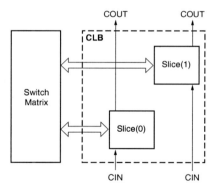

Figure 3.7: Xilinx FPGA *configurable logic block* [394].

The routing architecture of common island style FPGAs is presented in
Figure 3.9. The functional blocks are connected to the routing facilities by
connect blocks (CB). A variant of a CB structure is presented in Figure 3.9.
The interconnect has the topology of a 2-dimensional grid with programmable
switching boxes (SB) on the junctions. To improve the propagation delays
for non-local connections, some of the horizontal and vertical lines connect

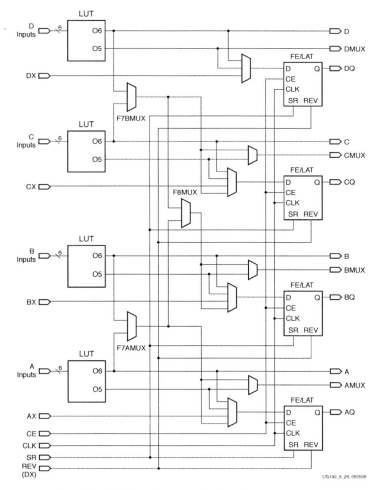

Figure 3.8: Simplified Xilinx Virtex-5 slice [394]. Four 6-input LUTs can be used as four pairs of 5-input LUTs.

distant SBs, skipping intermediate SBs. Figure 3.10 presents an example for regular and long lines having lengths of 1 and 2, respectively.

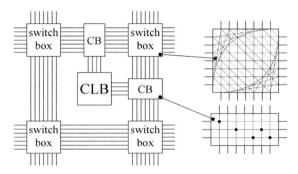

Figure 3.9: General FPGA interconnect architecture [141]. Configurable logic blocks are connected through connect blocks to switching boxes.

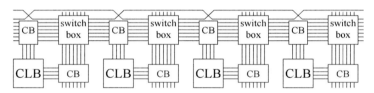

Figure 3.10: Local and global routing [141]: To minimize propagation delays, connections between distant CLBs can be implemented by wires spanning multiple SBs.

A different approach for minimizing the propagation delay is the hierarchical routing approach implemented by the historical Xilinx XC6200 FPGA family and by some newer FPGA devices. The XC6200 implements a uniform hierarchical routing approach which is based on the assumption that a well-routed circuit has mostly local connections [156]. Thus, the FPGA is divided into clusters of 4 × 4 CLBs or cells, where only local routing is available. Connections between clusters are organized hierarchically: a 4 × 4 group of clusters implements cluster to cluster communications by wires of length 4, connecting the cluster's border cells. Similarly, on the next hierarchy level, a 4 × 4 group of 4 × 4 groups of clusters is connected by wires of length 16. This scheme is applied recursively forming larger groups and using longer wires. Figure 3.11 illustrates the routing scheme.

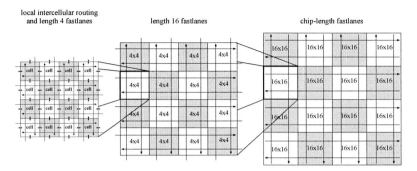

Figure 3.11: XC6200 hierarchical routing.

Extended logic elements.   In addition to CLBs, modern FPGAs provide specialized functional elements such as, e.g., memories, arithmetic operators, and processor units. While such elements can be implemented using CLBs, a dedicated circuit is faster and more resource efficient. The following list summarizes some of the specialized functional elements of modern FPGAs:

- **Block memory:** FPGA's on-chip memory is typically implemented in two ways: as distributed RAM using LUT memory cells and as block RAM (BRAM) using dedicated memory elements. Xilinx' BRAMs are realized as cascadeable and dual ported RAMs with parametrizable data port widths. Additionally, BRAMs can be used as FIFOs and content addressable memories (CAM).

- **Arithmetic/logical units:** The realization of complex arithmetic functions, such as multiplication, using CLBs is not very efficient [156]. To speed up the computation and to reduce resource costs, modern FP-GAs provide arithmetic/logical units distributed on the chip. The functional set of the so called *DSP blocks* is typically limited to addition and multiplication. DSP blocks of recent Xilinx Virtex FPGA devices additionally compute some Boolean and comparator functions [393, 394]. Connected by fast communication lines, DSP blocks can be efficiently cascaded for wide arithmetic computations.

- **Processors** combine memories and arithmetic/logical units into a computational pipeline. Some Xilinx Virtex FPGAs implement ARM and IBM PowerPC variants running at multiples of 100 MHz. The processors contain instruction and data caches and are powerful enough to run full-fledged operating systems. In addition, the FPGA internal configuration port is accessible within the processor address space. This encourages the design of run-time reconfigurable hardware systems.

- **I/O blocks:** An FPGA's versatility is reflected by the broad range of I/O functions it implements. From simple high-impedance pull-up and -down pins to differential buses and high speed transceivers with dedicated serial/parallel converters, FPGA I/O blocks implement a large number of different communication standards. Additionally, multiple clock interface pins allow for external frequency sources.

- **Clock networks:** Modern FPGAs implement multiple clock distribution networks for coherent clock bases across the chip fabric. The clock networks can be driven by integrated frequency synthesis components, external clock sources, and user defined logic.

Hardware description languages (HDL). In contrast to procedural software programming languages, which are inherently single-threaded, HDLs are able to model the parallelism and time behavior of concurrent hardware components. While initially introduced to capture and simulate circuit behavior, HDLs were quickly extended to the procedure of circuit synthesis for manufacturing and configuring electronic devices.

A circuit is described in prominent HDLs such as VHDL and Verilog by its behavior and its structure. The behavioral description notes the input–output relations without getting specific about the underlying implementation, whereas the structural description specifies the functional elements and their connections, typically expressed by a schematic or its textual equivalent. HDLs support a hierarchical design and composition process: a circuit can be partitioned into modules at different functional levels.

The design flow of FPGA circuits typically follows the sequence presented in Figure 3.12. After specifying the requirements, a circuit can be described by its structure and behavior in a HDL. Afterward, the *synthesis* step breaks the description down to basic elements such as gates and registers while obeying some restrictions on, e.g., the circuit size. The logic function of the circuit is also minimized during the synthesis step. For this, the circuit description is mapped to the *register-transfer-level* (RTL) representation. In the RTL, the circuits are formalized as a transfer function between register stages [156]. RTL captures Boolean equations, memories, and connectivity elements [79]. After the synthesis is completed, a circuit's building blocks are rewritten to match the actual hardware components of the FPGA. The *mapping* allows also for restructuring the circuit for an efficient use of FPGA resources. The subsequent *place & route* step tries to arrange the mapped building blocks and route the wiring. The automatic procedure typically uses a heuristic, as the mapping has to consider device limitations on, e.g., the amount of building blocks, their spatial locations on the device, the routing capacity, and signal propagation delays. The designer may also add additional limitations on timing, placement, and routing. In the final step, the FPGA binary program, called the *bitstream*, is derived from the placed and routed circuit. Loaded into the FPGA, the bitstream configures the FPGA to implement the goal function.

Figure 3.12: FPGA design tool flow. In the logic synthesis step, a circuit description is transformed into a netlist. This step often also includes logic minimization. Functional simulation can be applied after logic synthesis to verify the circuit behavior. In the technology mapping step, the netlist elements are mapped to functional elements of a concrete reconfigurable device. Afterwards, the circuit gets placed and routed. At this stage, circuit analysis may also reveal temporal aspects of the circuit. In the final bitstream generation step, the FPGA configuration string is created.

Reconfigurable computing. The intriguing property of FPGAs is their reconfigurability, allowing for the implementation of arbitrary Boolean functions of an appropriate size even after an FPGA has been manufactured. Initially used for prototyping and low volume productions, FPGAs quickly gained attention as a general computation platform [302]. Their inherent parallelism and the raw speed of a hardware implementation promoted their popularity. FPGA configuration methods can be divided according to whether the reconfiguration and computing are mutually exclusive and whether a device can be reconfigured completely or partially.

- **The multi-context FPGA** concept manages several configurations in the device's shadow memory to quickly switch the currently computed function. Having the drawback of additional configuration data storage and control, reconfiguration of multi-context FPGAs is very fast, taking only few cycles [156]. Furthermore, the loading of a new configuration does not interfere with the computing of the currently instantiated function. Especially, for high performance applications with large functions, which are partitioned into multiple FPGA-sized procedures, fast switching is essential. Despite the performance of multi-context FPGAs reconfiguration, today's major share of the FPGA market is covered by single-context FPGAs. Resource efficient and therefore cheap, single-context FPGAs match the common use case of sporadic reconfiguration, where timing constraints are not tight.

- **Partial reconfiguration** allows modifying a fraction of the FPGA configuration without touching the remaining area. Along with the instantiation of new functions, the method is also used to speed up the update of an existent solution by renewing only the area that must change.

An early partially reconfigurable device was introduced 1990 by Algo-tronix [25,188] and developed further by Xilinx [71,391] as the XC6200. It offers fine grained reconfiguration at the CLB and wire level. The architecture details and the complete reconfiguration procedure were made publicly accessible. Today, Xilinx supports partial reconfigura-bility for the Virtex FPGAs. Details of the internal circuitry and the bitstream format are not fully available to the public. However, Xilinx provides specialized tool flow chains such as PlanAhead [392] and the early access partial design flow [235] to generate partially reconfigurable bitstreams.

Atmel is another manufacturer building reconfigurable logic devices. With the FPSLIC family, Atmel combines an embedded processor and a reconfigurable fabric on a single die [34]. While only incomplete information from the manufacturer is provided on the reconfiguration details of the FPGA, the bitstream format is almost fully unfolded and published [243]. Similar to the XC6200 devices, the FPSLIC family allows for fine-granular reconfiguration on the CLB and wire level.

With partial reconfiguration, while being a comprehensible concept, there are multiple issues to be considered: the configuration time is proportional to the size of the reconfigured area. For applications where reconfiguration should be executed frequently and where the latency of reconfiguration is restricted, this reconfiguration time, of up to some milliseconds, might become significant. Additionally, generating partial bitstreams is computationally demanding, requiring the preprocessing and storing of all the partial bitstream variants for potential future floor-plans.

With the ability for reconfiguration, FPGAs became general under the func-tional aspect. Dynamic reconfiguration extends FPGAs coverage additionally to run-time adaptable functions. With the internally accessible configuration interface, FPGAs allow creating self-contained and compact adaptable hard-ware systems.

3.2.2 Programmable logic array Evolvable Hardware

Higuchi et al. [163] demonstrated one of the earliest works on combining reconfigurable hardware devices with genetic algorithms to create on-line adaptable embedded systems. The authors employed an electrically erasable and reprogrammable sum-of-product GAL16V8 device from Lattice. Intro-duced in Section 3.2.1.1, the device is capable of computing up to 8 sums of products on up to 16 inputs and their negations [160]. The generalized structure of GAL16V8 is illustrated in Figure 3.13. It consists of two switch

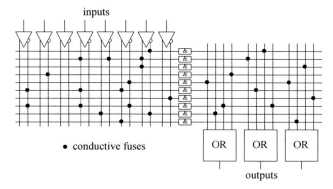

Figure 3.13: Generalized programmable logic array architecture employed in the experiments of Higuchi et al. [163]

matrices selecting the inputs for the intermediate AND gates and the AND outputs for the closing OR gates. The GAL's logic function is given by configuration matrices, which are treated in [163] as genotypes and exposed to the effects of evolutionary operators. The authors verified their concept on a 4-bit multiplexer, a 3-bit counter, and a 4-bit state machine. In follow-up work [181], a streamlined custom chip EHW implementation was presented, comprising a hardware GA, two larger programmable logic arrays with their associated input vector memories, and a NEC V30 processor. The device was used to evolve a muscular activity classifier for a motorized upper limb prosthesis control. An even more sophisticated concept was introduced by the authors in [160]: a fully parallelized hardware GA with a pool of reconfigurable PLAs, allowing for a substantial reduction in computation time.

3.2.3 Unconstrained Evolution

Digital circuits are perceived predominantly from the deterministic perspective. However, Boolean gate circuitry is build upon regular transistors with unique analog switching behaviors, connected by wires of different lengths, capacitances, and propagation characteristics. A design space considering the analog facets of digital circuit elements is by far more complicated than its synchronous counterpart and would hardly be considered by human designers. However, when using automatized design tools, this domain becomes more accessible.

Thompson presented, in a series of publications [351–355], his work on unconstrained evolution. Initially motivated by the construction of an evolvable robot controller, he focused on circuits that derive their frequency domain behaviors from unique transistor properties and propagation delays in latter

53

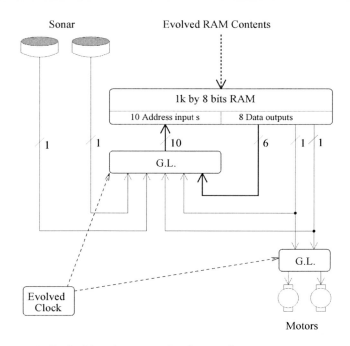

Figure 3.14: Evolvable robot controller [351, 352]: The robot comprises two ultrasonic range sensors, two genetic latches (GL), a transition state memory, and an evolved clock generator. The ultrasonic signal generator pings at 5 Hz asynchronously to the remaining robot circuitry. Sonar return echos are wired through GLs and the behavior memory directly to motor drivers. Evolution may configure the GL latches to wire-through and latching modes.

publications.

We start with Thompson's earliest work. Figure 3.14 presents the concept of an evolvable robot controller. The controller comprises two ultrasonic sonars, catching echos of continuously transmitted ranging impulses with a frequency of 5Hz. The detected signals propagate through two genetic latches (GL) and a behavior state machine directly to the motor drivers for the left and right wheels. An evolvable frequency generator provides the system clock. Evolution takes place at three locations: the basic robot behavior is realized by an finite state machine (FSM) implemented by a memory device. The memory content is subject to evolution. The GA also determines whether a signal wired through a genetic latch will be clocked or proceed directly to the GL's outputs. The third entity that is subject to the genetic algorithm is the evolvable clock generator.

The focus of Thomson's earliest publications is the evolution of wall avoidance [351, 352]. Based on the introduced simulative results for the evolvable frequency generator, Thomson implemented the idea on a real FPGA in [353]. The configuration bitstream of a Xilinx XC6212 [391] FPGA became the subject of GA operators, acting at the bit level. As presented in Section 3.2.1.3, the XC6200 FPGA family allows this kind of bitstream manipulation without consequences for the chip integrity. In the first experiment, the author studied the evolvability of 1 kHz, 10 kHz, 100 kHz, and 1 MHz frequency generators. To this end, 10 × 10 cells in the upper left FPGA corner were used to implement candidate solutions. The fitness was determined by evaluating the output frequencies for a period of one second. Similar to results from the initial publications, no secondary frequency sources were used. The behavior of the evolved frequency generators was based solely on signal propagation delays and transistor properties. The experiments showed convergent behavior for all four settings.

For the second experiment, Thompson extended the previous circuit setup by an input pin, as shown in Figure 3.15 (a). The GA's objective function was redefined to differentiate between 1 kHz and 10 kHz input frequencies. To this end, one of the frequencies was applied to the input pin for one-half second and a candidate solution's frequency response was measured on the output pin. The measurement was repeated in random order for both frequencies, so that every frequency was measured five times. Figure 3.15 (c) shows the input frequencies and their responses for the best solutions in the denoted generations. The analysis of the best evolved tone discriminator is done by Thompson et al. in [355, 357]. The circuit is presented in Figure 3.15 (a). To identify the nodes contributing to the discriminator's function, in the first step all nodes are excluded that do not lie on the signal propagation paths connected to the output pin. The result is presented in Figure 3.15 (a). In the next step, a search algorithm tests all nodes as to whether they contribute to the circuit's output, by setting their function to a constant. Figure 3.15 (b) shows nodes that cannot be clamped without affecting the computed function. Gray colored nodes are relays.

Figure 3.16 presents a schematic equivalent to the circuit in Figure 3.15 (b). The schematic can be divided into three parts. The authors discovered that output changes happen only after the input signal switches low. Thus, they focus their investigation on this time window. During an input "1", the gates of parts A and B become non-oscillating, configuring part C multiplexer to choose input's "1". Part C inverter chain realizes a 9 ns non-inverting time delay, forming during a high-going input circuit's output. The authors also observed that the circuit responds correctly to short (200 μs) high-going pulses setting the output to "1", while long high-going pulses reset the output to "0". The circuit "decides" in roughly 200 ns after a falling edge of the input,

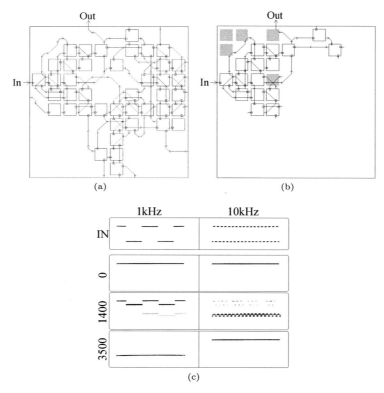

Figure 3.15: Evolving a 1 kHz / 10k Hz tone discriminator [353, 354]: Evolution takes place in 10×10 cells in the upper left corner of the XC6212 FPGA. Figure (a) shows the best solution wires and nodes connected by a path to the output pin. Cell functions, while being also subject to evolution, are omitted for clarity. Figure (b) pictures constant function nodes in gray that cannot be clamped without affecting the circuit's fitness. Figure (c) illustrates the fitness development for the best individual in the initial, the 1400th, and the 3500th generation.

how long the high-going pulse was. This can not be explained exclusively by Boolean logic behavior, as during an input ' '1", Parts A, B, and C as well, are in static states. After exhaustive PSPICE simulations and a circuit reimplementation by discrete elements, the authors found the initial dynamics of part A occurring after a falling input edge as decisive. They assume that

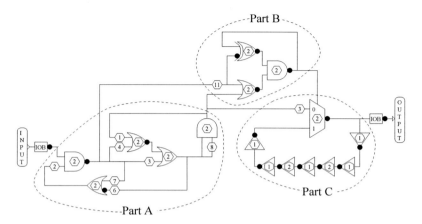

Figure 3.16: Evolving a 1 kHz / 10 kHz tone discriminator [353,354]: Boolean logic equivalent schematic of the solution shown in Figure 3.15 (b).

some FPGA implementation details such as "slow charge/discharge," "unknown parasitic capacitances," and "subtle property of the VLSI medium" might relate to the length of the high-going input and therefore affect the circuit's decision.

In following work [356], Thompson and Layzell refined the tone discriminator experiment by diversifying the fitness evaluation. To this end, a candidate solution was evaluated by four FC6212 FPGAs, bonded in different packages, powered by different kinds of power supplies and at different voltages. Additionally, the location of the reconfigurable area was altered and a 6 MHz clock provided an external frequency source. The goal of the experiment was to evolve a robust design that would be independent of the underlying hardware platform. In fact, the authors successfully evolved a tone discriminator circuit that was operable on all FPGAs and could be correctly simulated by PSPICE. However, while being a design lying completely in the Boolean logic domain, the circuit has utilized variable delay components with an implementation that had not been fully understood and analyzed by the authors. Additionally, the simulation showed the existence of transient spikes in the circuit.

The initial tone discriminator experiment shows impressively the potential of circuit evolution. The aspects are two-fold: An innovative circuit of only 32 cells was evolved, able to differentiate between events from a 200,000 times slower time domain. However, as all the degrees of freedom on an FPGA were open to evolution, transistor properties, circuit placement, the FPGA's technology and manufacturing process, the kind of power supply, the interaction with the connected instruments, the temperature and electromagnetic interdependencies with the environment, are unique and may play a pivotal role for the evolved function. The solution evolved in the second tone discriminator experiment, while still able to explore the unconstrained design space, is much closer to conventionally engineered solutions. Still, the circuits from both experiments demonstrate properties and design principles a human engineer is not yet able to employ efficiently.

From the conceptual point of view, the authors outline the following conclusion. In both tone discriminator experiments, the evolution was able to explore the complete and unconstrained design space. The genotype used by the GA modeled the deterministic world of an FPGA configuration bitstream. However, for the complete genotype definition, implicitly given properties of the evaluation platform and its environment had to be considered. In the first experiment, the evolution found a solution in the unconstrained search space while in the second experiment, where the evolution was also able to explore the search space beyond Boolean logic circuits, the evolution discovered a deterministic solution. This solution, however, employed design elements a human designer would avoid. The authors concluded that the discovered circuit might lie in a Boolean logic region that is "beyond the scope of conventional design rules" [356] and that unconstrained evolution does not necessarily require new design domains in order to create innovative solutions beyond the world of human creativity.

3.2.4 The POEtic Tissue Project

The POEtic Tissue Project (the 'P,' 'O,' and 'E' come from the concepts of phylogeny, ontogeny, and epigenetics, to be explained below) is a joint project of the universities of York, Barcelona (UPC), Glasgow, and EPFL, and extends the idea of evolutionary electronic hardware with the aspects of organic growth and learning. The Evolvable Hardware principle is understood basically as the development through inherited changes of the genotype. The ways biological entities such as viruses, single- and multi-cellular organisms, and other life forms develop through time can roughly be specified by three mechanisms:

- Replication and specialization of cells, creating larger structures such as organs and complete organisms. This process is known as ontogeny and morphogenesis.

- Learning, as the interaction with the environment creates immunological, cognitive, and behavioral patterns. Learning is also the nongenetic inheritance of acquired characteristics. The area of learning is subsumed under the category of epigenetics.

- Development through inherited changes of the genotype is summarized under the category of phylogeny.

Phylogeny, ontogeny and epigenesis span the biologically inspired POEspace of development. The goal of The POEtic Project is to investigate all these mentioned biological development principles on an electronic platform. Consequently, POEtic tissue is realized by a grid of regular cells. Populations, organisms, and organs are composed within the POEtic world from these cells, as shown in Figure 3.17 (a). A single cell itself divides into "molecules," as illustrated in Figure 3.17 (b), universal and reconfigurable POE elements are able to implement the function of a LUT, a shift register, a memory element, a configuration bitstream pipe, and an intercellular communication interface.

The POEtic tissue classification within the POE space is shown in Figure 3.18. It is a logic subdivision partitioned by the cellular separation. Each cell is a self-contained system able to carry the genotype of the entire tissue. The creation of an individual begins with the selection of a set of genes. This is done in the "genotype" layer, shown in Figure 3.18. The following step of organism growth by differentiation and specialization is realized in the "mapping" level. Finally, "learning" as the acquisition of knowledge during the cell's lifetime is applied in the "phenotype" level.

The cellular reconfigurable architecture of the POEtic tissue project was used to investigate biologically inspired design principles in the examples of self-healing and repair [141, 227], organic growth [372], and routing [349, 350]. More information can be found in [197, 285, 345, 346].

3.2.5 Evolvable Components

One of Sekanina's main research subjects in the area of Evolvable Hardware is that of virtual reconfigurable architectures. In his book, *Evolvable Components: From Theory to Hardware Implementations,* he proposes a component-style view and the decomposition of Evolvable Hardware to allow circuit designers to use and benefit from modularized and self-contained adaptive elements. To this end, general EHW building blocks such as the genetic algorithm, evolution control, input data memories, and a computation model are encapsulated in a component, leaving non-general elements such as the fitness evaluation and calculation as well as the triggering of the re-evolution to the expertise of the application designer. To demonstrate his approach, Sekanina presented a universal evolvable component implementation and verified it on multiple benchmarks from the image processing domain.

The basis for Sekanina's evolvable component is an adopted computational model of a generalized FPGA. It comprises a two-dimensional array of functional nodes embedded into an interconnect. Only feed-forward connections

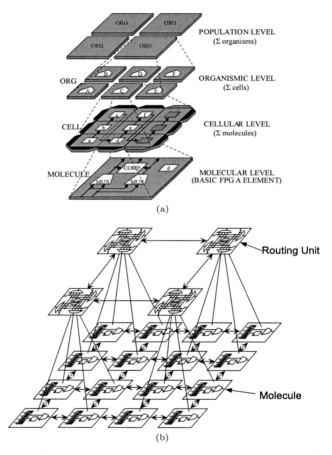

Figure 3.17: POEtic tissue: Figure (a) shows the abstraction layers [372] and Figure (b) a cell decomposition and its communication infrastructure [350].

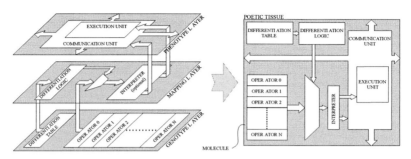

Figure 3.18: POEtic tissue [372]: POEtic tissue within the POE taxonomy.

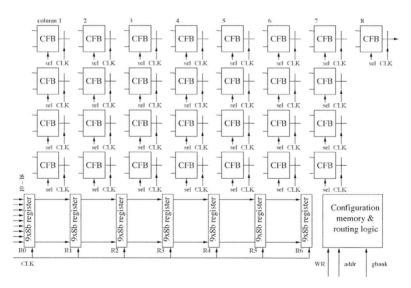

Figure 3.19: Evolvable components [300]: Adoption of a general FPGA as a computational model. In a pipelined architecture, Configurable Functional Blocks may use results from the previous column and values of the primary inputs. The primary outputs are taken from the CFBs in the last column.

61

are allowed, restricting the design space to combinatorial logic. Any node might connect to primary inputs and nodes in the previous l columns. Primary outputs might connect to any nodes and to primary inputs. The precise formalization is done with the help of the Cartesian genetic programming (CGP) model, described in Section 3.4.

Sekanina's concrete implementation of a virtual reconfigurable circuit (VRC) is shown in Figure 3.19. It is a pipelined realization with 29 configurable functional blocks (CFB), each operating on two 8-bit wide inputs. The architecture comprises nine 8-bit primary inputs and one 8-bit primary output. A CFB in column i might operate on the results computed in column $i-1$ and on the primary inputs. The architecture's output is provided by the CFB in the last column. The pipelining stages are defined by CFBs columns. The primary inputs are pipelined synchronously to the stages by auxiliary register banks. The functional set of a CFB is presented in Figure 3.20.

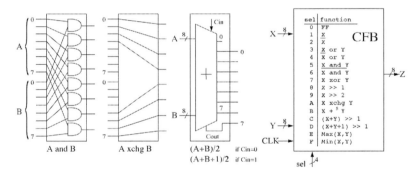

Figure 3.20: Evolvable components [300]: A configurable functional block operates on two 8-bit inputs. The functional set is listed in the right-hand table.

The combination of the general genetic unit and the VRC with application-specific circuitry for image processing application is presented in Figure 3.21. The genetic unit comprises an evolutionary algorithm with a mutation unit, genotype memory, and a random number generator. Additionally, a state machine controls the configuration and pipelined fitness evaluation of the VRC.

When considering image filtering to, e.g., reduce noisy pixels, a filter's quality is typically quantized by the visual difference between a noise free image and its filtered version, to which noisy pixels are added beforehand. Image differences are measured in Figure 3.21 by accumulating the absolute differences between the original noise free and the filtered pixels. Figure 3.22 helps

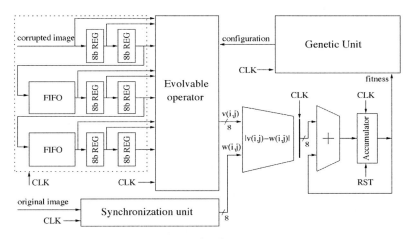

Figure 3.21: Evolvable components [300] for image processing applications. The general genetic unit and reconfigurable functional array components are combined with application-specific image row buffers, marked by a dashed box, and the fitness calculation circuit in the lower right corner.

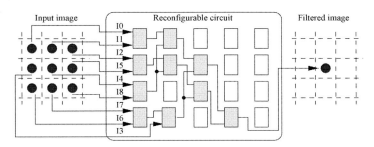

Figure 3.22: Evolvable components [300]: Image processing with the reconfigurable functional array. The filtered value for the central pixel of the input image is computed considering the pixel values of its neighbors.

clarify the input data processing of Figure 3.21. For a given pixel, the image filter model uses its neighbor pixels to compute the filtered pixel value. As illustrated in Figure 3.22, to filter the central pixel of a region in the left-hand input image, six directly neighboring pixels are provided to the VRC, which then computes the filtered value. When the image is stored linearly, pixel by pixel and row after row, accessing it in the same order requires the introduction of row buffers, to be able to extract and provide a contiguous image area to the VRC. In Figure 3.21, the extraction of a 3×3 image area is therefore realized by two line buffers.

Figure 3.23: Evolving a salt and pepper filter [240]: The upper row shows original images after randomizing 5% of the pixels to black and white. The lower row shows the filtered images. The filter was trained on Lenna image.

The presented VRC and the complete architecture from Figure 3.21 can operate at 134.8 MHz. With a pipelined VRC configuration and a fitness evaluation time for a 254×254 pixels image of roughly $(254 - 2)^2 \cdot 134.8\,\mathrm{MHz}^{-1} \approx 0.48$ ms, the genetic unit in Figure 3.21 has enough time to produce offspring individuals in parallel to the fitness evaluation. Thus, the complete architecture can run the evolution at the highest frequency possible. The system clearly shows the performance benefits of a register-reconfigurable architecture. While built upon generalized components, adaptation to application domains is possible just by defining the data interfaces, the fitness metric computation, and the re-evolution triggering.

Sekanina and his coauthors applied the presented architecture to evolve a wide range of image filters [299, 306, 310, 312, 322, 377]. Figure 3.23 illustrates noised and filtered images from [240]. The evolvable filter was trained using the Lenna image and tested on the remaining images. Apart from the image processing applications, Sekanina applied the concept of evolvable components to sorting networks [301, 303, 305] and arithmetic circuits [307].

3.2.6 The Functional Unit Row Architecture

Glette and Torresen presented a run-time reconfigurable EHW architecture tailored to signal classification [127]. To facilitate online evolution, the classifier architecture can be controlled in its function through configuration registers, similar to Sekanina's VRC approach [309]. A GA has been developed for the execution on a PowerPC 405 core of the Xilinx Virtex-II Pro FPGA family [127] and on a MicroBlaze soft processor core available for a greater number of Xilinx FPGA devices [131]. A more hardware-specific implementation, which saves resources by utilizing lower level FPGA reconfiguration abilities, has been explored in [366].

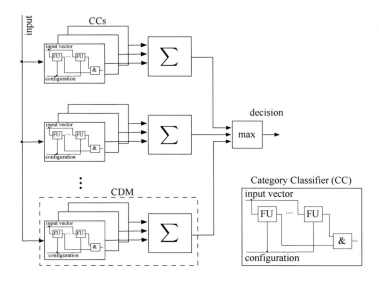

Figure 3.24: High level structure of the functional unit row architecture.

Glette's *Functional Unit Row* (FUR) architecture has a general high level structure illustrated in Figure 3.24. The input pattern is presented to a

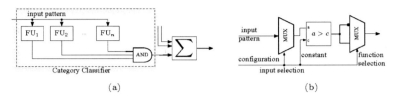

(a)   (b)

Figure 3.25: Category classifier (CC) and functional unit architectures. CC outputs (Figure (a)) are connected to an n-input AND gate. Multiple CCs with a subsequent counter for activated CCs make up a category detection module (CDM). The CDM with the highest number of activated CCs determines the FUR classification decision. A CC consists of multiple functional units (FU), which are the basic pattern matching elements of the FUR architecture (Figure (b)). An FU uses a data MUX selecting which of the input data to feed to the functions ">" and "$\leq$". The constant c with which the selected input data is compared, is given by the configuration lines. Then, a result MUX selects which of the function results to output.

number of subfunctions called *classifier circuits* (CCs). A CC is a function with a binary output indicating for an input vector a match or a mismatch to the trained category. Several CCs classifying the same category are grouped into a *category detection module* (CDM) and their outputs are fed into a counter summarizing the number of matches. The FUR's global decision is made by selecting the category with the highest number of matches. In case of a tie, the category with the lower index wins.

The FUR architecture belongs to the family of *ensemble classifiers*. The idea of an ensemble classifier is to train a set of diverse classifiers on the same training set and to combine the predictions. The FUR architecture can also be seen as an extension of the early EHW architectures of Kajitani (cf. Section 3.2.2) and Torresen [361]. Kajitani has used a single Boolean sum of products (SOP) function to realize a CDM, while Torresen has utilized a two stage scheme of multiple SOPs and a SOP subset selector for CDM implementation. The maximal number of activated SOPs in Torresen's architecture defines the global decision.

CCs in the FUR architecture decompose into multiple basic pattern matching elements—the *Functional Units* (FU) (cf. Figure 3.25(a)). The input data is presented to each FU on a common input bus. The outputs of FUs of a certain CC are fed into an AND gate. Thus, a CC reports a "hit" to the according CDM counter only if all its FUs indicate a "match."

The FUs are the reconfigurable elements of the architecture. Their configuration is captured by the genotype. As illustrated in Figure 3.25 (b), the FU

Table 3.1: Mutation probability distribution for the FUR architecture [127].

number of mutations	0	1	2	3
selection probability	0.1	0.6	0.2	0.1

configuration encodes the input vector and function selection as well as the function parametrization. The choice of the FU function is not restricted, however, ">" and "$\leq$" are selected as these functions have been shown to work well throughout a set of experiments [127]. Altogether, the FU transfer function for an input data a, a constant c, and the function selection bit s is defined by:

$$FU(a, c, s) = \left\{ \begin{array}{lll} s & : & \text{if } a > c \\ \bar{s} & : & \text{else.} \end{array} \right.$$

In this specific FU configuration, FUR's classification principle is closely related to the classification principle of decision trees. Decision trees realize decision boundaries with sections of straight lines that must be parallel to the axes of the input space spanned by all input data elements. FUR replaces DT's hierarchical decision trees by enumerable decision forests. In Section 7.2, the similarity of both classification principles will be demonstrated by similar recognition performances.

The FUR architecture implements n-point recombination and mutation schemes. For an efficient implementation, the mutation operator first selects the number of mutations n and then randomly selects n mutation locations within the genotype. The probability distribution of n is given by Table 3.1.

The authors propose a specialized evolution scheme for the FUR architecture. Each CDM is evolved separately, allowing for parallel execution. The evolution of a CDM is done incrementally. That is, a single CC is evolved from scratch until it reaches some classification accuracy or a maximal generation number. After that, the first CC is fixated and a randomly initialized second CC is added to the CDM. The evolution now tries to improve the CDM's overall classification accuracy by evolving the second CC and stops if some classification accuracy or a maximal generation number is reached. This scheme is repeated until the evolution of a complete CDM is finished. The authors motivate the incremental evolution scheme by its faster convergence due to the reduced genotype size undergoing evolution and the FUR's ability to operate already after even one CC in each CDM has been evolved.

Figure 3.26 displays the FUR run-time adaptation architecture. The architecture splits into a CPU running the evolutionary algorithm and two FUR implementations. The first implementation is used by the EA to evaluate the fitness of candidate solutions while the second implementation runs the best solution on real world data. The FUR architecture has been evaluated on different benchmarks such as face recognition [128, 130, 131], sonar return

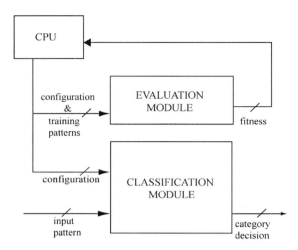

Figure 3.26: The FUR hardware implementation structure [127].

classification [129], and the categorization of electromyographic signals [7,9]. Its performance has been proven to be similar to that of state of the art methods such as neural networks and support vector machines.

In our work, we use the FUR architecture as a reference EHW system for comparison with our methods (cf. Section 7.1). Additionally, we use the FUR architecture to investigate run-time resource adaptation techniques in Section 7.2.

3.3   Analog Evolvable Hardware

Field programmable analog arrays (FPAA) are the analog world equivalent of FPGAs. Modern FPAAs share with FPGAs the basic structure of functional blocks embedded in a configurable interconnect. The functional nodes, the *Configurable Analog Blocks* (CAB), contain an amplifier, which can range from a single transistor to a complex operational amplifier. For some architectures, as will be presented later in this section, the node characteristics are configured by selecting the amplification element from a pool of amplifiers with different configurations. More popular, however, is the amplifier parametrization by tuning the surrounding circuitry, consisting of adjustable resistors and capacitors. FPAA manufacturers produce CABs tailored to some applications such as high precision and linear sensor processing and power efficient and high speed arithmetic calculations. Applications subject to rough conditions such as high radiation doses and temperature changes are an intriguing area for FPAAs. Here, radiation hardened FPAAs reduce the certification costs by providing a platform for analog designs. Custom circuits on the contrary need to undergo the complete qualification process for every new design. Additionally, circuitry that is capable of compensating for large temperature changes can be placed outside a temperature stabilized electronics box, next to the sensors and actuators, saving on wiring and weight.

The evolution of configurable analog devices is presented in Figure 3.27. It covers different flavors including gain amplifiers, filters, potentiometers, capacitors and mixed signal devices. The following sections present three architectures with functional elements consisting of single transistors, transistor arrays, and operational amplifiers. Each section also summarizes the architecture's application within the EHW domain.

3.3.1 Heidelberg Field Programmable Transistor Array

The architecture developed by Langeheine et al. [211] belongs to the family of the *Field Programmable Transistor Array* (FPTA) devices. It consists of 16×16 CABs surrounded by 64 I/O blocks, as shown in Figure 3.28. The chip supports only local routing, thus, CABs are connected to each other and to the I/O cells through ports on their north, east, south, and west borders. A CAB implements a pool of transistor geometries from which one transistor is selected. Transistors may be 0.6, 1, 2, 4, and 8 μm long, and 1, 2,..., 15 μm wide. A transistor's gate, source, and drain can be connected to, respectively, any of the CAB's routing channels, to V_{dd}, and to GND. In addition, each CAB has a unity gain buffer for monitoring the east, south, drain, and source voltages. CABs implementing P- and N-channel transistors are arranged in a checkerboard order. The routing matrix of a block uses six switches to implement a parametrizable interconnect between cardinal communication ports. The architecture of a CAB is presented in Figure 3.29. Its configuration requires 22 bits: 7 bits for the transistor geometry selection, 3×3 bits for transistor terminals routing, and 6 bits for the routing matrix. The complete configuration stream sums up to 768 bytes, when using 3 byte for configuring a single CAB.

Creating solutions for analog circuit domain needs is typically more complicated than designing digital circuits. Moreover, tools for analog design are not as versatile and powerful as their digital world counterparts. This lies in the complexity of the design space where the component properties depend on a large set of factors, such as the manufacturing process, component geometry, tolerances, parasitic influences, temperature effects, and aging. Therefore, analog circuits often require, for their initial and recurrent calibration, compensation for such drifting factors. Human designers com-

Nanjing U. FPACA [178]

2006 — MaZet MTI04 [242]

Georgia Tech FG-FPAA [147], Melexis MLX90308 [244], Analog Dev. AD855x [29]
2004 — U. KL FPMA [208], IMTEK FPAA [39], Fares bipolar FPAA [116]

TI PGA309 [347]
Anadigm FPAA dpASP [28]
2002 — TU Gdansk FPAA OTA-C Filter [265], Cypress PSOC Mix. Sig. Arch. [86]

Heidelberg FPTA [211]

2000 — PAMA-2000 [211]

Lattice ispPAC [216]
U. Sussex Evolvable Motherboard [218], ALD EPAD [21]
1998 — Palmo [266], U. John Hopkins FPMA [339], Higuchi EHW [259]
Zetex TRAC FPAA [409], Faura FIPSOC FPMA [118], Motorola DPAD2 FPAA [53]
JPL FPTA [331], Fraunhofer FPAD [41]
Premont et al. CCII-FPAA [276], Sinencio et al. CM-FPAA [108]
1996 — Pilkington Switch-C FPMA [411], Kutuk-Kang Switch-C FPAA [204]

U. Toronto MADAR FMPA [69], Analog Dev. Var-Gain Amp. [21]
1994 — Analogix Bipolar FPAA [272], Chang et al. MFSDB [64],IMP EPAC [176]

1992 —

Lee & Gulak, transcond. FPAA [220]
1990 — Lee & Gulak, sub-thresh. FPAA [219], Xicor Digital Pot. [390], IMP Prog. Filter [135]

1988 — Sivilotti Proto-chip [321]

1986 —

1984 — Vall & Tsividis ASP [374]

GAP-01 [275]

Figure 3.27: Evolution of the FPAA: Time-line combined from [99, 207] and [209]. Work marked by bold is described in this section. Acronyms. FPMA: Field programmable mixed-signal arrays, FPTA: Field programmable transistor arrays, PSOC: Programmable system on chip, OTA: Operational transconductance amplifier, and FPAD: Field programmable analog device.

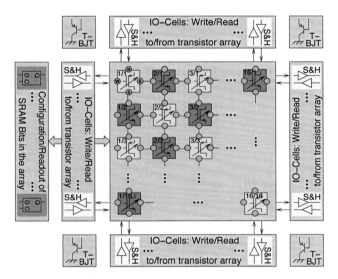

Figure 3.28: Heidelberg FPTA [211]: The architecture consists of 16×16 CABs implementing P- and NMOS transistors. For local routing, CABs connect on their north, east, south and west borders.

pose complex solutions typically from catalogs of well known circuits with widely understood behavior, for instance, filters, amplifiers, frequency multipliers, and synthesizers. While one of the goals of the Heidelberg FPTA is raising the evolvability of analog designs by means of sophisticated algorithmic methods [367, 368], its central motivation is the search for surrogate solutions for fundamental engineering designs and for new design principles [210–212, 214, 367].

The Heidelberg FPTA has been used to evolve ring oscillators [211], Boolean gates such as AND, NAND, OR and XOR [212, 213, 368], DACs [214], and operational amplifiers (OA) [367, 369]. We will introduce this last, as it includes elements relevant to our work.

Operational amplifiers are basic elements in analog circuit design. While there exist multiple implementation variants, the authors aim in their work at the discovery of new operational amplifier circuits [367]. An important condition is the creation of generalizable circuits, which behave the same in the simulation as in the real physical devices. The complexity of analog circuit design is reflected in the selected optimization algorithm. An OA is described by a vast set of parameters. It contains, e.g., the maximal operat-

71

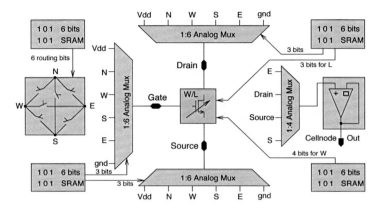

Figure 3.29: Heidelberg FPTA, CAB architecture [211]: A transistor's gate, source, and drain can be connected to any of the CAB's routing channels. A transistor's geometry is parametrizable by a length of 0.6, 1, 2, 4 and 8 μm and a width of 1, 2,..., 15 μm. A unity buffer supports monitoring the east, south, drain, and source voltages. The routing matrix implements parametrizable interconnects between the north, east, south, and west ports.

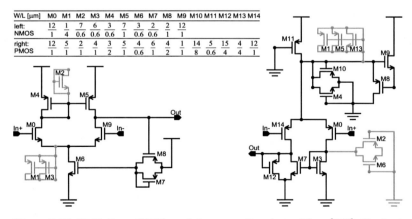

Figure 3.30: Heidelberg FPTA evolving operational amplifiers [367]: Evolved N- and PMOS operational amplifiers. Gray transistors are clamped inactive. The evolution succeeded in evolving understandable and device independent circuits.

ing frequency, slew rate, harmonic distortion, and phase shift. The authors note nine different OA parameters and formalize them as the optimization objectives for a Pareto based MOEA. To apply a general GA scheme, the authors define mutation and crossover operators acting on the two-dimensional FPTA grid. An additional enhancement of their NSGAII based [98] *MO Turtle-GA* is the specialized selection scheme. The authors divide the objective set into two subsets. While the non-domination set decomposition follows the NSGAII scheme, the differentiation within a non-dominated set prioritizes those individuals excelling in the objectives from the subset of the primary objectives.

Figure 3.30 shows the evolved N and PMOS operational amplifiers. The table in the upper left corner presents that transistor's geometries. Transistors drawn in grey are clamped inactive. The evolution's success is measured by the number of objectives in which the best evolved solution outperforms a human designed reference OA. In 20 runs, the evolution was able to evolve one NMOS and one PMOS operational amplifier that were better in 5 and 6 objectives than the reference OA, respectively. In further work, Trefzer raised the number of evolutionary runs to 50, finding solutions better than the reference OAs in 9 and 6 objectives for the NMOS and PMOS cases, respectively [369].

3.3.2 NASA Field Programmable Transistor Array

Originally developed by Stoica [331, 332, 336], the NASA FPTA has a similar architecture to that of the Heidelberg FPTA. It is a reconfigurable analog device comprising a two-dimensional mesh of transistor cells. Reconfiguration is done by setting conductive switches between the transistors and passive elements of a cell. Extracellular routing connects the cardinal neighbor blocks on their north, east, south, and west borders bidirectionally. Altogether, three versions of the NASA FPTA were developed [338]. The essential difference from the Heidelberg FPTA, apart from the number of active transistors employed simultaneously by a CAB, is the realization of the reconfiguration, which for the NASA FPTA is based on the programmable routing and adjustable passive element nominals, leaving the transistors immutable. The versatility of the NASA FPTA originates in its topology, allowing for the implementation of a set of common analog circuits, such as two- and three-stage operational amplifiers, logarithmic photo detectors, and Gaussian computational circuits [406].

In 2007, Stoica et al. [334] presented a successor reconfigurable adaptable architecture for analog circuits tailored for space applications. By analyzing the existing solutions, the authors created an architecture comprising coarse granular building blocks such as high voltage and low-offset operational amplifiers, high speed comparators, and current sources able to implement a wide range of popular circuits. The authors propose that their device demonstrate in the $-180°$C to $125°$C temperature range a component drift of less than 1% to 5%. Additionally, the architecture allows tuning the component parameters online, emphasizing its adaptable behavior.

The motivation for the NASA FPTA is two-fold: At first, the creation of robust electronics for harsh environments is a complicated task with a costly certification procedure. Optimizing the weight of airborne and space vehicles requires placing the sensory front-end electronics outside a central and temperature stabilized box to reduce the cabling. With a potentially very large temperature spectrum, the circuit components have to have mutually agreed upon characteristics to compensate for each other's temperature drifts. Such a design task is cumbersome but can be solved by automatic tools. An optimization process typically uses simulation to derive the characteristics of the candidate solution. Precise simulation, however, tends to become complex and computationally expensive. Opting for a universal reconfigurable analog circuit device offers two crucial benefits: A candidate solution can be evaluated directly on the target hardware. This is often much faster than a simulation, and is perfectly precise. Additionally, a universal reconfigurable device needs to pass mechanical, structural, and some other tests only once, reducing the time and costs of the final certification procedure. Stoica reports in his initial work [331, 332] that the evolution of circuits for the FPTA-0 was carried out on 256 computing nodes running a parallel genetic algorithm package PGAPack and a SPICE 3F5 circuit simulator. Later on, a board-level streamlined evolvable system comprising a TI 320C6701 DSP running a genetic algorithm and an FPTA-2 reconfigurable device reduced the computation time by roughly four orders of magnitude [337].

The second motivation for the NASA FPTA is the potential to create circuits with the ability to compensate, using the very same and uniform method, for degrading effects in silicon and component characteristic drifts during the complete system life time. Long term (100+ years) space missions face, apart from ionizing radiation, also silicon aging. Additionally, exploration missions to the surfaces of, e.g., Neptune, Triton, and Pluto, need to cope with temperatures as low as -220°C and even lower. The surface temperatures of Venus, in contrast, climb as high as 470°C [405, 406]. A system that uses the very same adaptation method to autonomously compensate for these challenges and to approach situations that have not been considered before the mission starts, offers an intriguing adaptivity concept.

Designed for space applications, the NASA FPTA device family has been evaluated in experiments investigating functional recovery under temperature drifts and radiation effects. The experimental scheme commonly used in the published work starts with an engineered or evolved solution created at regular temperature and radiation dosages. Afterward, the temperature is changed dramatically or the radiation is set to a high dosage. Then the

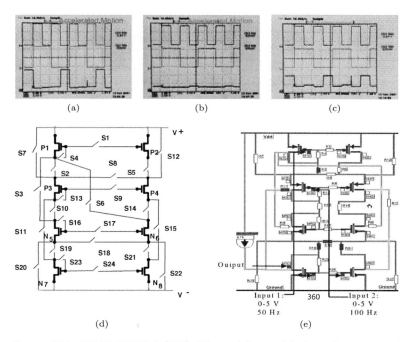

Figure 3.31: NASA FPTA-0 [338]: Figure (a) and (b) show the input and output behavior of a regular NOR gate implemented on the NASA FPTA-0 device at 27°C and 326°C, respectively. After observing degradations at 326°C, a genetic algorithm is started, recovering the NOR function. This is demonstrated in Figure (c). The corresponding FPTA-0 circuit is presented in Figure (e). Figure (d) shows the general NASA FPTA-0 transistor cell architecture [332].

evolutionary process is started, to recover the circuit functionality. In [333, 338, 405, 406] the authors report on high- and low-temperature experiments evolving Gaussian shape curve generators, low and high pass filters, half-wave rectifiers, operational amplifiers, controllable oscillators, NANDs, and NOTs. Figure 3.31 illustrates an example of an evolvable NOR. Engineered to operate at 27°C (Figure 3.31 (a)), the temperature is increased to 326°C, causing the circuit to fail (Figure 3.31 (b)). After starting the evolutionary optimization process, the behavior of a NOR is restored (Figure 3.31 (c)). The authors mentioned, however, that the solutions might become inoperable when the initial conditions are re-established and might therefore need re-evolution [338]. Besides experiments with temperature resistant circuits, the corrosive effects of radiation has been investigated on the examples of drivers, inverters, half-wave rectifiers, NAND gates, and 4 bit DACs [335]. In all the experiments, evolution successfully restored the functionality.

3.3.3 Lattice ispPAC

The lattice in-system programmable analog circuit (ispPAC) devices [216] offers reconfiguration on the super-transistor level. The chip family employs configurable elements, the PACblocks, comprising instrumental, wide band linear and rail-to-rail amplifier gain stages, precision active filters, and DACs. The on-chip building blocks can be cascaded by the means of the *analog routing pool* (ARP). Moreover, ARP allows routing PACblock signals to various chip pins. The PACblocks themselves have a fixed topology composed from PACells—amplifiers and programmable passive elements such as resistors, switches, and capacitors. Figure 3.32 (a) presents an exemplary ispPAC-10 architecture [217]. The chip implements four identical PACblocks. Each PACblock comprises two differential instrumental amplifiers, a summation amplifier with a switchable feedback resistor, and a programmable capacitor. Figure 3.32 (b) illustrates the PACblock architecture. The gain of the input amplifiers is adjustable from -1 dB to 10 dB in 1 dB steps and the capacitor is tunable within the 1 pF to 62 pF range in 128 steps. The analog routing pool allows cascading the PACblocks to higher-order transfer functions. Figure 3.32 (c) shows an example of the routing of a bi-quad bandpass filter [217].

The ispPAC-10 device has been used by Greenwood et al. [140] to investigate aging and fault injection effects on a third-order linear system possessing low-pass characteristics. To this end, the filter circuit, together with a subsequent reconfigurable compensator transfer function, were implemented on the device and connected to a computer driven signal generator and spectrum analyzer. While the transfer function's structure was fixed, the nominals of the capacitor and resistor were subject to evolution. In two separate experiments, the authors investigated the compensation of large and small bandwidth changes potentially caused by single but cardinal and continuous but marginal events, respectively. The fitness was defined as the square distance between the frequency responses of the reference and the evolved solutions. The differences are sampled at five frequencies, modeling the general frequency response shape. In the first experiment, the 44.25 kHz -3dB point of the reference low-pass was shifted to 53.0 kHz and 44.25 kHz, respectively. After 200 generations, the evolution found for the first case a compensating circuit with a frequency response similar to the original. The bandwidths of the original, defect, and compensated filters are shown in Figure 3.33. It was also possible to find a compensating circuit for the 44.25 kHz case. In the second experiment, the aging effects are simulated by successively changing

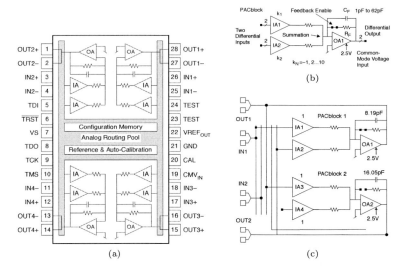

Figure 3.32: Lattice isppPAC 10 [216]: The architecture in Figure 3.32a is hierarchically decomposed into four PACblocks, which itself are combined of PACells—programmable amplifiers. PACblocks and chip pins are interconnected by an analog routing pool. Figure 3.32c shows an example of the routing for a bi-quad bandpass filter [217].

the low-pass's -3 dB point from 44.25 kHz to 51.0 kHz and 57.0 kHz. While it was possible to find a solution for the first change, the filter's re-evolution when changing the -3 dB point from 51.0 kHz to 57.0 kHz did not succeed.

The authors conclude that architectural restrictions of reconfigurable analog devices in general and of the isppPAC-10 device in particular had been selected carefully to give human designers and their methods powerful and versatile platforms. Evolution, however, might benefit more when able to utilize as many degrees of freedom as possible to find innovative solutions. Thus, it is argued, the experimental setup complexity could be reduced and the quality of the discovered circuits improved when stepping back from making architectural restrictions for reconfigurable devices based on assumptions of human creativity and engineering design principles.

3.4 Cartesian Genetic Programming

Cartesian Genetic Programming (CGP) is a variant of regular genetic programming and has the distinctive feature of utilizing a restricted directed

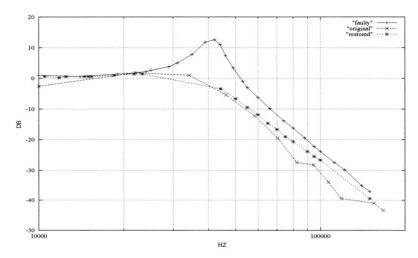

Figure 3.33: Compensating bandwidth changes with ispPAC-10 [140]: The evolution's goal is to evolve a compensating circuit tightly matching the frequency response of the original low-pass filter. The -3 dB point at 44.25 kHz of the original filter was shifted due to injected faults in the discrete component nominals to 53.0 kHz. The bandwidth change was successfully reverted by an evolved compensatory circuit.

acyclic graph (DAG) for genotype encoding. Introduced in 1998 by Miller, Thomson, and Fogarty [257], CGP was motivated by digital logic design for a generalized FPGA model that locates its functional nodes on a two-dimensional grid. To reduce the simulation complexity, only combinatorial circuits are considered by CGP. Routing cycles are avoided by only allowing feed-forward connections between the nodes. The term CGP comes from its initial node numbering scheme, indexing nodes by their Cartesian coordinates [252].

While CGP is primarily a formalization for a specialized computational model, it is also commonly associated with a simplified, mutation-only version of evolutionary strategies. This has two reasons: the crossover implementation acting on the genotype's logical structure cannot be realized straightforwardly, as it has to consider the nonfunctional restrictions of the phenotype. Additionally, the fitness landscape of digital circuits is often rough, favoring local-search related techniques.

This section presents CGP and its major revisions, as illustrated in the time line of Figure 3.34.

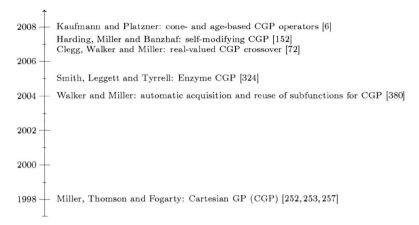

Figure 3.34: Evolution of Cartesian genetic programming.

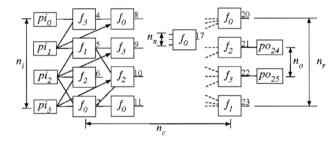

Figure 3.35: Cartesian genetic programming model and its parameters

3.4.1 The Representation Model

Formally, CGP consists of $n_c \times n_r$ nodes, n_i primary inputs, and n_o primary outputs. A node has n_n inputs and implements one out of $f_n = |F|$ different combinatorial functions on these inputs. While the primary inputs and outputs can connect to any of the node's inputs and outputs, respectively, the connectivity of the node's inputs is restricted. The input of a node at column c may only connect to the outputs of nodes in columns $c - l, \dots, c - 1$ as well as to the primary inputs. The levels-back parameter l restricts wiring to hardware friendly local connections. More importantly, as only feed-forward connections are allowed, the creation of combinatorial feedback loops is avoided. Figure 3.35 shows an example for a CGP model together with its parameters. The model in this example has five columns,

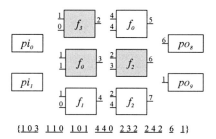

$$\{1\,0\,3 \quad 1\,1\,0 \quad 1\,0\,1 \quad 4\,4\,0 \quad 2\,3\,2 \quad 2\,4\,2 \quad 6 \quad 1\}$$

Figure 3.36: A CGP genotype and its mapping to a spatial structure. Nodes colored gray contribute to the primary outputs.

four rows, four primary inputs, and two primary outputs.

The CGP genotype consists of $n_c n_r$ node genes and n_o primary output connection genes. The genes are stored linearly, as shown in Figure 3.36. A node gene divides into n_n connections and a function selection gene. When configuring a phenotype's grid node, the first connection gene configures the first node input, the second connection gene configures the second node input, and so on. Linearly stored node genes are mapped to the two-dimensional grid columnwise. That is, the first node gene configures the upper left node of the grid. The second node gene configures the next grid node in the same column. When the configuration for all nodes in the first column has finished, the following columns are configured in the same way. After finishing the grid configuration, the first primary output connection gene configures the first primary output, the second primary output gene configures the second primary output, and so on. An example of such a mapping is shown in Figure 3.36.

Genotype size. The length of a genotype is constant and given by $n_c n_r (n_n + 1) + n_o$ integer values. The search space defining the bit length of a CGP genotype is estimated as follows: the node numbering, as presented in Figure 3.36, uses global addresses. However, the actual coding space of the node connection genes might capture only a subset of it. An input of a node in column i, $1 \leq i \leq l$, address n_i primary inputs and $(i-1) \cdot n_r$ nodes in the preceding columns. Thus, its effective coding requires $\lceil \log_2(n_i + (i-1)n_r) \rceil$ bits. Single connection genes in other columns are encoded by $\lceil \log_2(n_i + ln_r) \rceil$ bits. A primary output is encoded by $\lceil \log_2(n_i + n_c n_r) \rceil$ bits. A function selection gene accounts for $\lceil \log_2(f_n) \rceil$ bits. Altogether, when partitioning the CGP's encoding into $n_c n_r (n_n + 1) + n_o$ integers, the complete genotype, apart from

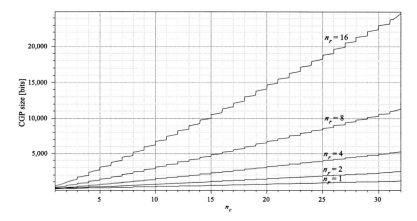

Figure 3.37: CGP upper size bound. Example of the different CGP genotype sizes when varying the number of columns (n_c) and rows (n_r). This CGP was configured with eight primary inputs, four primary outputs, an unrestricted levels-back parameter, and 4-input LUTs.

non-coding sequences, is

$$
\begin{aligned}
|CGP(n_i, n_o, n_c, n_r, n_n, l, f_n)| \quad = \quad & n_o \lceil \log_2(n_i + n_c n_r) \rceil + n_c n_r \lceil \log_2(f_n) \rceil \\
& + n_r n_n \big[(n_c - l) \lceil \log_2(n_i + l n_r) \rceil \\
& + \sum_{j=0}^{l-1} \lceil \log_2(n_i + j n_r) \rceil \big] \big]
\end{aligned}
$$

bits long. Some exemplary CGP genotype size developments depending on n_c, $n_r r$ and n_n are presented in Figure 3.37.

Evolutionary strategies for CGP. Miller uses throughout his work a variant of a $(1 + \lambda)$ evolutionary strategy that allows the parent to proceed to the next generation only if it is strictly better than all offspring. The offspring population typically amounts to either $\lambda = 1$ or $\lambda = 4$ individuals. The selection scheme is sketched in Algorithm 3.

An often used mutation operator for the CGP model is the *one-point muta-tion*, which randomly selects a node and modifies either the node function or one node input. If the function is mutated, a new function is randomly chosen from the function set. If an input is modified, one of the node's inputs is ripped up and reconnected to the output of a randomly chosen node in the previous columns or to a primary input.

Algorithm 3: `CGP-ES-Selection(p,Q)` - $(1 + \lambda)$ ES variant used by Miller [252]

> **Input:** parent individual p, offspring individuals Q
> **Output:** new parent individual
> 1 $Q' \leftarrow$ `select-best(Q)`   // select best offspring individuals
> 2 **if** p better than q, $q \in Q'$ **then**   // is p better as some $q \in Q'$?
> 3   **return** p // parent strictly better than all offspring individuals
> 4 **return random** $q \in Q'$ // return random best offspring individual

---

General DAG equivalency. The CGP model defines a directed acyclic graph. In reverse, any DAG $G = (V, E)$ can be mapped to an appropriately configured CGP model. To do this, one first has to identify all nodes in V that start and end a path. This set can be formalized as $I \subseteq V$, $\forall v \in V$: $(i, v) \notin E, i \in I$ and $O \subseteq V \backslash I$, $\forall v \in V : (v, o) \notin E, o \in O$. The nodes of I and O are associated with the CGP's primary inputs and outputs, respectively. The nodes on paths of length 0 are associated without loss of generality to primary outputs. For the remaining nodes, a distance is computed reflecting the maximal length required to reach a node on a path started from a node in O. This distance establishes a partial order by grouping nodes with equal distances into independent sets. Additionally, nodes with a distance i might only have edges to nodes in I and to nodes with distances greater than i. G can now be mapped to CGP with $n_c = n = |V \backslash \{I \cup O\}|$ columns, $n_r = n$ rows, $n_i = |I|$ primary inputs, $n_o = |O|$ primary outputs, and a levels-back parameter $l = n - 1$. This mapping places nodes with a distance i into column $n_c - i + 1$. This mapping scheme requires $n \times n$ grid nodes and can be improved by reducing the number of rows to one. The new mapping scheme places nodes with distance 1 into the highest and rightmost positions in the $n_c \times 1$ CGP grid. Nodes of distance 2 are placed next to the previously placed nodes. This procedure is iterated until all n graph nodes are placed in the $n \times 1$ CGP grid.

Single-line CGP. The CGP's orientation at the two-dimensional grid of a general FPGA entails fragmentation when evolving n to m functions with $m << n$. For instance, the computation of a general single-output function with 8 inputs requires a binary tree of depth 3. Such a tree would fit onto a grid with 3 columns and 4 rows. To avoid inhibiting the evolution, the actual grid size used during the optimization is configured to be slightly larger, comprising 4 columns and 5 rows. The search space describes 20 nodes, which is nearly three times as much as required to describe the tree. However, the CGP can be configured as a one-row only model with a levels-back parameter $l = n_c - 1$. The genotype length with a 50% overhead is now almost twice as small as the previous configuration. The one-row CGP is popular as it has proved to be less computationally complex [251, 399]. The drawback is the introduction of potentially non-local wiring, making the mapping of an evolved solution to hardware devices more complex.

Differences from GP. When comparing CGP with the regular GP, three differences are essential: A CGP's graph size is restricted by the genotype's length. While the actual fraction of the graph contributing to the primary outputs might acquire and release functional nodes and has therefore a variable size, the total graph size has a fixed upper bound. Avoiding excessive bloat in CGP (defined as the genotype's rapid growth in size over time), which is a common challenge in GP, here needs no measures to be taken. Miller investigated in [250] the existence and effect of bloat in CGP. He found that when using the standard CGP model and a one-point mutation, the presence and effects of bloat were negligible. The second cardinal difference from GP lies in the way CGP reuses partial solutions. While subtrees in standard GP may be referenced only once, no such restriction is imposed on subgraphs in CGP. A subgraph may be referenced multiple times, making the automatic reuse of partial solutions an inherent property of CGP. The last difference lies in the absence of a canonical CGP recombination operator. Moving genotype substructures in CGP needs to respect the non-functional phenotype restrictions. This makes the recombination complex and introduces limitations on the transferable grid areas. The straightforward recombination that swaps nodes at the same positions between genotype does not correspond to the subfunction transfer of a GP recombination. Attempts to create a GP-like crossover will be presented later on in this section. In Section 5.1 we will introduce a GP-like CGP crossover that transfers coherent subgraphs.

Non-functional genotype properties. An important property of CGP is its implicit coding of non-functional phenotype attributes. Genes within the CGP genotype do not explicitly encode their spatial position in the two dimensional grid. Their location is given by their order within the genotype and the corresponding mapping scheme specified by the CGP's parametrization. Moving a node's gene within the CGP genotype so that it is mapped to a different column might violate the levels-back parameter and introduce cycles. The main conceptual aspect of CGP that makes genotype manipulation difficult is that the CGP blends a general DAG representing a function with a spatial structure that expresses the non-functional phenotype characteristics. These non-functional properties introduce massive redundancies within the functional graph space. Additionally, the phenotype's spatial characteristics limit the graph space, and therefore limit the space of encodable functions. A criticism of CGP is that the encoding of non-functional phenotype characteristics might be a source of inefficiency. This has led to the development of a placement-free representation model [232, 233], which will be presented later on in this section.

Neutrality. The function computed by a Cartesian genetic program usually does not use all the grid nodes. The active nodes that lie in a subgraph indexed by some of the primary outputs may become inactive after mutation and then return to being active during evolution. While inactive nodes do not affect the computed function, their effect on the evolution and evolvability is pronounced. The point mutation modifies all genes with an equal probability, without considering their activity states. Mutations of active and passive genes are nevertheless treated differently, as active genes' mutations are subject to selection pressure while passive genes' mutations may pass without any restrictions. Therefore, guided search and randomization are the effects of active and inactive gene mutations, respectively. As the evolution progress, inactive nodes may also belong to clamped-off partial solutions. Hence, aside from being a source of randomness, inactive genes represent also an "evolutionary memory."

The interdependency of active and inactive genes in the context of a point mutation and the specific ES implementation have an additional aspect. A point mutation can be seen as a neighbor relation. For the flat fitness landscape regions typically found near local and global optima, the direct neighborhood under the mutation operator does not provide sufficiently diverse fitness values to determine an uphill fitness direction. Deprived of any orientation, the search benefits more from a forced yet unguided walk through the neighborhood, as implemented in Algorithm 3, than from the regular $(1 + \lambda)$ ES with a more local search horizon. The unguided walk has proved to be highly beneficial for CGP's evolvability [252] and has been referred to by Miller et al. as "neutrality." The random genetic drift on a equipotential fitness plateau has multiple mechanisms. In an analysis by Yu and Miller [400], the neutral mutation mechanism has be en decomposed by the redundancy types employed. Mutating active genes without changing the fitness demonstrate two types of redundancy. Semantically redundant elements such as $\mathtt{OR(false,}x\mathtt{)}$ and $\mathtt{AND(true,}x\mathtt{)}$ may be safely introduced and removed without affecting the fitness. Mutation may also switch between functionally redundant elements such as $\mathtt{OR(}x,y\mathtt{)}$ and $\mathtt{NAND(}\bar{x},\bar{y}\mathtt{)}$. These implicitly given redundancy types are exploited by the evolution [400]. Inactive genes form the explicitly given syntactically redundant elements. The evolution explores this space without an immediate impact on the fitness. The authors extended the selection scheme presented in Algorithm 3 by a customizable neutral drift and showed that the evolution reaches the optimization goal faster and more frequently when opening the bounds of neutral drift as much as possible. In this context, the authors have classified evolutionary search as "a sequence of neutral walks and fitness improvement steps."

Hardware aspects of CGP. CGP's versatility originates from its concept of a two-dimensional functional block arrangement including a directed data flow. Two properties make CGP particularly suitable for FPGA based autonomous adaptive systems. CGP can be parametrized to precisely match LUT-based FPGAs. Additionally, CGP encodes placement that reduces the mapping complexity of a candidate solution to routing and bitstring generation. There are, however, some drawbacks. On-chip evolution is a challenging task as autonomous systems have limited resources for circuit synthesis [130, 190]. With the lack of open FPGA bitstream architectures, custom routing and bitstream generation tools are research challenges on their own. For that reason, several researchers have resorted to *virtual FPGAs*: architectures with configurable registers [127, 300, 308, 413, 414]. For reasons of resource efficiency, virtually reconfigurable CGP architectures utilize coarse granular and application tailored functional blocks and routing elements [271, 371]. Higher level functions such as adders and multipliers have been used for data compression [289], cell scheduling [228], and robot navigation [252]. Fine granular CGP is used mostly for benchmarking and for some applications such as pattern recognition [153] [6, 9, 10], signal processing [240, 289, 299, 311, 322, 343], computer design [87] [11] and robot navigation [151].

Challenges of CGP. CGP has three major challenging points:

- *Scalability:* For larger and real world applications, the CGP model in combination with a fine grained logic lacks scalability. The excessive chromosome lengths lead to extremely large search spaces. To tackle scalability, a number of approaches have been proposed, which can be classified along three dimensions: The first dimension corresponds to the level of the hardware representation. To improve scalability, we should give up structural models that are too hardware friendly, and move towards behavioral models. Orthogonal to that, we see the dimension of object granularity. We can evolve hardware using gates and wires, arithmetic functions and buses, and eventually complete intellectual property cores and networks on chip [228, 289, 306]. The third dimension relates to incorporating knowledge into the evolutionary process. We can either evolve in a blind manner or try to leverage general, domain, or application specific knowledge [74, 362, 380].

- *Implicit genotype coding:* The phenotype's implicitly coded spatial structure introduces redundancies and hampers structural evolutionary operators. In the next section we will present an attempt to redefine CGP for a context free genotype encoding. In Chapter 5 we will also present our work on structural operators for CGP.

- *Genotype-to-phenotype mapping complexity:* While this is not exactly a challenging point of CGP, the absence of efficient and open synthesis tools for mapping CGP genotypes to the LUT-based FPGAs required for virtually reconfigurable architectures reduces CGP's attractiveness fro compact and autonomous adaptable systems [127, 302].

3.4.2 Enzyme Cartesian Genetic Programming

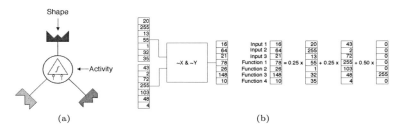

(a)   (b)

Figure 3.38: Enzyme GP [233]: Figure (a) presents a functional node within Enzyme GP. Evolutionary operators act on node shapes—signatures assigned to inputs, outputs, and the computed function. A node's output shape is a linear combination of inputs and function shapes. The computation is illustrated in Figure (b) [57]. The primary input and output nodes lack the function shape elements. Additionally, the primary input, respectively, output nodes have no input, respectively, output shape components.

The drawback of implicit position encoding within the CGP genotype motivated Smith et al. [324] to adopt the context free GP idea of Lones [232]. Lones's Enzyme GP mimics the "metabolic pathway, and the role of enzymes which express computational characteristics" by employing two concepts. The inputs and outputs of a functional node carry signatures as illustrated in Figure 3.38 (a). If an output signature of a node A closely matches an input signature of node B, then A and B may establish a connection. The output shape of a node is a linear combination of inputs and function shapes, as presented in Figure 3.38 (b). Consequently, the output shape represents to some extent a node's subtree. The primary input and output nodes lack function shape elements. Additionally, the primary input nodes have no input shape components, and the output nodes, no output shape components. The second concept concerns phenotype creation. Starting with the primary outputs, the primary input and free nodes with output shapes most tightly matching the primary output nodes' input shapes are identified and docked. This is iterated until no dangling inputs remain. An example is shown in Figure 3.39. A mutation operator changes the function and inputs shapes of a node.

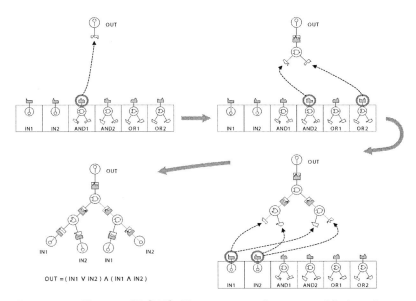

Figure 3.39: Enzyme GP [232]: Phenotype creation starts with the primary outputs showing unmatched inputs. Elements with the best matching output shapes are identified and connected to the dangling inputs. This scheme is repeated until no unmatched inputs remain.

Enzyme CGP adopts from Enzyme GP the way connections are established. Placed in Cartesian ordering, functional nodes posses, similar to Enzyme GP, shapes characterizing the inputs and outputs. The node inputs connect to the best matching outputs of nodes in the previous l columns and to the primary inputs. The resulting graph may have nodes and primary inputs with dangling outputs and nodes and primary inputs supplying multiple successive nodes and primary outputs. An Enzyme CGP genotype can be mapped to an identically parametrized CGP genotype. While Enzyme CGP is still not completely context free, it enables drawing wires in a more meaningful way establishing a similarity metric on the function and wiring of a subgraph.

Smith et al. [324] verified Enzyme CGP on a denoising image filter application, obtaining similar performance to that of regular CGP.

3.4.3 Recombination for Cartesian Genetic Programming

The structural GP crossover has no direct equivalent in CGP. The reasons lie, as described in Section 3.4.1, in the implicit coding of non-functional genotype properties by the phenotype. A GP-like crossover for CGP would have to operate only on graph structures.

There have been some attempts to introduce GP-like crossover for CGP. In [184] Kalganova and Miller compare the performance of three types of recombinations: swapping *i)* single connection and function selection gene, *ii)* all genes of a node, and *iii)* genes of all nodes in a row or column. The authors found that there are no pronounced differences between the recombination types. In later work, Miller et al. [252] questioned the general effectiveness of this kind of geometrical recombination.

In a later work, Clegg and Miller [72] adopted the recombination principle from floating point GA by computing a gene of an offspring individual as a linear combination of parent genes at the very same genotype position. Although this recombination type still does not operate on graph substructures, the authors could show that this kind of recombination significantly improves the convergence in the initial evolution phases.

Cai et al. [57] present a study on crossover effects in the Enzyme CGP model. Enzyme CGP qualifies wires by similarity signatures, reflecting to some extent the functions and wirings of the indexed subgraphs. The signatures are also used to establish connections between matching outputs and inputs. When transferring nodes of different parents to an offspring, the similarity signatures of a node indicate to what kind of functions and subgraphs the node likes to be connected to. While this crossover type does not operate on coherent substructures, it introduces a "soft" notion of subfunction transfer. The authors show on the example of even-3 parity benchmark and a 2-point crossover significant reductions of computational effort compared to regular CGP.

The search for an efficient CGP crossover operator is essential, as it opens the doors for global search algorithms. Conventional genetic algorithms rely on information drift among individuals. This is, e.g., a prerequisite for efficient Pareto based multi-criteria optimizers. In Section 5.1, we define structural CGP crossover. To this, we select functionally connected nodes from parent individuals to compose an offspring.

3.4.4 Automatic Acquisition and Reuse of Subfunctions in Cartesian Genetic Programming

Automatic acquisition and reuse of subfunctions was applied to CGP by Walker and Miller in 2004 [380]. The modules within CGP are defined as compositions of regular grid nodes and extend CGP's functional set F. In order to avoid potential bloat, hierarchical modules are not considered by the authors. The description of a module follows the syntax of CGP. Modules may have a variable number of inputs and outputs with at least two inputs and one output. Similar to CGP, the module size has an upper bound. The syntax of the CGP genotype has been extended to embed a list of module descriptions. Additionally, grid nodes indicate whether they are computing a regular function or referring to a module. The method relies on a single-row formalization of CGP. The authors called this model "Embedded CGP" (ECGP).

The automatic acquisition and reuse of modules is governed by three operators: *compress, expand,* and *module mutation.* Compression replaces a number of nodes by a newly created module. All inputs to module nodes that originate from non-module nodes or primary inputs become module inputs, and all outputs of nodes in the module that target non-module nodes or primary outputs become module outputs. The function and routing of nodes within the module remain unchanged. Hence, applying the compress operator to a chromosome neither changes its fitness nor its function. Importantly, nodes with subsequent node numbers in the one-row CGP configuration are selected to form a new module. As a node can connect to any previous node and to the primary inputs ($l = n_c - 1$), the compress operator selects nodes randomly. Expand is the reverse process, and replaces a module with its primitive nodes, again leaving the node functions and the routing unchanged. To leverage the evolution of useful modules, expand is twice as likely to occur as compress.

Module descriptions are treated as separate and self-contained sub-genotypes or chromosomes which are stored in a list at the end of the CGP genotype. When creating a module, the compress operator transfers the module's description to the modules list. The contributing grid nodes are replaced by a single type I node referring to the module. Regular grid nodes that do not refer to a module are referred to as type 0 nodes. Additionally, modules can also be introduced by a point mutation. While mutation cannot create a new module description, it can replace a node's function with a reference to one of the already created modules. Such nodes are referred to as type II nodes. Only type I nodes can be expanded and only type II nodes can be mutated by the point mutation operator. Modules that are not referred to are removed from the modules list. The module descriptions themselves are modified by the module mutation operator, which is essentially a standard CGP mutation operator except that it operates on module descriptions rather than on the overall chromosome and can also add and remove modules' inputs and outputs. As no direct input to output connections within a module are allowed, a module's number of outputs are bounded by the number of the module's nodes, and its inputs, by n_n times the number of the module's nodes. Whenever unconnected inputs appear during the alteration of a module's inputs and outputs, they are reconnected by applying the appropriate mutation operator. That is, unconnected inputs when adding an input and removing an output of a module are fixed by the regular point mutation. Unconnected node inputs within a module may occur when removing a module's input. In this case, the module mutation reroutes the dangling input within the module.

ECGP's performance has been extensively compared to that of CGP and other kinds of evolutionary algorithms. In [380], Walker and Miller demonstrate, with the example of an even parity function, that with increasing input sizes, ECGP dramatically outperforms CGP. In a follow-up work, those authors applied ECGP to the Hierarchical if-and-Only-if (H-IFF) and the Lawnmower benchmarks. While for the Lawnmower benchmark, ECGP scales by a factor of up to 1.8 better than CGP, on the H-IFF benchmark, CGP outperforms ECGP when the benchmark size increases. ECGP's module size became an additional focus in this work. The authors showed that ECGP is sensitive to the modules' sizes and that slight variations may lead to significant differences in the performance. This was confirmed in subsequent work [382] on the H-IFF and symbolic regression benchmarks.

The introduction to CGP of the automatic acquisition and reuse of subfunctions provided dramatical improvements in evolvability when applied to the evolution of Boolean circuits [380–382]. The benchmark set comprising even parity functions, adders, and multipliers, is considered to have a reasonable quantity of redundant structures that can be capsuled and reused. Despite its success, module acquisition in ECGP is done without considering the inner structure of the genotype. From the circuit design perspective, useful modules compute one or few results. A module's inner nodes, hence, contribute to a common output function and are therefore connected. Additionally, modules group related nodes in order to minimize routing. A new ECGP module creation scheme grouping functionally related nodes into modules may come closer to how human designers decompose and construct a circuit. The extraction and reuse of sub-DAG modules also becomes more similar to GP's subtree crossover.

In Section 5.2, we introduce automatic subfunction acquisition for CGP acting on meaningful substructures. To this end, we consider compact subgraphs as cones and fan out-free cones for module creation. Once structured module acquisition has been implemented, these methods can also be used to realize a structural crossover operator.

3.4.5 Self-modifying Cartesian Genetic Programming

Self-modifying CGP (SMCGP) is a developmental form of CGP [152]. The SMCGP genotype differs from a CGP genotype by using relative indexing and regular, primary input, primary output and "self modifying" node types. The latter encode an instruction telling the genotype expression operator to, e.g., add, delete, move or duplicate nodes, shift connections, and change node functions. Relative indexing allows relocating genotype regions efficiently while preserving the routing. The original genotype is considered as a generator element, which needs to be expressed. To this end, fitness evaluation can be divided into a development phase and an evaluation phase. In the first phase, all self modifying nodes are expressed once and a partial fitness is calculated. This is repeated until no more self modifying nodes remain, or until the maximal number of iterations has been reached. In the following phase, the fitness is obtained by combining the previously computed partial fitness values.

The motivation for SMCGP is the evolution of generalizable solutions. That is, solving some benchmark for a concrete n, where n is the input width, the hope is to be able to generalize the solution for case $n + 1$. SMCGP facilitates this by initially solving a small instance of the given benchmark and successively increasing and solving the next bigger instance, while using the previously found solution. For the example of an even n parity function, SMCGP evolves first an even 2 parity, then reuses the solution and evolves an even 3 parity. This is continued until a solution for a concrete even n parity function is found. During the evolution the generalization is partially verified, as for increasingly large n testing all input combinations becomes impractical. The general behavior is later verified symbolically by induction. To this end, the "generator" genotype needs to be simple enough to be processed by a computer algebra system or to be understood by a human.

Using SMCPG, general solutions for the even parity, adder, and π approximation have been found [150]. For unstructured benchmarks, such as the classification of proteins, SMCGP is on a par with CGP.

3.5 Chapter Conclusion

In this chapter we have illustrated the paradigm of Evolvable Hardware and presented some of the most astonishing and dominant work in this area. We have also selected some examples showing the challenges of EHW and helping us motivate our work, and putting our work in perspective. This chapter also motivates our choice of Cartesian genetic programming. CGP closely mirrors, with its two-dimensional node arrangement embedded into a feed-forward network, the architecture of today's fine- and coarse-granular reconfigurable devices.

To realize our idea of an EHW system able to react both to gradual and radical changes (cf. Section 3.1), we will not only introduce new algorithmic methods, as described in Section 2.5, but also create a novel and adaptable EHW pattern matching architecture (cf. Section 7.1), introduce architectural adaptation for the compensation of resource requirement fluctuations (cf. Section 7.2), and validate our approach with the optimization of processor caches (cf. Section 7.3).

Chapter 4

Digital Logic Evolution Framework and Experimentation Toolbox

Continuous hardware evolution is a rather novel research area without established experimental tools. We have therefore created our own set of instruments allowing us to carry out experiments and to develop new models and algorithms. We have created our tools to have versatile yet simple software interfaces and equipped the tools with the flexibility to modify all major algorithmic and architectural elements. From the algorithm engineering perspective, the toolbox facilitates a clear decomposition of evolutionary algorithms, evolutionary operators, and genotype encodings, so as to emphasize code reuse. To verify circuit evolution in a computationally limited environment, we have implemented a subset of our methods for an embedded processor without an operating system. All experiments in this thesis, except the experiments with the Functional Unit Row Architecture, have been carried out using our toolbox.

Our toolbox has two parts: an algorithmic part and a tools parts. Within the algorithmic part, programming interfaces for the creation of generate-and-test optimizers, evolutionary operators, and genotype encodings are defined. This is described in Section 4.1. Programs from the tools section help illustrate the search process, plot the results, carry out a step by step algorithm analysis, tune parameters, and distribute the execution of the experiment. This part is presented in Section 4.3. Section 4.4 concludes this chapter.

4.1 Framework Core Architecture

Once the concept of a novel evolutionary algorithm has been found, the algorithm performance needs to be compared with established methods. This is required since today's formal analysis tools cover only a subset of `generate-and-test` schemes. To demonstrate an EA's performance empirically, it first has to be

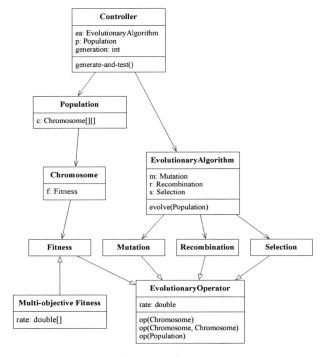

Figure 4.1: Framework core architecture.

formalized within an optimization framework. For sound statistical results, the algorithm then needs to be applied to a benchmark for a sufficient number of rounds. While our research focuses on hardware evolution, we have created a general framework for evolutionary optimizers. In designing this framework, we have put an emphasis on the following elements:

Simplicity: To minimize the implementation effort, we keep the data structures and the algorithm interfaces easy to understand and as simple as possible. Additionally, logging, experiment execution control, and the experiment save and restore mechanism are transparent to the algorithm designer. The framework's architecture, which is mainly defined by the data structure dependencies of a generic evolutionary algorithm, is presented in Figure 4.1. It has the following parts.

- **Controller** class: Loads the configuration files and instantiates the population as well as the evolutionary algorithm classes. After the initial steps, **Controller** executes the generate-and-test loop until a termination condition holds. The termination condition can be specified by time, generation number, or a functional quality threshold.

- **Population** class: Stores a two-dimensional field of **Chromosomes**. The **Population** class implements sorting, finding the best individual and logging.

- **Chromosome** class: This is a container class for the genotype data structures. It also holds a reference to the **Fitness** class. **Chromosome** also implements the **Fitness comparable** interface, allowing **Population** to sort a set of **Chromosomes** according to, for instance, the Pareto dominance metric. The genotype-to-phenotype mapping is implemented by **Chromosome**.

- **Operator** class: Defines a template for evolutionary operators acting on single genotypes, pairs of genotypes, and sets of genotypes. It also implements a real valued **rate** variable. The following operators inherit the **Operator** class:

  - **Fitness**: This class has the task of keeping the performance values for its **Chromosome** valid. That means that the **Chromosome** class invalidates its fitness each time the genotype is modified. The very next time the fitness of **Chromosome** is accessed, the **Fitness** class reevaluates it. While in its basic version the **Fitness** class supports only a single real valued fitness metric, the multi-objective **Fitness** implementation supports also Pareto based, ϵ-dominance, hyper-volume, kth nearest neighbor, and lexicographic ordering. Any new performance metric definition typically need only extend the **Fitness** operator.

  - **Selection**: This class picks a single or a set of parents from the parent population according to the selection strategy. Popular selection schemes are, e.g., the *fitness proportional* and *tournament* selections.

  - **Recombination**: This operator typically takes a pair of individuals and returns their recombined offspring. The **Recombination** class is independent of a genotype's encoding in the genetic algorithm scheme, as the genotype is represented by a plain bitstring. However, when improving the recombination efficiency, the operator is often applied to the genotype's logical structures. In this case it becomes dependent on the implementation of the **Chromosome** class.

– **Mutation**: The **Mutation** class takes a parent individual and returns its mutated version. Similarly to the **Recombination** operator, **Mutation** is independent of the implementation of the **Chromosome** class but may become dependent when acting directly on a genotype's inner structures.

Algorithm 4: Example of the $(1 + 1)$ evolutionary strategy implementation.

```
01 public class OnePlusOneES extends EvolutionaryAlgorithm {
02
03   public Population evolve(Population parent_population){
04     LinkedList<Chromosome> child = new LinkedList<Chromosome>();
05     Population child_population = new Population();
06
07     // create new child by cloning and mutating the parent
08     child.add(m.op(parent_population.get(0)));
09
10     // offspring individual selection: do not use the
11     // selection operator, compute directly
12     // return child if it has the same or better fitness than the parent
13     if (child.get(0).getFitness() >= parent_population.get(0).getFitness())
14         child_population.add(child.get(0));
15     else
16         child_population.add(parent_population.get(0).clone());
17
18     return child_population;
19   }
20 }
```

- **Evolutionary Algorithm** class: For each iteration of the **generate-and-test** scheme, **Controller** calls **EvolutionaryAlgorithm** with a **Population** as argument. **EvolutionaryAlgorithm** has the task of creating and returning a new offspring population by means of the **Selection**, **Recombination** and **Mutation** operators. Algorithm 4 presents an implementation of the $(1 + 1)$ evolutionary strategy. The algorithm uses a mutation operator to create a new offspring individual and implements the selection scheme directly. The fitness evaluation for the offspring individual is triggered in line 13.

While the architecture presented in Figure 4.1 determines the core structure of our optimization framework, it does not illustrate the complete architecture. Hidden from the algorithm designer, the framework implements a configuration file parser, framework composition by dynamically loading the algorithm classes according to the configuration file, logging functions, snapshot management for a step by step execution, a replay functionality, a versatile graphical user interface, and a remote network control.

```
# evolve a 2x2 bit adder using (1+1) Evolutionary Strategies

evolutionaryAlgorithmClass=moves.logic.OnePlusOneES
mutateClass=moves.CGP.CGP_Mutate
mutationRate=0.015

populationClass=moves.logic.Population
populationsize=100

chromosomeClass=moves.CGP.CGP_Chromosome
# CGP domain parameter
ni=4
no=3
l=2
nn=2
nr=4
nc=6

initChromosomeClass=moves.CGP.CGP_InitChromosome
init=random

fitnessClass=moves.CGP.Testfunctions.bool.CGP_BoolFitness
expression=(i & 0x03) + ((i & 0x0C) >> 2)
fitnessType=reciprocal_square_error

# terminate when correct solution is found, i.e., fitness >= 1.0
bestFitnessClass=moves.logic.BestFitness
```

Figure 4.2: Configuration file for the $(1 + 1)$ evolutionary strategy evolving a 2×2 adder.

Versatility: The data and algorithm dependencies presented in Figure 4.1 are implemented in such a way that they can be instantiated independently from each other. For situations like distributed experiment execution and incremental evolution, the ability of partial architecture instantiation facilitates adapting a framework to nonstandard operation modes.

Reusability: The basic architecture of our framework emphasizes a clear decomposition of evolutionary algorithms, genotype encodings, and evolutionary operators. With a strict decomposition, the implementation effort for novel methods can be dramatically reduced since the remaining components can be reused without any adaptation. Isolation is however not mandatory. For instance, efficient evolutionary operators often act on logical genotype structures and therefore need precise information about the genotype encoding. Within our framework, algorithm designers may freely decide how rigorously the component subdivision is implemented.

Configurability: Simple and self-explanatory configuration methods accessible to text manipulation tools like `sed` and `awk` are essential for the efficient and flexible generation of experiments. In particular, large scale algorithm comparisons employing multiple benchmarks make automatic setup generation a valuable method. With this in mind, we selected a plain text file format as the configuration method for our framework. Figure 4.2 gives an example of setting up the previously defined $1 + 1$ evolutionary strategy (cf. Algorithm 4). Each line of the file can either be a comment, an attribute definition, or empty. A comment starts with a "#", and "`<attribute>=<value>`" defines an attribute and its value. At first, the configuration file is loaded and parsed into a list of attribute names and keys. When the framework's default `EvolutionaryAlgorithm` class is instantiated, it checks whether the re is an "evolutionaryAlgorithmClass" attribute specifying a user defined EA. In this case, the user defined class is loaded, instantiated, and returned. During the instantiation, the user defined class finds its own class name in the "evolutionaryAlgorithmClass" attribute, skips the loading of itself, and proceeds with loading and configuring its variables. It also tries to instantiate the framework's default `Mutation`, `Recombination`, and `Selection` classes.

Since each of the framework's core classes implements the presented configuration scheme, the complete architecture illustrated in Figure 4.1 creates itself automatically by instantiating the default `Controller` class, parametrized with a configuration file.

Portability: The need to execute our framework and the developed algorithms on a wide range of platforms, caused us to select `Java` as the programming language. Available for high performance embedded, desktop, and cluster systems, `Java` also has a lot of additional benefits. It facilitates the use of sophisticated and efficient algorithms by providing extensive standard libraries, simplifying dynamic memory management, and allowing for the platform independent creation of graphical user interfaces. All of this helps produce simpler code and significantly reduces programming errors and development time.

4.2 Representation Models and Algorithms

One of the design goals presented in the previous section was the decomposition for code reuse of genotype representations, evolutionary algorithms, and evolutionary operators. However, dependencies between the these areas are often induced for reasons of efficiency. Figure 4.3 shows the genotype representation models implemented and the encoding independent evolutionary algorithms and operators. The dependencies in Figure 4.3 occur only between evolutionary algorithms and evolutionary operators. For instance, the OMOEAII implements its own cutoff, selection, and recombination operator, while the μGA algorithm relies on a special combination of population sets. Additionally, almost all multi-objective optimizers implement their own fitness metrics, typically differing in their techniques for calculating diversity and dominance.

Most frequently, the dependencies occur between genotype encodings and evolutionary operators. That is, operators such as mutation, crossover, and module aggregation, may work directly on genotype structures and cannot be reused without modification on representation models with a different topology. Figures 4.4 and 4.5 are grouped by genotype encoding and show which operators are implemented specifically for the corresponding representation model.

In the following two sections, we describe the methods shown in Figure 4.3 as well as in Figures 4.4 to 4.5 in more detail.

4.2.1 General Methods

Our framework implements the lookup table and Xilinx DSP48E based versions of Cartesian genetic programming. Additionally, it implements and extends the embedded Cartesian genetic programming model. The Java class dependencies for these representation models are illustrated in the upper left corner of Figure 4.3. The model implementations will be discussed in the next section. The remaining classes in Figure 4.3 are independent of the genotype encoding.

The evolutionary algorithms are the central components in Figure 4.3. We have implemented the

- generic GA and ES schemes: Both methods realize the generate-and-test procedures presented in Sections 2.1.2 and 2.1.3 without relying on a specific genotype encoding.

- SPEA2, TSPEA2, NSGAII, and IBEA: These algorithms have identical architectures. The major difference between SPEA2 and TSPEA2, presented in Sections 2.2.3 and 2.2.2, is the density metric. While SPEA2 uses the Euclidean distance to the kth nearest neighbor, NSGAII relies on the hypercube volume bound by the very next neighbors to establish a density index. TSPEA2 extends SPEA2's selection scheme and will be presented in Section 6.1.

  IBEA eliminates density estimations based on the value of the objective function. But SPEA2, TSPEA2, and NSGAII do compute their density rankings using objective values such as functional quality, area, and delay. The latter metrics are often defined in a non-linear way. Thus, the density values computed in different objective areas are difficult to compare. The IBEA algorithm family therefore relies only on Pareto

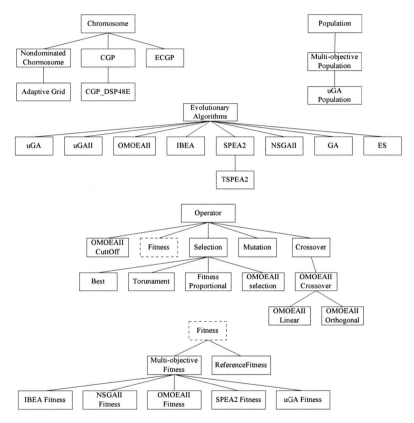

Figure 4.3: Representation models and representation model independent operators and algorithms.

based ranking for parent selection. Zitzler et al. presented I_{HD} and $I_{\epsilon+}$ IBEA variants in [416].

- μGA and μGAII: Presented in [78, 277], these algorithms follow the original idea of Goldberg [133], who observed that a small number of individuals in a population are often sufficient for a convergent optimization process. [78] combined the idea of Goldberg with the Pareto front diversity technique of Knowles and Corne [194]. The μGA algorithm was later extended to adaptive exploration and exploitation balancing in [277].

  The μGA and μGAII algorithms rely on three populations: an external population for non-dominated and diverse individuals, a working population, and an immutable population with randomized solutions. Additionally, a small short-term population is made up from the working and random population to serve as an input to a genetic algorithm. The μGA and μGAII population architecture is implemented by the μGA-Population class in Figure 4.3. The diversity technique of Knowles and Corne, which subdivides the hyperspace into a grid and adaptively refines it, is implemented by the AdaptiveGrid class.

- The OMOEAII scheme: Presented in [408], OMOEAII defines an orthogonal grid on the original fitness surface and computes a reduced fitness landscape by evaluating the solutions on grid junctions. With this, OMOEAII is able to minimize the number of fitness evaluations and has been demonstrated to be efficient for applications with independent objectives. The OMOEAII algorithm also implements specialized OMOEAII-mutation and OMOEAII-linear-crossover as well as the OMOEAII-orthogonal-crossover operators.

The remaining classes in Figure 4.3 are the general Tournament, FitnessProportional and Best selection classes, a Reference fitness class and the optimization algorithm specific IBEAII, NSGAII, OMOEAII, SPEA2 and μGA fitness classes.

4.2.2 Methods Specific to a Genotype

Cartesian genetic programming Based on Lookup Tables. Figure 4.4 shows the fitness, mutation, and recombination evolutionary operators implemented specifically for Cartesian genetic programming. One-point mutation as well as one-point, two-point, and uniform mutation operators are described in Section 3.4. Additionally, we have implemented multiple fitness evaluation classes. The first fitness evaluation class, the Boolean method, is able to realize a general mathematical function $c^*()$ given by a text string in the configuration file. With this, for an input range $I \subseteq \mathbb{B}^{n_i}$, an evolved circuit c, and employing the Hamming as well as the weighted Hamming functions

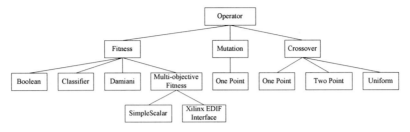

Figure 4.4: Evolutionary operators for lookup table based Cartesian genetic programming.

$h()$ and $wh()$, the `Boolean` class implements the following fitness evaluation methods:

- Hamming distance:

$$f_h(c, c^*, I) = 1 - \frac{1}{n_o|I|} \sum_{i \in I} h(c(i), c^*(i)),$$

- squared Hamming distance:

$$f_{h^2}(c, c^*, I) = 1 - \frac{1}{n_o^2|I|} \sum_{i \in I} h(c(i), c^*(i))^2,$$

- weighted Hamming distance (i.e., the difference between two bit strings at position i is weighted with 2^i):

$$f_{wh}(c, c^*, I) = 1 - \frac{1}{(2^{n_o} - 1)|I|} \sum_{i \in I} wh(c(i), c^*(i)),$$

- absolute numerical distance:

$$f_n(c, c^*, I) = 1 - \frac{1}{(2^{n_o} - 1)|I|} \sum_{i \in I} (|c(i) - c^*(i)|),$$

- fitness counter (special case of f_h):

$$f_c(c, I) = \frac{1}{|I|} \sum_{i \in I} c(i),$$

- reciprocal square Hamming error:

$$f_r(c, c^*, I) = \frac{1}{1 + \frac{1}{n_o|I|} \sum_{i \in I} h(c(i), c^*(i))}.$$

In our experiments, we preferred the reciprocal square error scheme, as it continuously decreases the selection pressure towards the final optimization phase, thus reducing the impact of stagnation.

The `Classifier` class uses the fitness counter function f_c of the `Boolean` class and additionally implements a parametrizable cross validation scheme, a loader, and efficient memory management for labeled feature vectors. To improve the overall evolution time for classifier architectures, the class also supports classifier architecture decomposition and distributed fitness evaluation.

The `Damiani` class realizes the evolution of hashing functions. At first presented by Damiani, Liberali, and Tettamanzi in [87], the goal of the class is to evolve a function build upon 4-input lookup tables organized in an 8×8 grid targeting the most uniform mapping of k keys to i indices with $k >> i$.

For evolving efficient memory-to-cache mapping functions, the `SimpleScalar` class implements an interface for the *SimpleScalar* systems simulator [35]. The `SimpleScalar` class is able to execute a remote *SimpleScalar* instance via `ssh` and to filter the output of *SimpleScalar* for execution cycles, miss- and hit-rates, memory access values, and any other computed metric. For cluster experiments, we extended *SimpleScalar* by Linux's true randomness source `/dev/random`. We also added the ability to load and use up to four CGP functions for computing memory-to-cache address mappings, covering all split and uniform configurations for a two leveled cache.

Finally, the `Xilinx-EDIF-Interface` class implements a realistic area and propagation delay estimate using the Xilinx place and route tools. To this end, the class creates for a CGP description a `JHDL` [40] class hierarchy, which is then exported as an EDIF netlist to a file. Afterward, Xilinx's `ngdbuild`, `map`, `par`, and `trce` tools estimate the circuit size and delay. Compared to the straightforward area and delay computation presented in Section 6.1, the higher precision when using the Xilinx tools comes at the price of high computational complexity. The `Xilinx-EDIF-Interface` class is also able to transform a CGP genotype into a bitstream using `bitgen` and `promgen`. We have implemented the EDIF exporter specifically for the CGP genotype model, as ECGP and other, LUT-based genotype encodings can be mapped to the plain CGP genotype.

Embedded Cartesian genetic programming. The ECGP model implements the `compact` and `extract` operators for the automatic acquisition and reuse of subfunctions in addition to the regular evolutionary operators. We have created new recombination and module acquisition methods, which we will present in Chapter 5. In Figure 4.5, these classes are represented by the cone–base recombination as well as the cone- and age-based selection classes. The remaining classes in Figure 4.5 have implementations similar to

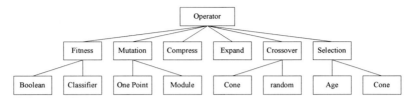

Figure 4.5: Evolutionary operators for embedded Cartesian genetic programming.

the corresponding CGP classes. The module mutation class has the additional functionality of adding and removing module inputs and outputs and is described in Section 3.4.4.

4.3 Experimentation Support and Tools

The creation of new evolutionary methods is typically an iterative process with interleaved phases of designing and testing. Handy experimentation tools including automatic performance evaluation are key to this phase. The efficiency of the experimentation tools is even more essential when comparing multiple algorithms on numerous and large benchmarks, exploring fitness landscapes, and tuning parameters. We have therefore created a visual tool that helps analyze the dynamics of novel methods as well as command line tools for efficient experiment generation and distributed execution.

We have already presented the configuration file format of our framework. In the next two sections we will introduce the graphical user interface for experiment tuning and analysis and the command line interface for unsupervised and distributed experiment execution.

4.3.1 Visualization and Analysis

The graphical user interface of our framework comprises the views *Calculation*, *Snapshot*, and *Statistics*. Figure 4.6 presents the *Calculation* view. It becomes visible after a user loads an experiment configuration file. In this view, the user can modify the parameters, save the configuration back to the file, and start the experiment. When starting an experiment, some of the parameters will become immutable, while others can still be modified. The reason for this is that the user can stop an experiment at any time to change, for instance, the mutation and the recombination rates. However, changing CGP's grid geometry would require the reinitialization of all dependent components, and is therefore locked. An experiment can be started to run continuously by pressing the "Start" button or can be executed to stop

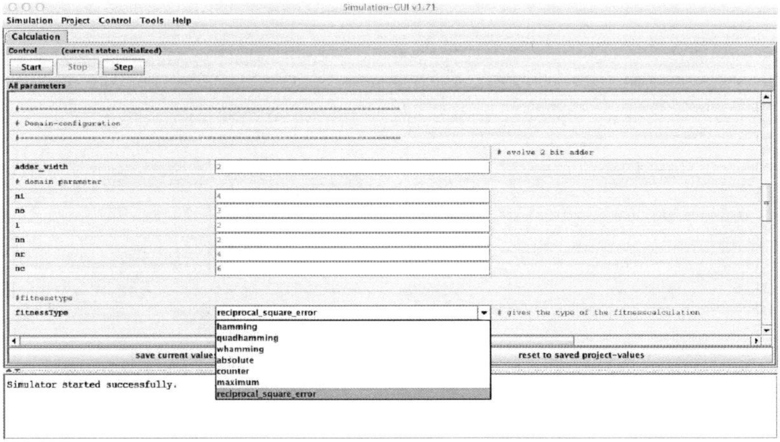

Figure 4.6: Graphical user interface: Configuration pane.

after the creation of a new generation by pressing the "Step" button. Once a button has been pressed, the *Snapshot* and *Statistics* views become visible.

In the *Snapshot* view, presented in Figure 4.7, the user can plot and test evolved individuals. An individual can be selected from the complete experiment history, the last generation, and from the periodically made backups. When an individual is selected, a helper class extending the `GuiChromosomePanel` gets the task of rendering the genotype into a two-dimensional picture. If no such helper class for a particular genotype is implemented, the genotype's textual representation is shown in the view. For the CGP model, we have implemented a visualization illustrated in Figure 4.7. The user can select between plotting all, only the active, and no wires at all, in addition to being able to toggle the node's coloring scheme, indicating to which primary inputs and outputs a node is connected by a path. Furthermore, the graphical user interface relays the user inputs to the helper class. With this, the user is able to toggle the primary input pins, highlighting the signal propagation through the CGP network. Finally, the *Snapshot* view allows exporting the visual genotype representation to a graphics file.

The *Statistics* view, presented in Figure 4.8, filters the experiment output log and plots variables such as the fitness and the most recent non-dominated set online. Any other variables within the log stream identifiable by a keyword can be added to the plot.

The handling of the graphical user interface has been tailored to minimize

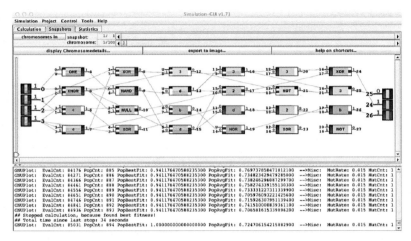

Figure 4.7: Graphical user interface: Genotype view.

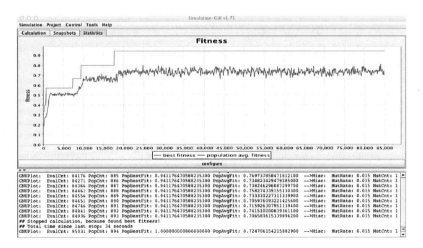

Figure 4.8: Graphical user interface: Statistics plot of an experiment.

the time a user spends preparing and configuring an experiment. Once a configuration file has been loaded, it can be reloaded and saved as a modified version by a single "click." With the selection of an experiment file, the user also defines the base directory for the experiment log files. For every run of the experiment, the graphical user interface automatically creates a unique log directory storing all configuration and log files in it. With this, an *a posterior* analysis will find all the necessary files in one place. The graphical user interface also allows replaying the statistics of previously executed experiments and illustrating the evolved individuals.

4.3.2 Command Line Tools and Distributed Simulation

When the implementation of a new method has been completed and the first parametrization has been set, the next steps require testing the new method on a larger scale. For this purpose, our framework implements multiple tools. The `ConfigCreator` tool allows creating a set of experiment files with algorithm parameters, determined within some intervals and discretized with a given granularity. The tool is also able to prepare all experiment files for the `Condor` [113] batch processing system to distribute the computation on a cluster.

Our second tool, `CalculationConsole`, implements its own job scheduler using standard Unix command line tools, avoiding any additional software. This dramatically simplifies the execution of an experiment on a large and heterogeneous compute network, as neither installation privileges nor specialized programs are required. Similar to the first experiment distribution tool, the second tool takes a set of experiment configuration files, the benchmark executables, and a list of computing nodes. It determines for every computing node the number of computing cores and distributes the experiments so that every core processes one experiment. The tool is able to monitor processing activity and to react properly to machine losses by reinserting broken experimental runs into the job queue.

Once all experiments have completed running, the next set of tools can help evaluate the results. The `evaluate_results` tool extracts the average, best, and worst fitness developments from a set of experiments and creates the appropriate `GNUPlot` data and drawing files. Similarly, the `evaluate_ce` tool generates `GNUPlot` drawings for the computational effort (cf. Section 2.4.1). For pattern recognition experiments, an additional set of tools can merge the partial classification results, create cross validation tables, and generate `GNUPlot` drawings showing the overfitting effects.

4.4 Chapter Conclusion

This section presented our framework's software architecture and tools for efficient experimentation with evolutionary hardware design and optimization. Our goal in creating this framework was a flexible and efficient implementation of new hardware representation models and evolutionary algorithms and an automatic and distributed experiment execution. All experiments presented in the following sections, except the experiments on the functional unit row architecture in Section 7.1, were conducted using our framework.

Chapter 5

Evolvable Hardware Abstraction Models and Operators

The choice of a suitable hardware representation model, i.e., the encoding of a hardware circuit by a chromosome, is paramount for successful evolutionary design techniques. The selection depends, as presented in Chapter 2, upon multiple factors. At first, the application and representation model abstraction levels need to be phased. For instance, the design space of a pattern matching application operating on binary encoded numbers typically consists of arithmetic functions able to process binary encoded data types. Matching this application to a gate based representation model without data type conversion adds an additional complication to the evolutionary search. The harmonization of the abstraction levels for this concrete case can be made in two ways: either by demultiplexing the binary encoded data types or by extending the representation model by buses and arithmetic functions for binary encoded number processing. The representation model abstraction level may be raised further if this helps reduce the search complexity. And this is the second trade-off: lower level representations, while often having a rather simple genotype-to-phenotype mapping, suffer early on from exponential growth of the design space. Higher level representations, on the other hand, have a more complex genotype-to-phenotype mapping but are often more tractable for EA operators. In summary, the selection of an appropriate representation model needs to balance the abstraction level and the correlative search efficiency against the complexity of the genotype-to-phenotype mapping.

The next crucial point when opting for a representation model is its ability to incorporate context and general knowledge. The incorporation can be done constructively by shaping the representation model and the evolutionary operators. Knowledge can also be implemented implicitly by letting the selection operator favor candidate solutions with the desired properties. Context knowledge can be divided into application and application domain specific areas. An example of the first case is Torresen's attempt to evolve a multiplier [364] by restricting the functional set of nodes connecting to primary inputs to the AND function, favouring the computation of all input bit products. Examples for the second case are the multi-chromosome and multi-objective approaches for input and output decomposition [73, 383] and cone based structural operators [6], presented later on in this chapter. Approaches for general knowledge incorporation are the developmental and modularization techniques presented by Walker et al. [380] and Harding et al. [150].

We selected Cartesian genetic programming (CGP) for our work because of three major factors: first, CGP closely reflects the nature of the data flow of combinatorial circuits. Secondly, it is versatile in capturing fine granular LUT- and wire-based elements as well as highly complex buses and IP cores. And the third factor is CGP's simplicity in expressing directed acyclic graphs. Obviously, these factors can be criticized. CGP's focus on combinatorial circuits requires additional architectural elements to implement sequential circuits. Its generality necessitates a greater effort to tailor it to a concrete application and probably a larger search space. The representational simplicity comes with the drawback of complex structural operators. However, the combination of all three factors makes CGP an excellent choice for autonomous embedded systems.

The complexity of structural evolutionary operators is in our view the most substantial criticism of CGP. The difficulty involved with the structural operators for two-dimensional CGP is that modifying and transferring the subgraphs of functionally related nodes requires the rearrangement of the entire genotype. Thereby, the geometrical and interconnection limitations have to be respected. When switching to a one-dimensional model consisting of a single row and dismissing the levels-back parameter, CGP emphasizes structural operator implementations. However, this also shifts CGP's focus away from hardware friendly local connections towards a general DAG oriented model.

Our first contribution is the formalization, implementation, and evaluation of a structural crossover for one-row Cartesian genetic programming in Section 5.1. The goal is to establish a meaningful information drift among individuals by considering subgraphs of functionally dependent nodes. The second contribution of this chapter is the extension of meaningful subfunction extraction to the concept of automatic discovery and reuse of (sub)functions (ADF) and its comparison with age based module creation. The first method shares the idea of structural crossover, that encapsulating meaningful substructures may be more beneficial than selecting modules out of random nodes. The second method is motivated by the creation of biological organs as structures persisting without significant modifications for a long period of time, and thus implicitly contributing to an individual's success. Both methods are presented and compared in Section 5.2.

5.1 Structural Crossover for Cartesian Genetic Programming

The straightforward implementation of a CGP crossover acts on the geometrical structure of the phenotype. The drawback is, as described previously and in Section 3.4.3, that the phenotype's geometry only indirectly reflects the underlying communication structure. To simplify the GP like graph based CGP crossover implementation, we define our method only for the one-row CGP model and allow wires of any desired length. This also extends the applicability of the operator to the ECGP model. When implementing a CGP crossover naively, the resulting operator randomly selects a continuous block of nodes and transfers it to the offspring genotype. This is shown

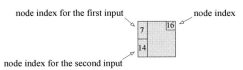

Figure 5.1: Cone based CGP crossover: Node legend.

in Figure 5.2 (a). A block of 5 nodes is randomly selected for the transfer. As connections in the CGP genotype are created randomly, nodes in a block are not necessarily connected, and from point of view of the underlying graph the naive crossover transfers randomly sampled nodes. Figure 5.2 (b) highlights the corresponding subgraphs. The basic idea of our method is to select a connected subgraph of a specific shape and rearrange the genotype so that the naive crossover becomes effective in transferring meaningful subfunctions. As a subgraph shape we select cones for two reasons: cones are a widely used concept in circuit synthesis, especially in the area of LUT mapping for FPGAs (cf., for example, [82]). Given a node n_r in the DAG, a cone rooted at n_r consists of n_r itself plus some predecessor nodes, such that for any node n_i in the cone, there exists a path from n_i to n_r that is entirely in the cone. Note that while a cone has a distinct root node n_r, it can have several outputs. The rationale behind cone based crossover is that many useful substructures in classically engineered circuits are cones, e.g., the sum and carry functions of a full adder. The second reason for selecting cones is their efficient computation. To define a cone, its root node is selected randomly in the first step. Next, all nodes lying on paths between primary inputs and the root are collected by a depth-first search or breadth-first search. When sorting the node list in decreasing order with respect to node indices, the first $n-1$ nodes together with the root node define a cone of size n. One subtlety in generating cones is that we have to avoid what is called *reconvergent paths* in logic synthesis. Returning to the previous example, this would be a path between a cone node n_i and the root n_r which is not entirely in the cone.

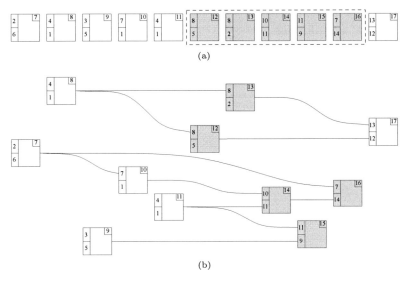

(a)

(b)

Figure 5.2: Naive CGP crossover implementation: Random selection of a continuous block of nodes as shown in Figure (a) does not reflect the underlying graph structure, shown in Figure (b).

This can not happen when applying the presented cone creation strategy, as otherwise there would exist a node n_j, $i < j < r$, with n_j being outside the cone. But as all nodes lying on a path to n_r and having an index k, $i < k < r$, are added to the cone before adding n_i, no such n_j exists.

5.1.1 The CGP Crossover Algorithm

Our crossover implementation comprises the following steps:

- We first select a donor and a recipient individual. Then, we form cones by randomly selecting root nodes and a common cone size between n_{min} and n_{max}. Depending on the actual DAGs, the resulting recipient cone can be smaller than the donor's cone. Additionally, selected cones can contain modules. Figure 5.3 illustrates the selection of a donor cone of size $n = 5$ using a graph (Figure 5.3 (b)) and a CGP representation (Figure 5.3 (a)).

- In the next step, both genotypes are rearranged so that the cones form compact blocks. To this end, cone nodes are moved directly after the

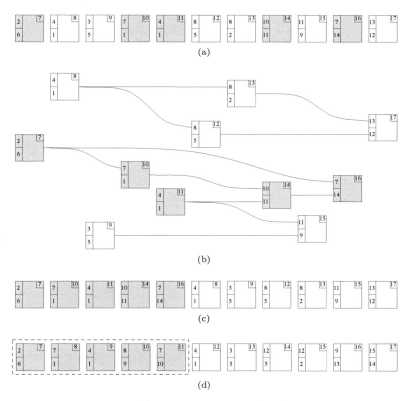

Figure 5.3: Cone-based (E)CGP crossover, the rearrangement of the genotype: Figure (a) shows the CGP genotype and Figure (b) its graph representation. Cone creation starts in this example with the selection of a random root node, node 16 on our case, and the cone size of, e.g., 5. Then, cone nodes are rearranged by placing them directly after the first cone node without changing the relative order, as shown in Figure (c). No feedback wires are introduced in this step. After this, the correct indexing is reestablished in Figure (d). The naive CGP crossover can be applied on this cone transferring a meaningful subfunction.

cone node with the smallest index. In Figure 5.3 (a), the first cone node has index 7. Therefore, cone nodes 10, 11, 14, and 16 are placed directly behind node 7 in Figure 5.3 (c). The cone node order remains unchanged. The rearrangement does not introduce feedback wires, as non-cone nodes (nodes 8, 9, 12, 13, and 15 in Figure 5.3 (a)), lying in the original genotype between the first and last cone nodes (nodes 7 and 16), may have inputs connecting to cone nodes but do not contribute to any cone node input. The rearrangement finishes with reestablishing the correct indexing. Figure 5.3 (d) shows the resulting genotype containing a compact block of functionally related nodes ready for the naive crossover. The recipient genotype undergoes a similar rearrangement, preparing the target for the transfer.

- The third step is the formation of two sets, set p that contains those nodes of the donor's cone which have output connections to nodes outside the cone, and another set q that contains those nodes of the recipient which contribute to nodes within the recipient's cone. Then, all inputs of donor cone nodes connecting to non-donor nodes, and all inputs of recipient genotype nodes connecting to recipient cone nodes, are set dangling.

- The fourth step transfers the donor cone to the prepared location of the recipient genotype, forming a new recombined individual. This process preserves all node types. Specifically, nodes in the donor cone which are modules remain modules. The relevant module descriptions are copied to the offspring individual's modules list. The modules list is updated as recipient modules may become inactive during the transfer.

- In the final step, the dangling inputs of the transplanted cone, respectively, the recipient genotype, are randomly connected to the nodes in list q, respectively, p. If the resulting genotype still contains unconnected inputs, they are connected randomly to preceding nodes.

While the mechanism of our cone based crossover is defined the same way for CGP as for ECGP, the effects are slightly different. For the CGP model, the cone based crossover transfers only the selected subgraph to the offspring individual. In contrast, in the ECGP model, the cone based crossover may also migrate module descriptions, creating a new way of informational drift among individuals.

5.1.2 Evaluation

We evaluated our cone based crossover on the design of even parity, multiplier, and classification circuits. While the first two benchmarks do not strictly match the application profile of EHW functions, they are commonly used to verify and compare the performance of new methods [199, 380, 381]. Additionally, we included classifiers for electromyographic signals as a benchmark. In this application, sensors attached to the skin collect the electric signals of contracting muscles to control a prosthetic hand [183, 361] [7, 9]. The test data was recorded from four muscles of a volunteer's forearm. A sequence of eight contractions (movements), each with 20 repetitions, was measured. The typical signal for a movement is composed of a nine seconds relaxation phase and a five seconds contraction phase. From the last two seconds of the contraction phase, we removed the DC offset and applied RMS smoothing to obtain the feature vectors. The resulting dataset consists of 144 strings of 200 bits each. Based on that data, we evolved a classifier circuit for the movement "open hand." As we want to investigate and compare the computational effort for evolving a classifier and not the generalization capabilities of the representation model, we measured the classifiers' fitnesses on the training data set and defined it to be sufficient when the classification rate on training data exceeds 85% and 95%. A more detailed description of EMG signal classification architecture, the signal acquisition setup, and the feature extraction scheme is presented in Section 7.1.2.

Table 5.1: ECGP, mutation, and crossover parameters for the parity, multiplier, and classification benchmarks. M denotes the number of fitness evaluations per generation.

	parity	multiplier	EMG classifier
genotype length	50 nodes	200 nodes	
number of inputs n_i	3/4/5	4/6	200
number of outputs n_o	1	4/6	1
functional set	2-LUT AND NAND OR NOR	4-LUT AND AND_{inv} OR XOR	4-LUT any function
M for $1 + 4$ ES / GA-5/ GA-50	4/4/47		
mutation rate	0.03		
one-point mutation probability	0.6		
compress/expand probability	0.1/0.2		
module mutation probability	0.1		
module size	2...8 nodes	2...10 nodes	
crossover probability	0.01		
crossover cone size	2...20 nodes		

The ECGP model parameters, including the genotype length, the number of inputs and outputs, and the functional set for the nodes, are shown in Table 5.1. We chose ECGP for the experiments as it is faster for the selected arithmetic benchmarks than the one-row CGP [380, 381]. For the parity function, we used 2-input LUT nodes but restricted the functional set to a few Boolean functions. For the multipliers, we used 4-input LUTs but again restricted the function set to the functions AND, OR, XOR, as well as AND_{inv}, which is an AND with one input inverted. Finally, for the EMG classifiers, we used 4-LUTs without any restriction on the node function.

The regular EA method of CGP and ECGP is a variation of the $1 + \lambda$ ES with $\lambda = 4$ [252]. We presented the exact algorithm in Section 3.4. For a comparison of ES with EAs employing a crossover operator, we implemented a standard elitism based GA with binary tournament selection. The elitism rate is 5%, but at least one individual is picked. We executed two GA configurations, using population sizes of 5 and 50. This covers a population size identical to, and another significantly larger than, that of the reference ES. In the first case (GA-5), the best individual proceeds directly to the next generation. For a population size of 50 (GA-50), the three best individuals proceed directly to the next generation which leaves us with 47 remaining fitness evaluations.

Mutation is applied with a probability of one, but splits into three cases. We either apply one-point mutation, module creation/deletion, or module mutation. The mutation rate denotes the percentage of mutated nodes in a circuit (or in a module). Modules are twice as likely to be dissolved as created, something which increases the pressure towards useful modules. The actually used rates and probabilities can be found in Table 5.1. The cone based crossover operator considers cones with a size of up to 20 nodes (primitive nodes and modules). The application probability is 1%. Higher mutation rates have had negative effects on the convergence speed.

Table 5.2: Computational effort for cone based crossover: $1 + 4$ ES versus GA with populations of 5 and 50 individuals. Bold numbers indicate improvements over the $1 + 4$ ES.

	$1 + 4$ ES	GA, |population|=5		GA, |population|=50	
	absolute	absolute	relative	absolute	relative
2×2 mul	$66,623$	$64,111$	-3.8%	$102,593$	$+54.0\%$
3×3 mul	$8,840,574$	$2,518,964$	-71.5%	$39,064,742$	$+341.9\%$
3-parity	$81,122$	$382,036$	$+470.9\%$	$186,898$	$+130.4\%$
4-parity	$477,880$	$6,294,678$	$+1217.2\%$	$6,482,504$	$+1256.5\%$
85% EMG	$18,260$	$19,859$	$+8.8\%$	$28,825$	$+57.9\%$
95% EMG	$510,147$	$576,988$	$+13.1\%$	$695,794$	$+36.4\%$

The experimental results are presented in Table 5.2, which shows the computational effort both in absolute numbers and relatively to our reference implementation of the $1+4$ ES. A negative relative effort denotes an improvement. From the experimental results, we can make the following observations: comparing the $1+4$ ES to a GA with a population size of 5, we conclude that the GA is better for 3×3 multipliers, on par or slightly worse for 2×2 multipliers and for EMG classifiers, and dramatically worse for the parity function. This points to the effectiveness of the cone based approach for multipliers and to its inefficiency for single-output as well as random logic circuits. Increasing the population size to 50 increases substantially the computational effort for every case. It has to be noted that a GA with a population size of 50 also evolves correct circuits but needs far more fitness evaluations.

5.2 Automatic Acquisition and Reuse of Structural and Age Based Modules

In Section 3.4.4, the mechanism of the original ECGP compress operator is described as the random selection and compaction of a contiguous node interval within the one-row CGP genotype. As argued in Section 5.1, the corresponding graph structure is basically random. This is illustrated in Figure 5.2. Our implementation of CGP subgraph selection for the recombination operator can be adopted for the automatic acquisition and reuse of modules. This follows more closely Koza's original idea of functionally related substructures for module acquisition in GP. Additionally, inspired by the biological principle of organs, we compare structural with age based module creation.

5.2.1 Age Based Module Creation

Age based module creation aggregates primitive nodes (i.e., nodes not referring to a module) that have persisted in the genotype for a larger number of generations. The rationale behind age based module creation is that aged nodes are likely to contribute directly or indirectly to an individual's success, and should therefore be preferred over randomly selected nodes.

We assign to each primitive node n_i an attribute age(n_i). The age is incremented by one in each generation, and set to zero when the node is selected for mutation or compression. The age of primitive nodes within modules remains unchanged: modules themselves do not have an age.

We form module candidates by aggregating primitive nodes, restricting the number of nodes by lower and upper bounds n_{min} and n_{max}. The average age of a module candidate m_j is then given by

$$\text{age}(m_j) = |m_j|^{-1} \sum_{n_i \in m_j} \text{age}(n_i).$$

In our implementation we use two-stage binary tournament to select which module will actually be created. That is, we generate a module candidate by the following procedure: first, we select a random primitive node n_i and a number of primitive nodes $n, n_{min} \leq n \leq n_{max}$, also randomly. Then, we extend the module from n_i to nodes with smaller node numbers until we hit a module or aggregate exactly n primitive nodes. We create another module using a different random primitive node n_j and draw the one with higher average age. If both modules have the same average age, we draw one module randomly. This step is repeated once to derive the final module.

We also experimented with module candidate selection demonstrating maximum average age. This requires the formation and evaluation of a larger number of module candidates. However, picking the module with maximum average age proved inferior to the two-stage binary tournament scheme for all benchmarks. An explanation for this is the fact that maximizing the average module age tends to generate small modules with nodes of great age.

5.2.2 Cone Based Module Creation

Our cone based module creation strategy targets, similar to the cone based crossover, the reordering of the genotype in such a way that the regular ECGP compress operator becomes effective in selecting meaningful graph substructures to form a module. To this end, we adopt the genotype reordering scheme used by the cone based crossover and described in Section 5.1 and illustrated in Figure 5.3. The scheme decomposes into following steps:

- Similar to the cone based crossover scheme, a cone root node n_r and size n_s are randomly selected in the beginning. As ECGP does not capture hierarchical modules, n_r may only have a primitive type. Additionally, the module size n_s is restricted to values between n_{min} and n_{max}.

- In the next step, the predecessor list of n_r is determined and sorted with respect to node indices in descending order. The list is cut after the $n_s - 1$ node or directly before the first appearance of a module node. Together with the root node, up to n_s nodes are now selected to form a module. All selected nodes are primitive and no reconvergent paths can arise, as shown in Section 5.1.

- The genotype rearrangement is identical to the scheme employed for the cone based crossover. All module nodes are moved directly behind the node with the lowest index without changing the relative order (Figure 5.3 (a), Figure 5.3 (c)). Afterwards, the correct indexing is reestablished (Figure 5.3 (d)).

- In the next step, the regular ECGP compress operator puts the module's genes in a separate genotype within the modules list and replaces the former module nodes in the ECGP genotype by a single node of Type I. As the indexing of the ECGP genotype becomes inconsistent again, the node numbering is recomputed.

5.2.3 Evaluation

We compare the age- and cone-based module creation on the same benchmark set and under the same conditions as employed for the cone based crossover experiments in Section 5.1.2. The parametrization of the ECGP representation model, the ES, the mutation operator, and the benchmarks are summarized in Table 5.1. We additionally extend the parity benchmark with the 5 even parity function.

The experimental results are presented in Table 5.3. The table shows the computational efforts and the ratio between our techniques and the regular, random module creation, for random-, age-, and cone-based module creation. A negative relative effort denotes an improvement.

Table 5.3: Computational effort for random-, age-, and cone-based module creation for ECGP. Age- and cone-based module acquisition is compared to random module acquisition.

	random	aging		cone	
	absolute	absolute	relative	absolute	relative
2x2 mul	66,623	51,961	**−22.0%**	49,052	**−26.4%**
3x3 mul	8,840,574	6,001,917	**−32.1%**	3,638,120	**−58.9%**
3-parity	81,122	49,160	**−39.4%**	87,915	+8.4%
4-parity	477,880	494,295	+3.4%	265,796	**−44.4%**
5-parity	1,825,645	1,385,244	**−24.1%**	1,112,691	**−39.1%**
85% EMG	18,260	14,743	**−19.3%**	23,855	+30.7%
95% EMG	510,147	314,311	**−38.4%**	873,319	+71.2%

Age based module creation is highly effective. For six out of the seven benchmarks, age based module creation lowers the computational effort from the previous method, with improvements ranging from some 20% and 40%. The one exception is the 4-parity function, where the computational effort increased slightly by 3.4%.

The overall results for the cone based module creation technique are somewhat inconclusive. However, looking at the different benchmarks we note that for the evolution of multipliers and for larger parity functions, cone based module creation proves highly beneficial. In contrast, for evolving EMG classifiers, the cone based approach does not work at all. Intuitively, the identification of cones as useful subcircuits is hampered if the function is rather small, is a single output function, or consists potentially of random logic functions. In the first case, there is no sufficient potential for creating cones, in the second case, there is no re-usability of a cone for different outputs, and the third case has an insufficient amount of repetitive structures. Multipliers are highly regularly structured functions that are neither particularly small nor single output. From the experimental data, it is clear that cone based module creation is effective for multipliers, in particular, it is more effective than age based module creation.

5.3   Chapter Conclusion

In the introduction of this thesis we proposed a unified adaptation method for Evolvable Hardware that relies on modern Pareto based multi-objective algorithms such as NSGAII and SPEA2. Information drift among candidate solutions, typically implemented as a recombination operator, is a prerequisite for these algorithms. While a meaningful recombination operator can be implemented in a straightforward manner for genetic programming, in Cartesian genetic programming, the implicit genotype coding makes it a challenging task.

In this chapter, we introduced cone based structural crossover for Cartesian genetic programming. With this, we are able to use Pareto based multi-objective evolutionary algorithms to adapt hardware to both gradual and radical changes. Furthermore, we extended the structural CGP operators by cone based automatic acquisition and reuse of subfunctions, which proved to be very effective for regularly structured multiple output circuits such as multipliers. Finally, we introduced age based automatic subfunction acquisition and reuse. This operator proved to be very successful for functions with a more randomized inner structure, such as the pattern matching elements of a classifier.

Chapter 6

Efficient Multi-Objective Optimization for Cartesian Genetic Programming

Adapting to radical resource changes as well as to slowly emerging environmental changes by the very same method is an intriguing idea. It can be solved elegantly by modern, Pareto based multi-objective evolutionary optimizers, as described in Section 1.1 and illustrated in Figure 1.2. We reprint that figure in Figure 6.1. Multi-objective optimization has been previously applied to Evolvable Hardware basically to explore aspects of scalability and digital circuits design principles. For instance, Coello Coello et al. [73, 77] uses a circuit input space decomposition to define a multi-objective function. To this end, for a circuit with n inputs, the population is subdivided into 2^n subpopulations. Each subpopulation has a separate goal, evolving solutions satisfying a single input–output relation of the target function. Once a candidate solution achieves this, the fitness function starts to count the overall number of correctly mapped input–output relations. In the last stage, when a candidate solution matches the goal function completely, the fitness function tries to minimize the number of functional blocks. Their approach does not scale as the population grows exponentially in the number of inputs. However, the authors do not promise the evolution of large circuits but focus on revealing design principles employed by human and automatic designers.

A multi-stage fitness definition, as previously presented, is a common approach for multi-objective circuit evolution. The intuition behind this is the evolution a functionally correct circuit first before optimizing for the remaining secondary objectives, such as size and delay. Similar to the method of Coello Coello, Kalganova and Miller [184] define a two-stage fitness function accounting for a solution's number of gates after the goal function has been implemented correctly. While multi-stage fitness for multi-objective evolution can be implemented with minimal additional effort, it has two drawbacks. Compensating for radical resource changes needs a pre-evolved and an up to date set of solutions with diverse system-related objectives. The

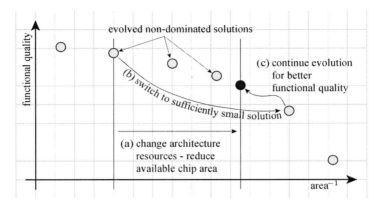

Figure 6.1: Adaptation to radical changes by the means of Pareto based multi-criteria optimization.

design of efficient diversification scheme is a nontrivial task. The second issue reflects the characteristics of EHW applications domains that do not have a correctness property but rather define an optimization goal as a continuous metric. In this case, the task of the optimization is the quick compensation for functional quality degradations. Radical requirement changes are compensated for by reselecting a system behavior with respect to secondary objectives, such as a circuit's size and operation frequency. Both arguments encourage the evolution of functional and system-related objectives simultaneously. Coincidentally, modern multi-objective EAs incorporate sophisticated diversification techniques, allowing them to implement the adaptation to gradual and radical changes by the very same method.

In this chapter we investigate multi-objective evolutionary optimization for Cartesian genetic programming. In Section 6.1 we focus on objective prioritization, mimicking the $1 + 4$ ES selection scheme by a genetic algorithm. In the following section (cf. Section 6.2), techniques based on the periodization of the population helps us to blend the efficiency of local search with the multi-objective optimization of global search techniques. Finally, Section 6.3 concludes the chapter.

6.1 Selection Schemes for Multi-Objective Cartesian Genetic Programming

For our experiments, we qualify digital circuits with regard to three objectives: their functional quality, their speed, and their required hardware area.

As in this section we rely on a benchmark set of logic and arithmetic functions with a completely defined behavior, we determine the *functional quality* for input vectors I as the reciprocal of the mean square error between the output vectors of an evolved individual c and a correct function c^*:

$$f(c) = \frac{1}{1 + \frac{1}{|I|} \sum_{i \in I} ham(c^*(i), c(i))^2},$$ (6.1)

where $ham(c_1, c_2)$ refers to the Hamming distance between two bit vectors c_1 and c_2. A correct circuit receives a functional quality of one.

We estimate the delay of a circuit by the number of logic blocks on its longest path. Given the CGP model, the delay is in the range $\{0, \ldots, n_c + 1\}$. A delay of zero means that the longest path of the circuit connects an input directly with an output. A delay of n_c means that the longest path traverses all logic blocks of the model, whereas a delay of $n_c + 1$ indicates that none of the outputs are connected to an input. The fitness with respect to circuit *speed* is determined as:

$$speed(c) = 1 - \frac{delay(c)}{n_c + 1}$$ (6.2)

The speed metric equals one for the fastest possible circuit (a circuit that maps primary inputs directly to primary outputs) and zero for a circuit that has no connection at all from primary inputs to primary outputs.

We quantify the size of a circuit not by the number of transistors required to implement its Boolean gates but by the number of uniform, reconfigurable functional blocks it uses. The number of logic blocks used by a circuit c, denoted by $used\_blocks(c)$, is in the range $\{0, \ldots, n_c \cdot n_r\}$. Based on this value, we define a circuit's fitness with respect to *area* as:

$$area(c) = 1 - \frac{used\_blocks(c)}{n_c \cdot n_r}$$ (6.3)

A circuit of minimal size, i.e., a circuit not using any logic block, receives an area of one, a circuit that utilizes all available logic blocks has an area of zero.

6.1.1 Objective Prioritization

When comparing the efficiency of single- and multi-objective optimizers, intuition suggests that the simultaneous optimization of multiple and potentially contradictory goals may result in slower convergence. While this is not always the case, as we will show later on, Figure 6.2 illustrates two examples where the functional quality develops far better when optimized by a single-objective EA. The diagrams compare, for the even 6 parity and a hashing

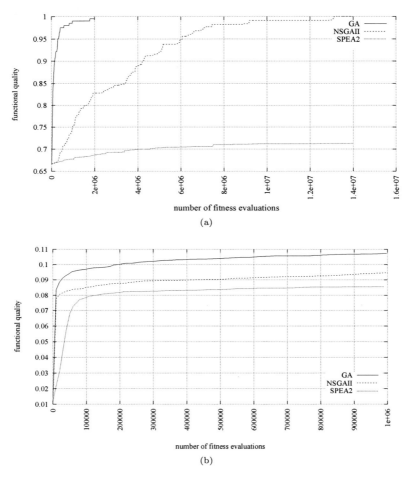

Figure 6.2: Development of the average functional quality: Comparing GA, SPEA2, TSPEA2, and NSGAII on evolving even 6 parity (Figure (a)) and a hashing function (Figure (b)). While SPEA2, TSPEA2, and NSGAII optimize additionally for small circuit size and delay, the plots show the development of functional quality only.

function, the average functional quality development shown by a regular, elitism based GA and the multi-objective SPEA2 and NSGAII. In addition to functional quality, SPEA2 and NSGAII optimize also for area and speed. The benchmark and the algorithm configurations will be given in detail in the next section.

Figure 6.2 allows the following observations: the choice of an MOEA is critical and may result in a dramatically different performance. That is, while in Figure 6.2 (b) the difference in the functional quality developments between NSGAII and SPEA2 is substantial but seems to be constant, for the parity benchmark NSGAII is far better than SPEA2 (Figure 6.2 (b)). Apart from mutual differences between MOEAs, both fall significantly behind GA regarding the functional quality. Particularly for the parity benchmark, the gap is dramatic. While this was anticipated, poor MOEA performance may render these methods infeasible for situations where the rate of change of the input data distribution exceeds an algorithm's adaptation capability and the overall computational effort becomes too large.

An efficient and general method of improving the performance of multi-objective EAs for CGP needs to be independent of the selected algorithm and the target application. Consequently, the representation model itself and the evolutionary operators are potential places for the implementation. For a constructive approach, we need to know which structural elements of a circuit are common to solutions with outstanding functional quality, small circuit size, and low delays. However, this properties typically depend on the function optimized. We therefore selected a non-constructive approach, guiding the multi-objective search to preferred solution subspaces by means of increased selection pressure.

In single-objective optimization, selection pressure is typically regulated by rating candidate solutions regarding some desired properties. This information is combined with the functional quality to select individuals for reproduction. When optimizing multiple objectives, a canonical way to improve the convergence of some objectives is to prefer individuals with the corresponding above average objective values for reproduction. In our case, to put an emphasis on functionally fit CGP circuits, area and speed are taken less into account when selecting parents. The potential drawback is that the functionally fit individuals may demonstrate larger circuit sizes and propagation delays than the individuals evolved by regular, Pareto based MOEAs. As we will show in the next section, the opposite is the case for CGP.

We select SPEA2 to demonstrate our method, as it possesses a standard structure common to many modern MOEAS, such as , e.g., NSGAII. Both algorithms are described in Section 2.2.2 and Section 2.2.3. A suitable place for implementing a selection pressure technique is the fitness metric definition employed to fill the working population. The archive is explicitly used to store nondominated and diverse individuals. Changing the archive filling scheme would modify the Pareto and diversity based dynamics of SPEA2. In contrast, modifying the parent selection scheme changes only the direction of search in the objective space.

The selection scheme for SPEA2's working population relies on a fitness definition which takes into consideration the sorting of nondominated sets and the diversity of the objective space. To increase the selection pressure towards individuals with above average functional quality, we replace the original fitness function by a linear combination of objective values. For every objective o_i, a weight w_i, $0 \leq w_i \leq 1$, $\sum_j w_j = 1$, denotes o_i's contribution to the overall fitness value. The complete fitness function is defined as $f = \sum_j o_j w_j$. More pressure towards functionally fit individuals can now be realized by increasing the appropriate weight and decreasing the weights of the remaining objectives.

Prioritizing individuals for reproduction by linearly weighting the objectives is a fundamental idea of first generation MOEAs [96]. In [367], Trefzer et al. applied a related scheme to a Pareto based algorithm. The authors modified NSGAII's reproduction scheme to select parents using a primary objective and a randomly chosen secondary objective. The algorithm was named *MO-Turtle GA* and was used to evolve analog circuits. In our initial experiments, we observed that functional quality develops best when experiencing the highest selection pressure. We have named this specifically configured SPEA2 variant, similar to the work of Trefzer et al., *Turtle SPEA2* (TSPEA2).

In the next section we investigate whether TSPEA2's observed behavior generalizes to other applications, and how the remaining objectives evolve.

6.1.2 Evaluation

We evaluate TSPEA2's performance on a common CGP benchmark set comprising even parity functions, binary adders, and multipliers [184, 253, 257]. Additionally, we employ a hashing function [87] as a circuit design benchmark. TSPEA2's behavior is compared to GA, SPEA2, NSGAII, IBEA $I_{\epsilon+}$, and IBEA I_{HD}. The two latter algorithms were designed by Zitzler and Künzli [416] to eliminate the implicit search emphasis introduced by diversity techniques operating on nonlinear objective space definitions.

The hashing function had been defined previously by Tettamanzi et al. [87]. The goal was to find a function $h : \mathbb{B}^{16} \to \mathbb{B}^8$ which maps a set M of 2^{12} keys to a set N of 2^8 indices in the most uniform way possible. The fitness function is defined as:

$$f(h) = \frac{1}{1 + \frac{1}{|N|} \sum_{i=1}^{|N|} (|\{j | j \in M, \ h(j) = i\}| - \frac{|M|}{|N|})^2}. \tag{6.4}$$

Similar to the classification benchmark in the previous chapter, the hashing fitness function is a graded metric with an optimum which might be unachievable when resources are limited. We configure the CGP model to conform to the parameters of the original paper [87] except for the functional set F, which may use any Boolean function with four inputs. The key set is created randomly.

Table 6.1: Benchmark configurations. S is the termination number, measured in fitness evaluations. GA may terminate earlier when finding a correct solution for the parity, adder and multiplier benchmarks.

	6-parity	7-parity	2 + 2	2 × 2	3 + 3	3 × 3	hashing
$|P|$				100			
n_c	12	14	50		200		8
n_r			1				8
n_i	6	7	4		6		16
n_o		1	4		6		8
n_n			2				4
l			∞				
F	AND, NAND, OR, NOR		AND, AND$_{inv}$, OR, XOR				any
$P(\text{mut.})$	0.03		0.01		0.002		0.004
$P(\text{rcmb.})$			0.9				
rcmb. type			two-point				uniform
S	$14 \cdot 10^6$		$20 \cdot 10^6$			$6 \cdot 10^6$	10^6

Table 6.1 summarizes the benchmark configurations. For the parity, adder, and multiplier experiments, we configured the CGP model as a single line of two-input gates (nodes). An 8×8 CGP array of 4-input nodes is used for the hashing function. All algorithms rely on a one-point mutation. Two-point crossover is employed for the arithmetic operators, and for the hashing function, a uniform crossover both with a recombination probability of 0.9. The function set for the nodes is not restricted for the hashing function experiment, i.e., the node function can be an arbitrary function of four inputs. For the parity benchmarks the function set is limited to AND, NAND, OR, and NOR. In particular, the XOR logic function is excluded, as otherwise the evolution of correct parity functions is not a challenge at all. The remaining benchmarks may use AND, AND$_{inv}$, OR, and XOR.

As we are interested in the asymptotic behavior of the functional quality of the algorithm's evolved circuits, we conducted several optimization runs for each benchmark. We stopped the evolution after a predefined number of fitness evaluations. For the parity function, this limit was set to $14 \cdot 10^6$ fitness evaluations; for the 3×3 multiplier, to $6 \cdot 10^6$ fitness evaluations; for the hashing function, to 10^6; and for all other experiments, to $20 \cdot 10^6$. The single-objective GA may stop earlier in case it finds a correct solution.

Results

We compare two aspects of the benchmarks. The functional quality performance is evaluated using Koza's "computation effort" (CE) metric [198], presented in Section 2.4.1. To be able to apply CE to the hashing benchmark, we terminate an evolutionary run when the fitness exceeds 0.1. The second aspect covers the development and shape of the nondominated sets. To compare the nondominated sets, we employ the methodology presented in Section 2.4.2. Thereby, we map a sequence of nondominated sets evolved by a particular algorithm and benchmark combination to quality numbers and n-attainments. In a second step we compare different sequences of quality numbers and n-attainments by nonparametric tests revealing the significance of differences in distribution. For every benchmark, we have compared the nondominated sets for all pairwise combinations of algorithm using Zitzler's $I_{\epsilon+}$, $I_{\epsilon*}^1$, and I_{HD}^1 indicators [419], Hansen and Jaszkiewicz's $R1$, $R2$, and $R3$ measures [149] and Pareto attainments [419]. The outcomes of the first six methods are inspected regarding distribution differences by the Mann–Whitney [236], Fisher [120], and Kruskal–Wallis (KW) [202] tests. The attainments are compared using the Kolmogorov–Smirnov (KS) test [196, 323]. As every test is applied to 20 algorithm pairs, the complete evaluation for all benchmarks amounts to 133 5×5 tables of significance numbers. We therefore present only the $I_{\epsilon+}^1$ indicator analyzed by KW, and the Pareto attainments evaluated by KS. The details of these tests are presented in Section 2.4.2. We will indicate whether other tests confirm or disagree with the outcome of these two tests.

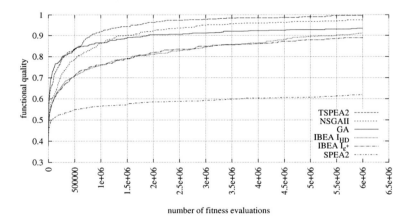

Figure 6.3: Development of the average functional quality: Comparing GA, SPEA2, TSPEA2, NSGAII, IBEA $I_{\epsilon+}$ and IBEA I_{HD} on the evolution of a 3×3 multiplier. The plot shows the development of functional quality only.

In the previous section, Figure 6.2 illustrated the development of the average functional quality for the even 6-parity and hashing function and the SPEA2, NSGAII and GA algorithms. The diagram demonstrates the dominance of the single-objective GA over the MOEAs. A counter-example is presented

Table 6.2: Computational effort and number of correctly evolved circuits for standard GA and some MOEAs. The computational effort (CE) is given in multiples of 10^6. SPEA2 could not evolve a sufficient number of correct circuits to determine the computational effort. P_s denotes the probability of evolving a correct solution during n runs. Bold numbers indicate the best performing algorithms.

	2 × 2 add			3 × 3 add		
	CE	P_s	n	CE	P_s	n
GA	**3.35**	0.74	43	**2.35**	0.53	41
SPEA2	−	0.05	37	−	0.0	33
TSPEA2	4.20	**1.0**	35	6.81	**0.85**	28
NSGAII	5.55	0.97	35	19.90	0.83	31
IBEA $I_{\epsilon+}$	5.49	0.82	40	79.44	0.60	35
IBEA I_{HD}	8.55	0.94	38	82.74	0.54	35

	2 × 2 mul			3 × 3 mul		
	CE	P_s	n	CE	P_s	n
GA	2.93	0.95	43	14.12	0.38	42
SPEA2	−	0.02	37	−	0.0	40
TSPEA2	**2.22**	**1.0**	33	**6.89**	**0.97**	37
NSGAII	3.58	**1.0**	35	14.84	0.73	38
IBEA $I_{\epsilon+}$	9.42	0.94	39	58.74	0.27	40
IBEA I_{HD}	9.14	0.97	39	80.27	0.25	40

in Figure 6.3. It displays the average functional quality development for the 3 × 3 multiplier. For this benchmark, TSPEA2 has the fastest convergence, followed by NSGAII, GA, IBEA I_{HD}, IBEA $I_{\epsilon+}$, and SPEA2. Table 6.2 confirms the results, attributing to TSPEA2 a 97% probability of evolving a correct solution. NSGAII follows with 73%, GA with 38%, IBEA $I_{\epsilon+}$ with 27%, and IBEA I_{HD} with 25%. This result clearly shows that some multi-objective optimizers can outperform the standard single-objective GA in evolving functionally correct circuits. GA's convergence performance shown in Figure 6.3 is very common to global search algorithms. Global search methods often possess fast rates of evolution in the initial exploration phases, but stagnate in the final search phases. The steeper convergence gradients of MOEAs in their advanced search stages for this particular benchmark may be caused by diverse populations, preserving the effectiveness of their EA operators.

The complete set of results for CE is presented in Tables 6.2 and 6.3. Apart from CE, the tables show the probability of correct circuit evolution and the number of experimental runs executed by each algorithm. SPEA2 did not succeed in evolving a sufficient number of correct circuits within the predefined number of fitness evaluations. Therefore, we did not compute its

Table 6.3: Computational effort and number of correctly evolved circuits for standard GA and the MOEAs. The computational effort (CE) is given in multiples of 10^6. SPEA2 could not evolve a sufficient number of correct circuits to determine the computational effort. P_s denotes the probability of evolving a correct solution during n runs. Bold numbers indicate the best performing algorithms.

	6-parity			7-parity			hash		
	CE	P_s	n	CE	P_s	n	CE	P_s	n
GA	**0.40**	**1.0**	68	**1.59**	0.98	66	**0.47**	**0.65**	38
SPEA2	–	0.0	48	–	0.0	44	–	0.0	38
TSPEA2	4.24	**1.0**	44	10.77	**1.0**	24	2.33	0.51	37
NSGAII	11.62	**1.0**	38	61.52	0.46	32	16.63	0.13	38
IBEA $I_{\epsilon+}$	0.57	0.84	65	124.06	0.16	65	9.11	0.20	39
IBEA I_{HD}	1.19	0.81	64	7.79	0.25	63	22.74	0.13	38

computational effort. Bold values indicate the best performing algorithm for a particular benchmark.

From the results, we observe that except for the hashing benchmark no algorithm has a higher probability of finding a correct solution than TSPEA2. Among the multi-objective optimizers, the computational effort of TSPEA2 is the best for all but the parity benchmarks. For the multiplier functions, TSPEA2 is even better in CE than the GA. Generally, the gap between TSPEA2 and the remaining MOEAs became larger for the adder and multiplier benchmarks, when the parity of the circuits increases from 2×2 to 2×3 bits. For the even 6-parity, both IBEA variants has a lower CE than TSPEA2 and NSGAII. Here, GA offers the best computational effort. The 7-parity is again mastered best by GA, followed by IBEA I_{HD}, TSPEA2, NSGAII, and IBEA $I_{\epsilon+}$. For the hashing function, TSPEA2 and IBEA I_{HD} switch places. Generally, the gap between TSPEA2 and GA never became as large as for the other MOEAs. While for the 6-parity benchmark TSPEA2 requires ten times more fitness evaluations than the GA to evolve a correct solution with a probability of 99%, NSGAII and IBEA $I_{\epsilon+}$ show factors of 60 and 77 for the even 7-parity function, and IBEA I_{HD} a factor of 42 for the hashing benchmark.

While TSPEA2 proves to be successful in solving its primary design goal of fast functional quality evolution, approaching and sometimes even exceeding the performance of a single-objective GA, the next section investigates the development of the remaining objectives and whether TSPEA2's nondominated sets are on a par with the results of other multi-objective algorithms. For instance, for the adder, multiplier, and 6-parity benchmarks, there is always at least one MOEA having a similar probability of evolving a correct circuit. Thus, it's interesting how the corresponding nondominated sets compare to the results of TSPEA2. For the 7-parity and hashing benchmarks, TSPEA2 has a far higher probability of evolving a correct circuit. This may indicate that TSPEA2 has a better developed nondominated set than its competitors.

Before discussing the significance tests for the differences of the distributions of the nondominated sets, Figure 6.4 shows an example of the objective space coverage for the hashing benchmark, achieved by 75% (Figure 6.4 (a)) and 25% (Figure 6.4 (b)) of the evolved nondominated sets. The functional quality and area^{-1} objective values are normalized and negated. A hypothetical optimal solution has, therefore, the objective coordinate $\vec{0}$. We omit the discussion of the attainment functions spanned by the functional quality and delay, as the effects and conclusions are almost identical.

Our first observation from Figure 6.4 is that all algorithms are able to evolve smooth nondominated sets. The sets contain many diverse Pareto points, offering a considerable range of circuits with different objective trade-offs. The next observation concerns the performance of TSPEA2. For nondominated set regions with low functional quality (e.g. 0.7 to 0.9) and small circuit size (e.g. 0.0 to 0.025), the competitors of TSPEA2 tend to evolve functionally better solutions. This is the case for circuits of size 0, i.e., consisting only of wires between primary inputs and outputs, and partially for circuits with one functional block, where in the 25% attainment, only IBEA $I_{\epsilon+}$ found functionally better solutions. All functionally dominant circuits with 2 or more blocks are found by TSPEA2. Functional quality prioritization gives TSPEA2, apart from functionally dominant solutions, also more freedom to explore circuit regions with inferior quality in the remaining objectives. This can be observed in Figure 6.4 (b), where TSPEA2 manages to find a more diverse set of solutions than the other algorithms, with area values between 0.05 and 0.17.

Table 6.4 and Table 6.5 present the evaluation of the comparisons of the nondominated sets using the unary $I_{\epsilon+}^1$ indicator as well as the attained functions. Again, the first method is evaluated by the KW test while the KS test is used to compare the attainment functions. For the KW test, a numeric value in column c and row r indicates that the H_0 hypothesis of identical distribution sequences is rejected. The number represents the one-tailed p-value indicating whether the algorithm in row r has a lower and therefore a better mean than the algorithm in column c. If the number is below $\alpha = 0.05$, we consider the distribution differences as significant. In contrast to the asymmetric KW test, the KS test verifies whether two sequences follow the same distribution or not. Therefore, a numerical value in column c and row r below $\alpha = 0.05$ indicates that the attained coverages of the algorithms in row r and column c are significantly different.

We draw the following conclusions from Table 6.4 and Table 6.5:

- While the nondominated sets of TSPEA2 are sometimes classified as different and significantly different from the nondominated sets of the other MOEAs, the KW test never evidences a higher $I_{\epsilon+}^1$ mean. Thus, we can conclude that no tested MOEA managed to evolve a significantly better nondominated set than TSPEA2 by means of the $I_{\epsilon+}^1$ indicator.

- For parity and hashing benchmarks, TSPEA2 significantly dominates all tested MOEAs according to the KW test. This is interesting, as for the 7-parity and hashing functions, we anticipated TSPEA2's evolving "better" nondominated sets as a consequence of its higher probability for correct circuit evolution. For the 6-parity function, however, all the MOEAs have similarly high probabilities of evolving correct circuits. The dominance of TSPEA2 for the parity benchmark lets us assume that parity circuit design space regions with high functional quality also demonstrate above average values in the remaining objectives. A possible positive correlation between the objectives can intuitively be explained by the fact that an "optimal" parity function also has the smallest possible circuit size and delay.

- SPEA2 is almost always considered significantly different and inferior in evolving nondominated sets.

Additionally to the $I_{\epsilon+}^1$ indicator, we have compared the nondominated sets using the $I_{\epsilon*}^1$ and I_{HD} indicators and the $R1$, $R2$, and $R3$ measures. The outcome has been inspected by the KW, Fisher, and Mann–Whitney tests. The results are, apart from minor deviations, almost identical to the results presented in Tables 6.4 and 6.5.

Conclusion

The multi-objective evolution of CGP circuits by modern MOEAs such as the NSGAII and SPEA2 can be significantly improved by introducing weights for the preferences and objectives into the selection scheme. Especially for potentially collinear objectives, TSPEA2 excels, sometimes even outperforming the single-objective GA. However, it is the regular effect of fixed linear weighting of the objectives that arranges that some fitness areas are explored more thoroughly than others. While for TSPEA2 this effect is not significant, it can still be observed. Altogether, if the evolution of the main objective in a short period of time is essential while it is acceptable to reach very good but not the highest values for the other objectives, TSPEA2 is a very useful solution. When unbiased exploration of the complete fitness landscape (which is therefore more robust) is important, as for instance when a good weighting scheme is unknown *a-priori*, other techniques have to be investigated.

In the following section we introduce a general methodology and a Pareto based local search style algorithm for an exploration without preferences of the fitness landscape.

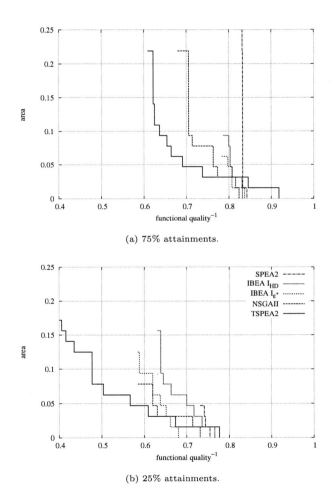

(a) 75% attainments.

(b) 25% attainments.

Figure 6.4: 75% and 25% attainments for the hashing benchmark. The objective values are normalized and negated, thus, a hypothetical optimal solution has the objective coordinate $\vec{0}$.

Table 6.4: Comparison of the nondominated sets. A dot denotes an accepted H_0. When the KW test rejects H_0 for the algorithm pair (a_{row}, a_{col}), a one-tailed p-value lower than $\alpha = 0.05$ indicates that a_{row} evolves significantly better nondominated sets than a_{col} regarding $I_{\epsilon+}^1$ (cf. Section 2.4.2). A star indicates significantly different nondominated set distributions at $\alpha = 0.05$ according to the KS test.

		SPEA2	TSPEA2	NSGAII	IBEAI$_{\epsilon+}$	IBEAI$_{HD}$
2 × 2 add	SPEA2		1.000	1.000	1.000	1.000
KW test	TSPEA2	0.0		·	·	0.0
	NSGAII	0.0	·		0.998	·
	IBEAI$_{\epsilon+}$	0.0	·	0.002		0.0
	IBEAI$_{HD}$	0.0	1.000	·	1.000	
2 × 2 add	SPEA2		*	·	·	*
KS test	TSPEA2	*		·	·	*
	NSGAII	·	·		*	*
	IBEAI$_{\epsilon+}$	·	·	*		*
	IBEAI$_{HD}$	*	*	*	*	
3 × 3 add	SPEA2		1.000	1.000	1.000	1.000
KW test	TSPEA2	0.0		·	·	0.0
	NSGAII	0.0	·		·	0.0
	IBEAI$_{\epsilon+}$	0.0	·	·		0.003
	IBEAI$_{HD}$	0.0	1.000	1.000	0.997	
3 × 3 add	SPEA2		*	*	*	*
KS test	TSPEA2	*		*	*	*
	NSGAII	*	*		*	*
	IBEAI$_{\epsilon+}$	*	*	*		*
	IBEAI$_{HD}$	*	*	*	*	
2 × 2 mul	SPEA2		1.000	1.000	1.000	1.000
KW test	TSPEA2	0.0		·	·	0.0
	NSGAII	0.0	·		·	0.0
	IBEAI$_{\epsilon+}$	0.0	·	·		0.0
	IBEAI$_{HD}$	0.0	1.000	1.000	1.000	
2 × 2 mul	SPEA2		*	·	·	*
KS test	TSPEA2	*		·	·	*
	NSGAII	·	·		·	*
	IBEAI$_{\epsilon+}$	·	·	·		*
	IBEAI$_{HD}$	*	*	*	*	
3 × 3 mul	SPEA2		1.000	1.000	1.000	1.000
KW test	TSPEA2	0.0		·	0.0	0.0
	NSGAII	0.0	·		0.0	0.0
	IBEAI$_{\epsilon+}$	0.0	1.000	1.000		·
	IBEAI$_{HD}$	0.0	1.000	1.000	·	
3 × 3 mul	SPEA2		*	*	*	*
KS test	TSPEA2	*		*	*	*
	NSGAII	*	*		*	*
	IBEAI$_{\epsilon+}$	*	*	*		*
	IBEAI$_{HD}$	*	*	*	*	

Table 6.5: Comparison of the nondominated sets. A dot denotes an accepted H_0. When the KW test rejects H_0 for the algorithm pair (a_{row}, a_{col}), a one-tailed p-value lower than $\alpha = 0.05$ indicates that a_{row} evolves significantly better nondominated sets than a_{col} regarding $I^1_{\epsilon+}$ (cf. Section 2.4.2). A star indicates significantly different nondominated set distributions at $\alpha = 0.05$ according to the KS test.

		SPEA2	TSPEA2	NSGAII	IBEA$I_{\epsilon+}$	IBEAI_{HD}
6 parity	SPEA2		1.000	1.000	1.000	1.000
KW test	TSPEA2	0.0		0.0	0.003	0.001
	NSGAII	0.0	1.000		0.999	0.989
	IBEA$I_{\epsilon+}$	0.0	0.997	0.001		·
	IBEAI_{HD}	0.0	0.999	0.011	·	
6 parity	SPEA2		*	·	*	*
KS test	TSPEA2	*		·	*	*
	NSGAII	·	·		*	*
	IBEA$I_{\epsilon+}$	*	*	*		·
	IBEAI_{HD}	*	*	*	·	
7 parity	SPEA2		1.000	·	*	0.021
KW test	TSPEA2	0.0		0.0	0.0	0.0
	NSGAII	·	1.000		0.005	·
	IBEA$I_{\epsilon+}$	1.000	1.000	0.995		·
	IBEAI_{HD}	0.979	1.000	·	·	
7 parity	SPEA2		*	*	*	*
KS test	TSPEA2	*		*	*	*
	NSGAII	*	*		*	·
	IBEA$I_{\epsilon+}$	*	*	*		·
	IBEAI_{HD}	*	*	·	·	
Hashing	SPEA2		1.000	1.000	0.999	0.990
KW test	TSPEA2	0.0		0.0	0.0	0.0
	NSGAII	0.0	1.000		·	0.001
	IBEA$I_{\epsilon+}$	0.001	1.000	·		·
	IBEAI_{HD}	0.010	1.000	0.999	·	
Hashing	SPEA2		*	*	*	*
KS test	TSPEA2	*		*	*	*
	NSGAII	*	*		·	*
	IBEA$I_{\epsilon+}$	*	*	·		·
	IBEAI_{HD}	*	*	*	·	

6.2 Evolutionary Algorithm Periodization

The methods and algorithms presented in this section have many motivations:

- The previous section presents objective selection schemes that significantly improve the efficiency of the multi-objective evolution of CGP circuits. Their excellent performance has been shown using many benchmarks, suggesting that they have good generalization capabilities. However, the weighting scheme used by TSPEA2 for its objectives needs to be balanced by a human designer each time there is a new set of goal functions, in order to obtain the highest possible performance. The demand for an unsupervised and preference-free multi-objective method for CGP is a challenge we address in this section.

- In our work, we have observed the dominance of evolutionary strategies with small λs for single-objective CGP compared to standard, elitism based GAs with larger populations. $1 + \lambda$ ES belongs to the family of local search algorithms, while the single- and multi-objective GAs presented in this work come from the global search family. A systematic approach for combining algorithms to blend their properties, their convergence behaviors, and their functionalities, is the next challenge approached by this section.

- Pareto based multi-objective algorithms introduce the nondominance order relation and diversity into their populations. When combined with non-Pareto approaches, these properties have to be respected. Pareto based ES that also implement a standard diversity technique, therefore, define the next challenge of this section.

- Finally, combining original algorithms with no or a small implementation effort is the last topic for this chapter to address.

When combining multiple algorithms into a single scheme, we are inspired by the work of Schwiegelshohn [298] and Ierardi [175] on periodic sorting networks (PSN) with constant depth. Sorting networks assume that each input element is located on a two-dimensional grid. Compare–exchange lines (CEL) between two grid nodes sort the adjacent elements in a single step. A concrete PSN scheme comprises two and more CEL layouts that are applied rotationally. For instance, Knuth's odd–even transposition sort is a PSN of depth 2. We have observed for some PSN algorithms that the grid's geometry plays an essential role in the convergence behavior [187]. Some geometries enable outstanding convergence in the initial search phases, while other excel in the intermediate or final stages. Applying the very same PSN scheme to a multi-geometry set of CEL layouts improves the overall convergence. We extend this idea for population- and generation-based heuristic optimizers by proposing a *periodized execution model* that blends the algorithms' properties, functionalities, and convergence behaviors in a simple and straightforward way. To this end, we define for a rotationally executed sequence of algorithms a repetition function specifying the number of generations each algorithm is iterated before proceeding with the next one.

6.2.1 The Periodization Model

Let $A = (a_1, a_2, \ldots, a_n)$ be the set of algorithms used in the periodization. As an illustrative example, consider $A = \{GA1, GA2, LS\}$. For a hypothetical periodized algorithm that executes a single step/generation of GA1, followed by two steps of LS, then a single step of GA2 and two steps of LS, the index sequence I for the algorithm selection is given by (a_1, a_3, a_2, a_3), and the repetition sequence F is $(f_1, f_2, f_3, f_4) = (1, 2, 1, 2)$. While in this specific example, F is a vector of constants, the number of repetitions can be adaptively adjusted based on the history of the optimization run $\mathcal{H}$. In particular, global search GAs with fast convergence in the beginning of an optimization run could be repeated more often in the early search phases, while local search algorithms that excel at improving nearly optimal nondominated sets could be used more intensively in the final optimization phase.

With t as the current generation number, $\mathcal{H}$ as the history of the current optimization run, $A = (a_1, a_2, \ldots, a_n)$, $n \in \mathbb{N}$ as the set of algorithms used in the periodization, $I = (i_1, i_2, \ldots, i_m)$, $m \in \mathbb{N}$, $i_k \in (1, 2, \ldots, n)$ as the set of indices for the selected algorithms in the execution sequence, and $F = (f_1, f_2, \ldots, f_m)$, $f_k(t, \mathcal{H}) \to \mathbb{N}$ as the number of repetitions for the algorithms in I, the complete *periodized execution model* P is defined as:

$$
\begin{aligned}
P &= A_I^F \\
&= (a_{i_1}^{f_1(t,\mathcal{H})}, a_{i_2}^{f_2(t,\mathcal{H})}, \ldots, a_{i_m}^{f_m(t,\mathcal{H})}).
\end{aligned}
$$

The history $\mathcal{H}$ can be large if considering the complete information of an optimization run, or more compact if considering, for example, only the dominated space of the current nondominated set. In our experiments, we choose $f_k(t, \mathcal{H})) := f_k(t) \equiv const$. For the general case, however, $\mathcal{H}$ changes with each generation. Accordingly, the number of algorithm repetitions $f_k(t, \mathcal{H}_t)$ computed in generation t for algorithm a_k may differ from the $f_k(t+1, \mathcal{H}_{t+1})$ computed in the next generation. Therefore, the repetition vector F needs to be updated after each generation. An example where this effect becomes relevant is when some algorithm is iterated until local convergence occurs. That is, if for l algorithm repetitions the best individual or the nondominated area does not change, the periodization scheme proceeds with the next algorithm. However, if the population can be improved, the algorithm is executed again for at least l generations.

6.2.2 Hybrid Evolutionary Strategies

Evolutionary Strategies in their original form rely solely on a mutation operator. The $\{\mu \overset{,}{+} \lambda\}$ ES uses μ parents to create λ offspring and selects μ new parents from all individuals in case of a '+' variant or from the new individuals in case of the ',' variant.

Our new hES local search style technique is a $1 + \lambda$ ES designed for periodization with multi-objective evolutionary algorithms. In particular, we include two concepts from the Elitist Nondominated Sorting GA II (cf. Section 2.2.2) in hES: the fast nondominated sorting and the crowding distance as a diversity metric. Fast nondominated sorting calculates nondominated sets for the objective space points. The *crowding distance* for a point is defined as the volume of a hyper-cube bounded by the adjoining points in the same nondominated set. Consequently, the crowding distance creates an order, denoted by $\prec_n$, on the points of a nondominated set. Our hES local search technique uses fast nondominated sorting to decompose parents and offspring into nondominated sets, and uses crowding distances to decide which of the individuals might be skipped in order to keep the nondominated set diverse.

In summary, the key ideas for our hES algorithm are:

1. A local search style algorithm is executed for every element of a given set of solutions. Exactly one individual, which is nondominated, from a parent and its offspring proceeds to the next population.

2. Offspring individuals that are mutually nondominated to their parent but have a different Pareto vector are skipped. This prevents unnecessary fluctuations in the nondominated set.

3. Neutral genetic drift, as presented by Miller in [252], is achieved by skipping a parent if at least one of its offspring holds an equal Pareto vector.

4. Parents and offspring are partitioned into nondominated sets and new parents are selected using NSGAII's crowding distance metric.

Algorithm 5 shows the pseudocode of our hES implementation `hES-step`. The algorithm starts with the creation of offspring in lines 1 to 4. To this end, for every individual in the parent population P_t, `hES-step` executes $1 + \lambda$ ES appending the newly created offspring to Q_t. The $1 + \lambda$ ES loop is implemented by the `ES-generate` in Algorithm 5. After the offspring are created, `hES-step` proceeds with the concatenation of parents and offspring by calling the `add-replace` procedure, listed in Algorithm 7. `add-replace` clones the parent population and successively adds offspring that have a unique Pareto vector to this population. An offspring with a

Pareto vector identical to its parent replaces the parent. Then, hES-step partitions the concatenated set R_t in line 6 into nondominated sets $\mathcal{F}_i$ using NSGAII's fast-nondominated-sort (cf. Algorithm 2). After that, starting with the dominant set $\mathcal{F}_1$, the algorithm partitions $\mathcal{F}_1$ by the parents into $G = \{G_1, G_2, \dots\}$. That means all individuals of G_i have the same parent p. Additionally, if $p \in \mathcal{F}_1$, then $p \in G_i$. Should a non-empty set G_i not contain the parent p, one of the least crowded individuals of G_i is selected to proceed to the next generation. Otherwise, the parent proceeds to the next generation. Once p or one of its offspring is transferred to the next generation, p and all of its offspring are skipped by hES-step from further processing.

Algorithm 5: hES-step(λ, P_t)—perform a single hES step

Input: λ, parent population P_t
Output: new archive P_{t+1}

1   $Q_t \leftarrow \emptyset$
2   **foreach** $p \in P_t$ **do**
3 | $Q_t \leftarrow Q_t \cup$ ES-generate(p, λ)
4   **end**
5   $R_t \leftarrow$ add-replace(P_t, Q_t)
6   $\mathcal{F} \leftarrow$ fast-nondominated-sort(R_t)
7   $P_{t+1} \leftarrow \emptyset$
8   **foreach** $\mathcal{F}_i \in \mathcal{F}$ **do**
9   crowding-distance-assignment$(\mathcal{F}_i)$
10     $\mathcal{G} \leftarrow$ group-ordered-by-parent$(\mathcal{F}_i)$
11   **foreach** $\mathcal{G}_j \in \mathcal{G}$ **do**
12   **if** *parent of* $\mathcal{G}_j$ *not already replaced* **then**
13   **if** $parent(\mathcal{G}_j) \in \mathcal{G}_j$ **then**
14 | $P_{t+1} \leftarrow P_{t+1} \cup \{$parent$(\mathcal{G}_j)\}$
15   **else**
16   sort$(\mathcal{G}_j, \prec_n)$
17           $P_{t+1} \leftarrow P_{t+1} \cup \{\mathcal{G}_j[0]\}$
18   **end**
19   mark parent of $\mathcal{G}_j$ as replaced
20   **end**
21   **end**
22 **end**

6.2.3 Evaluation

We experimented with several benchmarks to compare hES and the periodized variants of hES, NSGAII and SPEA2. At first, we used the standard benchmarks for multi-objective algorithms DTLZ{2,6} and ZDT6. These benchmarks are available with the PISA toolbox [49] and are described in [239]. Second, we compared our algorithms on the evolution of digital

---

Algorithm 6: ES-generate(p,λ)—generate λ offspring

Input: parent p, number of offspring λ
Output: offspring set Q
1   $Q \leftarrow \emptyset$
2   **for** $i \leftarrow 1$ **to** λ **do**
3      $p' \leftarrow \text{mutate}(p)$
4      $Q \leftarrow Q \cup \{p'\}$
5   **end**

Algorithm 7: add-replace(P,Q)—return copy of P joint by Q, replace parents in P by offspring in Q with equal Pareto vectors, avoid adding multiple offspring with equal Pareto vectors.

Input: sets P, Q
Output: set R
1   $R \leftarrow P$
2   **foreach** $q \in Q$ **do**
3   **if** $\nexists r \in R : r \preceq q \wedge q \preceq r$ **then**
4         $R \leftarrow R \cup \{q\}$
5   **end**
6   **if** $\exists r \in R : r \preceq q \wedge q \preceq r \wedge parent(\{q\}) == r$ **then**
7         $R \leftarrow R \cup \{q\}$
8         $R \leftarrow R \backslash \{r\}$
9   **end**
10   **end**

---

circuits, i.e., even 5- and 7-parity and 2×2 and 3×3 adders and multipliers. As in Section 6.1, besides the functional quality of a digital circuit, we selected the circuit's area and speed to define a multi-objective benchmark.

In our experiments we executed 20 repetitions for every combination of goal function and algorithm. For the hES, **ES-generate** produces 32 offspring for each parent. For the other benchmarks, Algorithm 5 was configured to have one offspring per parent.

Table 6.6 presents the configuration of the benchmarks DTLZ{2,6} and ZDT6. For these benchmarks, NSGAII and SPEA2 employ the SBX crossover operator [97]. The optimization runs were stopped after 10,000 fitness evaluations. Table 6.7 shows for the digital circuit benchmarks the CGP configurations, termination criteria, and population sizes. We limit the functional set to the Boolean functions presented in Table 6.8. To simplify the nomenclature, we use the following abbreviations:

$$\begin{array}{lcl} \text{hES} & \rightarrow & \mathbf{h} \\ \text{SPEA2} & \rightarrow & \mathbf{s} \\ \text{NSGAII} & \rightarrow & \mathbf{n} \end{array}$$

Table 6.6: DTLZ2, DTLZ6, and ZDT6 benchmark configurations.

no. objectives	2
number of decision variables	100
individual mutation probability	1
individual recombination probability	1
variable mutation probability	1
variable swap probability	0.5
variable recombination probability	1
eta mutation	20
eta recombination	15
use symmetric recombination	1

Table 6.7: CGP benchmark configurations. S is the termination number, measured in fitness evaluations. $|P|$ and $|A|$ denote the capacity of the parent population and the archive.

	5-parity	7-parity	2 × 2 add	2 × 2 mul	3 × 3 add	3 × 3 mul
$|P|/|A|$				32/100 for hES, 50/100 else		
n_c				200		
n_r				1		
n_i	5	7		4		6
n_o		1		4		6
n_n				2		
l				∞		
F				see Table 6.8		
$P(\text{mut.})$				0.1		
$P(\text{rcmb.})$				0.0 for hES, 0.5 else		
rcmb. type				one-point		
S	400.000	800.000	400.000	1.600.000	400.000	1.600.00

6.2.3.1 Periodization of hES for DTLZ2, DTLZ6 and ZDT6

To examine the effect of local search, we first execute the standard NSGAII and SPEA2 for a given benchmark in order to determine the reference performance. Then, we increase step by step the influence of local search by periodizing NSGAII with hES until only hES is executed. In terms of our periodization model (cf. Section 6.2.1), we investigate the six periodization schemes: $\mathbf{n}$, $\mathbf{s}$, $\mathbf{nh}$, $\mathbf{nh}^4$, $\mathbf{nh}^{10}$, and $\mathbf{h}$.

Table 6.9 shows the results of the KW test applied to the benchmarks DTLZ{2,6} and ZDT6 with respect to the unary additive epsilon indicator $I_{\epsilon+}^1$ at the significance level $\alpha = 1\%$. The results of the KS test are omitted

Table 6.8: CGP configuration: Functional set F.

Number	Function	Number	Function
0	0	10	$a \oplus b$
1	1	11	$a \oplus \bar{b}$
2	a	12	$a + b$
3	b	13	$a + \bar{b}$
4	$\bar{a}$	14	$\bar{a} + b$
5	$\bar{b}$	15	$\bar{a} + \bar{b}$
6	$a \cdot b$	16	$a \cdot \bar{c} + b \cdot c$
7	$a \cdot \bar{b}$	17	$a \cdot \bar{c} + \bar{b} \cdot c$
8	$\bar{a} \cdot b$	18	$\bar{a} \cdot \bar{c} + b \cdot c$
9	$\bar{a} \cdot \bar{b}$	19	$\bar{a} \cdot \bar{c} + \bar{b} \cdot c$

as they indicate differences significant at $\alpha = 5\%$ between the nondominated sets for almost all combinations of algorithm and benchmark.

Table 6.9: Comparison of the nondominated sets of DTLZ2, DTLZ6, and ZDT6. A dot denotes an accepted H_0. When the KW test rejects H_0 for the algorithm pair (a_{row}, a_{col}), a one-tailed p-value lower than $\alpha = 0.01$ indicates that a_{row} evolves significantly better nondominated sets than a_{col} regarding $I_{\epsilon+}^1$ (cf. Section 2.4.2).

		n	s	nh	nh^4	nh^{10}	h
DTLZ2	n		.	0.0	0.0	0.0	0.0
KW test	s	.		0.0	0.0	0.0	0.0
	nh	.	.		0.0	0.0	0.0
	nh^4	.	.	.		0.0	0.0
	nh^{10}	.	.	.	.		0.0
	h	.	.	.	.	.	
DTLZ6	n		.	0.0	0.0	0.0	0.0
KW test	s	.		0.0	0.0	0.0	0.0
	nh	.	.		0.0	0.0	0.0
	nh^4	.	.	.		0.0	0.0
	nh^{10}	.	.	.	.		0.0
	h	.	.	.	.	.	
ZDT6	n		.	.	.	.	0.0
KW test	s	.		.	.	.	0.0
	nh	0.0001	0.0027		.	0.0001	0.0
	nh^4	0.0	0.0	0.0014		0.0	0.0
	nh^{10}	.	.	.	.		0.0
	h	.	.	.	.	.	

The central observation for the DTLZ2 and DTLZ6 experiments is that the quality of the nondominated sets degrades with an increasing influence of local search. Starting with the periodization of NSGAII and hES, the KW test shows falling performance when increasing the number of hES iterations. The hES-only experiment results in the worst performance of all the algorithms. The KW test results are confirmed by the graphical interpretation of the 75% attained nondominated sets in Figure 6.5 (a) and Figure 6.5 (b).

For the ZDT6 benchmark, the influence of hES is not as one sided as for the DTLZ{2,6} benchmarks. The nh periodization outperforms SPEA2 and NSGAII. Further increase in the influence of hES in the nh^4 periodization lets it dominate all other algorithms. The nh^{10} periodization is on a par with SPEA2 and NSGAII, while the execution of hES alone, as with DTLZ{2,6}, falls behind. The 75% attainments pictured in Figure 6.6 (a) confirm this. Interestingly, despite the large gap between nh^{10} and the group of SPEA2 and NSGAII, the KW test finds no significant differences at $\alpha = 1\%$ between the corresponding indicator sequences. The KS test, similar to the results for the DTLZ{2,6} benchmarks, reveals significant differences at $\alpha = 5\%$ for all algorithm combinations except the NSGAII and SPEA2 pair.

The DTLZ{2,6} and ZDT6 benchmarks demonstrate the various kinds of impact that local search may have when periodized with global search algorithms. To gain an insight into whether the order of the algorithms in the periodization sequence influences the results, and into how an hES-less periodizations of SPEA2 and NSGAII compares to the regular SPEA2 and NSGAII, we fixate on the ZDT6 benchmark and apply 2- and 3-tuple permutations of the NSGAII, SPEA2, and hES algorithms. All the experiments were repeated 100 times and the execution was stopped after 200 generations.

Table 6.10 shows the results for 2-tuple combinations of NSGAII, SPEA2, and hES. The general observation taken from the KW test is that hES periodized with either NSGAII or SPEA2 outperforms standard NSGAII, SPEA2, and their combinations. Interestingly, the *hES-after-SPEA2* outperforms the *hES-after-NSGAII*, while *SPEA2-after-hES* does not. This shows that the performance of this particular periodization scheme may be sensitive to the initial order of the executed algorithms.

The KS test confirms the results observed before. There are basically two classes of algorithms, showing significantly different results: the class of algorithms periodized with hES, and the class of NSGAII, SPEA2 and their combinations. In contrast to the previous test, the differences between (hs) and (nh) are now identified as significant.

Next, Table 6.11 shows the results of 3-tuple combinations of hES with NSGAII and SPEA2. Analogous to the results achieved for the 2-tuple tests, all the periodized algorithms outperform (KW) and differ (KS) from NSGAII and SPEA2.

In summary, we can conclude that for the DTLZ{2,6} benchmarks, an in-

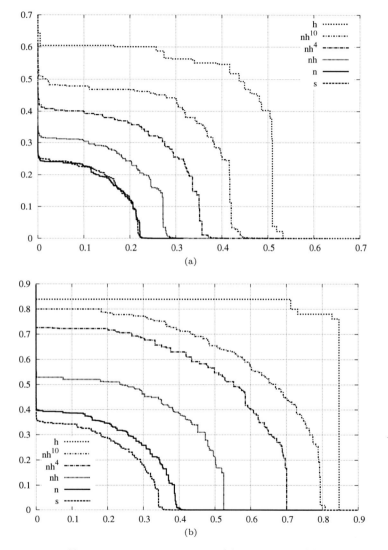

Figure 6.5: 75%-attainments for the DTLZ2 (a) and DTLZ6 (b) benchmarks. A hypothetical optimum is located at $\vec{0}$.

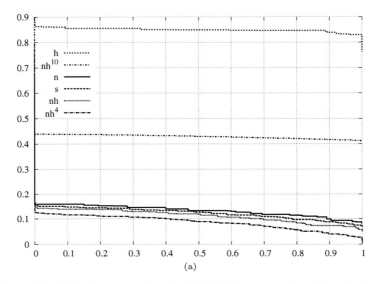

Figure 6.6: 75%-attainments for the ZDT6 (a) benchmarks. A hypothetical optimum is located at $\vec{0}$.

creasing impact of hES reduces the quality of the nondominated sets evolved, while for the ZDT6 benchmark, the schemes periodized with hES have the dominating results.

6.2.3.2 Periodization of hES for Digital Circuit Design

In contrast to the previous benchmarks, we optimize for three objectives in this section: the functional quality, the area, and the propagation delay. In total, each algorithm is executed 20 times for each pair of goal functions. Table 6.12 summarizes the number of runs that resulted in functionally correct solutions. The first observation is that for the parity, the 3×3 adder, and the 3×3 multiplier benchmarks, almost none of the algorithms managed to evolve functionally correct circuits. We focus therefore on the experiments involving the 2×2 adder and the 2×2 multiplier, when discussing the influence of local search on the evolution of correct circuits.

When comparing the motivations and methodologies in the current section with those of Section 6.1, several analogies become clear: in this section, we try to improve multi-objective circuit optimization by combining it with a single-objective local search technique, while in Section 6.1, we mimic the

Table 6.10: ZDT6 nondominated sets comparison for 2-tuple combinations of NSGAII, SPEA2 and hES to NSGAII and SPEA2. A dot denotes an accepted H_0. When the KW test rejects H_0 for the algorithm pair (a_{row}, a_{col}), a one-tailed p-value lower than $\alpha = 0.01$ indicates that a_{row} evolves significantly better than a_{col} regarding $I^1_{\epsilon+}$ (cf. Section 2.4.2). A star indicates significantly different nondominated set distributions at $\alpha = 0.05$ according to the KS test.

		n	s	nh	hn	sh	hs	ns	sn
KW test	n		•					•	•
	s	•						•	•
	nh	0.0	0.0		•		•	0.0	0.0
	hn	0.0	0.0	•		•	•	0.0	0.0
	sh	0.0	0.0	0.0091	•		•	0.0	0.0
	hs	0.0	0.0	•	•	•		0.0	0.0
	ns	•	•						•
	sn	•	•					•	
KS test	n		•	*	*	*	*	•	•
	s	•		*	*	*	*	•	•
	nh	*	*		•	*	*	*	*
	hn	*	*	•		•	•	*	*
	sh	*	*	*	•		•	*	*
	hs	*	*	*	•	•		*	*
	ns	•	•	*	*	*	*		•
	sn	•	•	*	*	*	*	•	

selection scheme of a single-objective algorithm within a multi-objective optimizer. In both sections we want to approach the performances of baseline methods by incorporating their key principles into a unified approach. However, there is a cardinal difference between remodeling a multi-objective algorithm and blending multiple independent algorithms into a single method. While in Section 6.1, the reference TSPEA2 is created to prioritize functionally fit individuals and therefore is expected to have a higher performance in evolving correct solutions, in this section, hES has no such alignment towards a specific objective being completely unbiased. Thus, a higher performance in evolving correct solutions is not self-evident. Fortunately, a consequence of a fair selection scheme is that no nondominated set deterioration is expected for hES.

Despite treating equally all objectives, hES is most effective in finding functionally correct solutions. While SPEA2 outperforms NSGAII for this particular CGP configuration on the 2×2 adder and multiplier benchmarks, increasing the influence of hES in the periodization with NSGAII produces even greater success rates. nh[4] and especially nh[10] periodization schemes reveal only a small gap with the hES-only performance. This insight is also partly confirmed by the results of the KW and the KS tests presented in

Table 6.11: ZDT6 nondominated sets comparison for 3-tuple combinations of NSGAII, SPEA2 and hES to NSGAII and SPEA2. A dot denotes an accepted H_0. When the KW test rejects H_0 for the algorithm pair (a_{row}, a_{col}), a one-tailed p-value lower than $\alpha = 0.01$ indicates that a_{row} evolves significantly better nondominated sets than a_{col} regarding $I_{\epsilon+}^1$ (cf. Section 2.4.2). A star indicates significantly different nondominated set distributions at $\alpha = 0.05$ according to the KS test .

		n	s	nhs	nsh	shn	snh	hns	hsn
KW test	n		·	·	·	·	·	·	·
	s	·		·	·	·	·	·	·
	nhs	0.0	0.0		·	·	·	·	·
	nsh	0.0	0.0	·		·	·	·	·
	shn	0.0	0.0	·	·		·	·	·
	snh	0.0	0.0	·	·	·		·	·
	hns	0.0	0.0	·	·	·	·		·
	hsn	0.0	0.0	·	·	·	·	·	
KS test	n		·	*	*	*	*	*	*
	s	·		*	*	*	*	*	*
	nhs	*	*		·	·	·	·	·
	nsh	*	*	·		·	·	·	·
	shn	*	*	·	·		·	·	·
	snh	*	*	·	·	·		·	·
	hns	*	*	·	·	·	·		·
	hsn	*	*	·	·	·	·	·	

Table 6.12: The number of circuits with perfect functional quality evolved during 20 runs.

	2×2 add	3×3 add	2×2 mul	3×3 mul	5-parity	7-parity
n	1	0	0	0	0	0
s	6	0	7	0	0	0
nh	7	0	8	0	0	0
nh^4	9	0	11	0	0	0
nh^{10}	11	0	14	0	0	0
h	12	1	15	0	0	0

Table 6.13: Non-dominated sets comparison: A dot denotes an accepted H_0. When the KW test rejects H_0 for the algorithm pair (a_{row}, a_{col}), a one-tailed p-value lower than $\alpha = 0.01$ indicates that a_{row} evolves significantly better nondominated sets than a_{col} regarding $I^1_{\epsilon+}$ (cf. Section 2.4.2). A star indicates significantly different nondominated set distributions at $\alpha = 0.05$ according to the KS test.

		n	s	nh	nh^4	nh^{10}	h
2 × 2 add	n		·	·	·	·	·
KW test	s	·		·	·	·	·
	nh	·	·		·	·	·
	nh^4	·	·	·		·	·
	nh^{10}	·	·	·	·		·
	h	·	·	·	·	·	
2 × 2 add	n		*	*	*	*	*
KS test	s	*		·	·	·	*
	nh	*	·		·	·	*
	nh^4	*	·	·		·	*
	nh^{10}	*	·	·	·		*
	h	*	*	*	*	*	
3 × 3 add	n		·	·	·	·	·
KW test	s	0.0067		·	·	·	·
	nh	0.0004	·		·	·	·
	nh^4	0.0011	·	·		·	·
	nh^{10}	0.0	·	·	·		·
	h	0.0	·	·	·	·	
3 × 3 add	n		·	*	*	*	*
KS test	s	·		·	· ·	·	*
	nh	*	·		·	·	*
	nh^4	*	·	·		·	*
	nh^{10}	*	·	·	·		*
	h	*	*	*	*	*	
2 × 2 mul	n		·	·	·	·	·
KW test	s	0.0		·	·	·	0.0
	nh	0.0	·		·	·	0.0013
	nh^4	0.0	·	·		·	·
	nh^{10}	0.0	·	·	·		·
	h	0.0016	·	·	·	·	
2 × 2 mul	n		*	*	*	*	*
KS test	s	*		·	*	*	*
	nh	*	·		·	·	*
	nh^4	*	·	·		·	*
	nh^{10}	*	*	·	·		*
	h	*	*	*	*	*	
3 × 3 mul	n		·	·	·	·	·
KW test	s	0.0006		·	·	·	·
	nh	0.0	·		·	·	·
	nh^4	0.0	·	·		·	·
	nh^{10}	0.0	·	·	·		·
	h	0.0002	·	·	·	·	
3 × 3 mul	n		*	*	*	*	*
KS test	s	*		·	·	*	*
	nh	*	·		·	·	*
	nh^4	*	·	·		·	*
	nh^{10}	*	*	·	·		*
	h	*	*	*	*	*	

Table 6.14: Non-dominated sets comparison: A dot denotes an accepted H_0. When the KW test rejects H_0 for the algorithm pair (a_{row}, a_{col}), a one-tailed p-value lower than $\alpha = 0.01$ indicates that a_{row} evolves significantly better nondominated sets than a_{col} regarding $I^1_{\epsilon+}$ (cf. Section 2.4.2). A star indicates significantly different nondominated set distributions at $\alpha = 0.05$ according to the KS test.

		n	s	nh	nh^4	nh^{10}	h
5-parity KW test	n		•	•	•	•	•
	s	0.0		•	•	•	0.0
	nh	0.0	•		•	•	0.0
	nh^4	0.0	•	•		•	0.0
	nh^{10}	0.0	•	•	•		0.0
	h	•	•	•	•	•	
5-parity KS test	n		*	*	*	*	*
	s	*		•	•	•	*
	nh	*	•		•	*	*
	nh^4	*	•	•		•	*
	nh^{10}	*	•	*	•		*
	h	*	*	*	*	*	
7-parity KW test	n		•	•	•	•	0.0054
	s	0.0		•	•	•	0.0
	nh	0.002	•		•	•	0.0
	nh^4	0.0	•	•		•	0.0
	nh^{10}	0.0	•	•	•		0.0
	h	•	•	•	•	•	
7-parity KS test	n		*	*	*	*	*
	s	*		•	•	•	*
	nh	*	•		•	•	*
	nh^4	*	•	•		•	*
	nh^{10}	*	•	•	•		*
	h	*	*	*	*	*	

Table 6.13. For the 2×2 adder, the KW test finds no significant differences in nondominated sets at $\alpha = 1\%$ while the KS test partitions the algorithms into groups of $\{n\}$, $\{s, nh, nh^4, nh^{10}\}$, and $\{h\}$ with significant differences in the evolved nondominated sets at $\alpha = 5\%$. For the 2×2 multiplier benchmark, NSGAII is dominated by all, and hES by SPEA2 and nh according to the KW test. The KS test splits the algorithms, similarly to what happened with the 2×2 benchmark, into groups of $\{n\}$, $\{s, nh, nh^4, nh^{10}\}$, and $\{h\}$. Additionally, in the group of $\{s, nh, nh^4, nh^{10}\}$ SPEA2 evolves different nondominated sets than it does for nh^4, nh^{10}.

The 3×3 adder and multiplier benchmarks split the algorithms into $\{n\}$ and $\{s, nh, nh^4, nh^{10}, h\}$ groups with different nondominated sets according to the KW test. The KS test reveals, similar to what happened with the

2×2 benchmarks, the same general tendency of differences between the nondominated sets evolved by the NSGAII, the hES, and the group of the remaining algorithms.

The general partitioning according to the quality of the evolved nondominated sets between NSGAII, hES, and the rest of the algorithms, is even more pronounced for the parity benchmarks, as now the KW test also confirms significant differences. That is, SPEA2, **nh**, $\mathbf{nh}^4$, and $\mathbf{nh}^{10}$ are better than NSGAII and hES for 5- and 7-parity functions and NSGAII is better than hES for the 7-parity function. The KS test finds significant differences between the three groups, also finding a significant difference between **nh** and $\mathbf{nh}^{10}$ for 5-parity.

In summary, we can state that periodizations of hES with NSGAII, as well as the non-periodized SPEA2, create, for almost all benchmarks, nondominated sets which are better than those of the non-periodized hES and NSGAII. Additionally, with the increasing influence of hES in a periodization scheme, the probability for the evolution of correct circuits increases.

6.3 Chapter Conclusion

Pareto based multi-objective optimization is fundamental for our holistic Evolvable Hardware approach. We have observed, however, state of the art MOEAs performing below average for the domain of CGP circuits. This has motivated our research on the scalability of MOEAs for CGP. At first, we redefined the selection of parents in SPEA2 by a linear objectives aggregation scheme leaving the Pareto diversity mechanism in place. We proved our new algorithm to be very efficient, sometimes outperforming even the single objective GA. The diversity of the evolved nondominated sets was on a par with, but sometimes significantly different than, the solutions from NSGAII and SPEA2.

For the following reasons we have been looking for a more systematic approach: Fixed and efficient objectives weighting scheme is not always known *a priori* and may change during the search process. The robustness of an evolutionary algorithm can therefore be improved by avoiding putting preferences into the selection operator. A selection scheme without preferences also allows exploring the complete fitness landscape. Finally, we were searching for a way to combine algorithms that already worked very well, and their properties, into a single scheme without implementing yet another new algorithm.

With the introduction of the algorithm periodization scheme and a Evolutionary Strategies variant able to cope with nondominated sorted populations, we have combined single objective local search style algorithms with multi-objective global search algorithms into one method without modifying the single algorithms themselves. Algorithm periodization can be used to explore the nature of the optimized function by varying the influences of the rotationally executed algorithms. More importantly, for the domain of CGP circuits, a carefully balanced periodization scheme has proved to be superior to the single algorithms of the periodization sequence.

Altogether, our methods can significantly improve the multi-objective evolution of CGP circuits in terms of convergence rates and sometimes in terms of the diversity of the nondomination set. In the next chapter, we will present Evolvable Hardware applications employing these methods and algorithms.

Chapter 7

Evolvable Hardware Applications

In this chapter we apply our methods, introduced in Chapter 5 and Chapter 6, to the applications of Evolvable Hardware pattern matching architectures and processor optimization.

In the first section (Section 7.1), we investigate their application to electromyography (EMG) signal classification. EMG signals are generated by contracting muscles. Today, muscle signal classification has become more and more popular for steering lower- and upper-limb prostheses. With the potential non-stationarity of EMG signals, Evolvable Hardware solutions are highly suitable for this application. EHW systems allow secure functional and temporal operation modes, are energy efficient, compact, and, most importantly, inherently adaptable to varying components. EMG's potentially non-stationary signal components could be induced by changing conductances of the electrodes attached to the skin, muscle fatigue, varying amputee conditions, and long term muscular characteristic variations, such as aging.

In Section 7.2, we extend our work on adaptable classifier architectures by investigating the behavior of the classification accuracy during and after changes in the available resources a classifier may use, and after the classifier size has been adjusted. we are motivated by our adaptation paradigm proposed in Section 1.1, relying on simulated evolution for gradual changes, and on pre-evolved solutions for radical changes. Observing the impact of architectural reconfigurations, we gain insights into the adaptation dynamics of an EHW classifier. We select the run-time reconfigurable functional unit row classifier of Glette et al. [127] for our experiments, and extract the magnitudes of any drops in accuracy and of the recovery behavior for both gradual and radical changes in architecture.

In our last contribution, we extend the notion of Evolvable Hardware to an application that has not been considered for adaptation in conventional engineering. In Section 7.3 we apply the concept of Evolvable Hardware to the evolution of the memory-to-cache address mapping functions of a processor. To this end, we introduce a small reconfigurable fabric within a CPU and subject it to evolution. Thereby we use a realistically sized embedded system with a multi-level cache and a cycle-accurate execution time fitness.

7.1 ECGP Based Architecture for Electromyographic Signal Classification

A prosthetic hand controller (PHC) is usually operated by signals generated by contracting muscles, i.e., electromyographic signals. The challenge of modern prosthesis control, which became relevant with the introduction of multi-functional prostheses, is that the conventional way of steering a prosthesis overstrains the amputee. It is very difficult for amputees to select from among multiple prosthetic device functions using a limited set of muscles and types of muscle contractions. To have improved control over motions using prostheses with more degrees of freedom, classification based PHCs are necessary. Additionally, it would be a great advantage to have access to PHCs which adapt themselves to changes in the user's EMG signal patterns. These EMG patterns are influenced by parameters such as muscle fatigue, skin conductivity, and the amputee's age. Currently, users are required to adapt to pre-defined EMG patterns, partly supported by periodic re-training sessions.

In the context of a PHC, Evolvable Hardware becomes an interesting approach, providing possibilities for self-adaptation, fast training, and compactness. The combination of evolutionary algorithms and reconfigurable hardware allows for automatically constructed hardware systems able to adapt their structure to specification changes. Learning to classify electromyographic signals is basically an incremental learning problem when it is applied in practice. In general, a learning task is *incremental* if the training examples that must be used to solve that task become available over time [126]. In our case, it would be possible that a disabled person using an intelligent prosthesis system carries out some exercises under the guidance of that system. The system records and processes the measured data, extending the available training data with new samples. The advantages of such an approach are obvious: First, the system would adapt to the behavior of the disabled person (and not vice versa). Second, the system would also be able to adapt to long term changes in the behavior of the disabled person. An interesting question is whether the classifier can then be trained incrementally instead of training it "from scratch." Updating and retraining the classifier using the most recent data may allow discarding old training data, as the essential knowledge that can be extracted from that data is already contained in the classifier's parameters. For support vector machines (SVMs) and other conventional classifier paradigms, which are used for comparison in this work, there are available incremental training techniques (cf., e.g., [215, 273, 317]).

In this section, we define an pattern matching architecture based on ECGP and compare it to the reference EHW classifier of Glette and Torresen, described in Section 3.2.6, and to conventional state of the art pattern matching algorithms. Among the conventional classifiers, we employ artificial neural networks and support vector machines, which are considered to be some of the most powerful classifier methods existing today. All experiments using the FUR architecture in this section (Section 7.1) were carried out by Kyrre Glette.

The two key insights we want to gain from our experiments are whether our and the FUR based EHW classifier are on a par with state of the art pattern matching algorithms, and whether EMG signals have a non-stationary nature requiring continuous adaptation.

To motivate the relevance of our work, the next section (cf. Section 7.1.1) presents the history and currently used control strategies of EMG-driven prostheses. As EHW based classifiers have been applied frequently to EMG signal classification, the section also summarizes related work in this area. Sections 7.1.2 and 7.1.3 describe the setup of our EMG sensor system and the signal processing as well as the feature extraction schemes. ECGP based and conventional approaches are given in detail in Sections 7.1.4 and 7.1.5. A description of the experiments, validation schemes, and the results is given in Section 7.1.6.

7.1.1 Classification of Electromyographic Signals

The first known prosthesis controlled by electromyography signals is the "Hüfner Hand" [67]. In 1948, Reiter implemented a prosthesis controller using one EMG channel to encode "open" and "close" movements of an artificial hand [284]. A quick contraction and relaxation triggered the "open" movement and a steady force contraction caused the prosthesis to gradually close the hand. Driven by the availability of compact electronic components, the area of prosthesis control gained more popularity in the 1960s and 1970s. Substantial effort went into defining strategies for robust selection of prosthesis actions from muscular activities [65,66,101,138,158]. The first commercial system was offered in the early 1960s [195]. In the following, we discuss modern EMG signal classification techniques with both conventional systems and Evolvable Hardware.

Modern conventional upper limb prosthesis control systems typically use rudimentary algorithms to derive information for steering the prosthesis. There are three popular methods of acting on the signal of a muscle, or more precisely, a group of muscles, which consider:

- the intensity of the muscular activity. For a single channel, typically two intensity thresholds separate three muscle states: relaxed, slightly contracted, and contracted, allowing the prosthesis to perform, for example, "open" and "close" movements [101].

- the muscular activity growth rate. Similar to the previous method, two thresholds for the speed of the performed contraction partition the channel output into three states [65].

- multiple groups of muscles, discriminating between contracted / non-contracted muscles, to encode the prosthesis action. For example, using two channels, up to three prosthesis actions and a neutral state can be selected.

For multi-functional prostheses, the control system can use quick co-contractions to switch between different activity modes (e.g., switching between the "grasping" and the "rotating" modes for an artificial hand). However, such a control mechanism is not intuitive and has to be learned by the user.

Pattern recognition algorithms enable a different way of extracting information from muscular activity. For example, instead of requiring the user to be familiar with the activation of some groups of muscles to trigger an "open" movement, pattern recognition algorithms are able to extract the natural hand "open" impulse from the superimposed EMG signals of the forearm. Pattern recognition methods allow for intuitive control and are also capable of discriminating between a larger number of distinct movements. However, multiple EMG channels are needed for the robust detection of multiple movements.

Early attempts to use pattern recognition algorithms were made by Finely [119], Herberts [158], and Graupe and Cline [138]. In today's literature on EMG signal classification, the signal processing chain is often broken down into three algorithmic components: *feature extraction, dimensionality reduction,* and *pattern classification.* The feature extraction step isolates application specific attributes from the EMG signal. Dimensionality reduction decreases the amount of data to obtain a more robust and accurate classification by selecting or projecting features. The final pattern classification step determines the predefined category to which the input data belongs. The complete processing chain has to be carefully balanced. In particular, the choice of a pattern recognition algorithm and the selected features contribute significantly to the recognition accuracy.

Feature extraction schemes for continuous prosthesis control act in a sliding window manner. That is, a feature set is calculated for each window of the data, where the windows are typically up to 300 milliseconds in length and are selected according to the classification rate of the prosthesis controller.

Historically, the development of computationally efficient algorithms has been of the utmost importance, since prosthesis controllers typically run on battery powered embedded systems. Here, feature extraction methods acting in the time domain (TD) are often regarded as being well-suited because of their simplicity. Examples of time domain methods widely used in EMG classification are mean absolute value (MAV) [110, 173, 182, 268, 403] [10], zero crossing (ZC) [110, 173], slope sign changes (SSC) [110, 117, 173], and waveform length (WL) [110, 117, 173].

EMG electrodes, being electrically only loosely attached to the skin surface, tend to act as antennas, collecting noise from power lines, adjacent electric and electronic prosthesis subsystems, and other electromagnetic sources. Time domain methods in general and methods using amplitude based features in particular have difficulties dealing with such noise and also with the effects of varying skin conductance. Consequently, a significant part of the related work concentrates on frequency domain based feature extraction to suppress noisy influences. The Fourier transformation (FT) and the short time Fourier transformation (STFT) [110, 186, 326] are among the most popular methods. Capturing information from the time and frequency domains, the wavelet transformation (WT) [110, 186] and the wavelet packet transformation (WPT) [110, 112, 326] have also been successfully studied for the recognition of EMG signals. Despite being computationally expensive, frequency domain feature extraction schemes are feasible on today's high performance embedded systems.

Reducing the dimensionality of the feature space while preserving essential information may increase a classifier's generalization ability. Additionally, irrelevant information that is skipped in this step reduces the amount of data to be processed by the classifier. Dimensionality reduction can be implemented as a feature selection that aims at maximizing the probability of a correct classification [112, 247]. For the classification of EMG signals, the *projection* of features is quite popular. Projection creates a new and generally smaller feature set by combining the original features in a linear or non-linear way. Some of the algorithms employed are principle component analysis (PCA) [112, 247], linear and non-linear discriminant analysis (LDA, NLDA) [70], and self-organizing feature maps (SOFM) [70].

The last step of the signal processing chain covers pattern recognition. A dominant part of the related work uses artificial neural network (ANN) classifiers [164, 171, 173, 263]. More recent work also has introduced support vector machines (SVM) for EMG signal classification [47, 316] [10], as well as Bayesian classifiers [109, 111, 112], fuzzy classifiers [62, 185], Gaussian mixtures [172], and hidden Markov models [61].

A compact overview of the methods for preparing, processing, and classifying EMG signals is given by Zecca et al. [407] and Parker et al. [269].

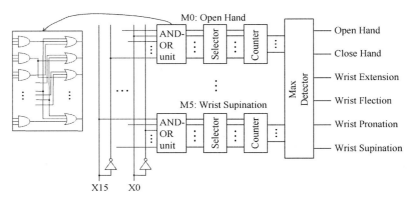

Figure 7.1: Evolvable hardware architecture for classification tasks introduced by Torresen in [361].

Classification of Electromyographic Signals with Evolvable Hardware

An early use of EHW for pattern recognition was reported by Higuchi et al. [160]. Their architecture, presented in Section 3.2.2, was originally applied to character classification but was later used for classification in a PHC [181, 183]. The configuration of the architecture was evolved using a genetic algorithm implemented on the same chip as the classifier, resulting in a compact and adaptable system. The controller was trained with feature vectors extracted from EMG data where one input signal consisted of four channels at a resolution of four bits. The classifier distinguished between six different kinds of movements. The classification performance was computed by dividing the EMG data into two halves and using one half as the training data and the second half as the test data. Although the results showed a classification rate for the evolved circuits competitive with that of artificial neural networks (ANNs), it was noted that the size of the employed dataset might be insufficient; this was indicated by the strongly varying classification rates. As a result of having the GA implemented entirely in hardware and on the same chip, the learning time (800 ms) for the EHW approach was significantly shorter than that of the ANN. Short training times are important for the user-friendliness of a PHC, especially if online adaptation is applied.

Using similar EMG data, Torresen [361] conducted experiments on incremental evolution using an EHW architecture. The two layer architecture consisted of AND-OR matrices followed by a selector layer. The AND-OR matrices were evolved in the first step followed by the evolution of the selectors. In addition, the best subsystems from different runs were combined into one

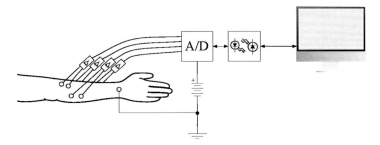

Figure 7.2: The EMG measurement system. The analog signal processing part is decoupled from the PC and powered by a battery. EMG signal amplifiers are placed close to the electrodes to reduce noise. Signal processing is implemented completely on the PC.

system. The results showed that a two step incremental approach can lead to a better generalization performance and shorter computation times than either traditional one-step evolution and ANN.

We have compared, in [9], the presented EHW architectures of Higuchi et al. [160] and Torresen [361] with the FUR architecture demonstrated in Section 3.2.6 and with our ECGP based classifier architecture, which we will introduce in this chapter. The results have shown that accuracy rates increase from the first-generation classifier of Higuchi et al., through the more sophisticated and complex architecture of Torresen, to the modern schemes of the FUR and ECGP based ensemble classifiers.

7.1.2 Recording Electromyographic Signals

We use two measurement systems for stationary and portable EMG signal recording. The stationary system comprises four components: EMG sensors (Tyco Arbo*, Ag/AgCl, 35 mm), amplifiers (Biovison [45]), A/D converters (N.I. [261]), and a standard computer. The system is shown in Figure 7.2 and continuously monitors four sensor channels with 14 bit resolution at a sampling rate of 6 kHz. Two important requirements for such a measurement system are the reduction of noise in the analog signal processing path and a reproducible biomechanical experimental setup. To reduce noise, we employ an optical bridge (Sonowin [325]) to galvanically decouple the signal amplifiers and the A/D converters from the computer that accumulates the data. A separate battery provides a stable power supply to the amplifiers and A/D converters. Moreover, the amplifiers are placed as near as 10 cm to the electrodes attached to the skin in order to minimize parasitic inductances. For portable EMG data acquisition, we use a MindMedia Nexus 10 Biofeedback

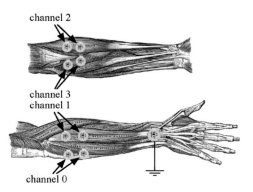

Figure 7.3: Sensor placement (muscle anatomy taken from [139]).

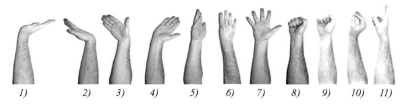

Figure 7.4: Motion classes: *1)* extension, *2)* flexion, *3)* ulnar deviation, *4)* radial deviation, *5)* pronation, *6)* supination, *7)* open, *8)* close *9)* key grip, *10)* pincer grip, and *11)* extend index finger.

System [258] to continuously monitor four EMG sensor channels with 24 bit resolution at a sampling rate of 2048 Hz.

We place the four electrode pairs on the top, bottom, medial, and lateral sides of the forearm with the reference at the wrist, as shown in Figure 7.3. The exact electrode positions are determined specifically for the test subject to obtain pronounced signals. A reproducible biomechanical experiment setup is an important requirement for such a measurement system. Thus, after the initial calibration we mark the electrode positions to be able to re-establish the experimental setup on different days.

In a single run of the experiment, the test subject has to perform a sequence of multiple different movements. Some of these movements are depicted in Figure 7.4. Each movement starts with a relaxation phase followed by a contraction phase, as shown in Figure 7.5(a). The EMG signal for the contraction part can be roughly divided into a one second phase at the onset

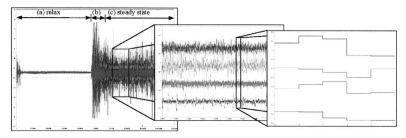

Figure 7.5: EMG signal preprocessing. The left figure shows the raw signals for all four channels, consisting of *a)* a relaxation phase, *b)* a transient phase with intensified activity, and *c)* a steady state contraction phase. The center figure presents the DC offset-compensated and rectified signals from the four channels in the steady state phase, and the right figure shows a single extracted feature vector using the $(200, 2, 5)$ scheme.

of the contraction, containing the transient components of the EMG signal, and a subsequent steady state phase, which corresponds to a constant force contraction. We use the steady phase for classification.

For the first experiment we use the stationary EMG measurement system to record the movements *1)* to *8)*, as presented in Figure 7.4, by three individuals on three consecutive days. In each of the nine sessions, an individual repeats the movement sequence 20 times. Each movement consists of a nine second relaxation phase and an eleven second contraction phase. The data is recorded at a sampling rate of 6 kHz. For the second experiment, recorded by Boschmann et al. [50] [10], we use the portable EMG measurement system to have a single individual collect data from all eleven movements presented in Figure 7.4 over 21 days. Similar to the previous setup, the subject records a single sequence of movements five to six times a day. In total, 121 sessions are conducted during different times of a day. Each movement starts with a relaxation part of about four seconds followed by a contraction part that lasts about five seconds. The sampling rate in this experiment is set to 2048 Hz.

The data from the first experiment is analyzed by the "Day1–3" and "2of3" evaluation schemes, and the data from the second experiment is analyzed by the "121" evaluation scheme. The definitions of these schemes will be given in Section 7.1.6.

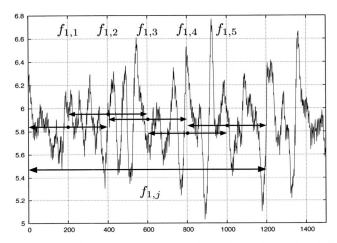

Figure 7.6: (200,2,5) feature extraction scheme for a single signal channel: Five average values over 2×200 samples defines a feature vector. An averaged window overlaps with the subsequent window for 200 samples.

7.1.3 Electromyographic Signals Processing and Feature Extraction

Signal preprocessing and feature extraction is done completely in the digital domain. Our method is inspired by the mean average value (MAV) scheme of Kajitani et al. [183]. We design the method to have an efficient computation procedure by subdividing the input signals into small and disjoint intervals. Partial solutions are computed for each interval and reused for feature vector extraction. This minimizes redundant computations.

The feature vector extraction scheme is defined by the triple (r, s, t), where r is the number of samples in the moving average window, s is the number of moving average windows used to compute a single feature value, and t is the number of values in the feature vector calculated for a particular channel. With k as the number of signal channels, p as an index of a signal sample, d_{ip}, $i = 1, \ldots, k$, as the DC compensated raw signal, and $j = 1, \ldots, t$ a single feature vector, $v \in \mathbb{R}^{kt}$ is calculated by

$$v = (v)_{ij} = -\log\left(\frac{1}{rs} \sum_{l=(j-1)r+1}^{(j-1+s)r} |d_{il}|\right).$$

Thus, a single feature vector in the (r, s, t) scheme consists of $k \times t$ values calculated over $r(s + t - 1)f^{-1}$ seconds, where f denotes the sampling rate.

To demonstrate a feature vector calculation, we given an example of computing a $(200, 2, 5)$ scheme for a signal sampled at 6 kHz. The first element of $v = (v_{1,1}, v_{1,2}, v_{1,3}, v_{1,4}, v_{1,5})$ is computed as $v_{1,1} = -log([200 \cdot 2]^{-1} \cdot [|d_{1,1}| + |d_{1,2}| + \cdots + |d_{1,400}|])$. Similarly, the remaining elements of v rely on means computed using the raw signal values with indices $(201, \ldots, 600)$, $(401, \ldots, 800)$, $(601, \ldots, 1000)$, and $(801, \ldots, 1200)$. Altogether, the first feature vector relies on data recorded over $200 \cdot (2 + 5 - 1) \cdot 6000^{-1} = 200$ [ms]. Figure 7.6 shows an EMG signal example and the according elements of v.

Our feature extraction scheme is tailored for the continuous operation mode of a prosthesis controller running on a small embedded system. With an update frequency of f_u for the feature extraction and classification chain, the window size r should be set to $f \cdot f_u^{-1}$ to allow the reuse of $(v)_{ij}, i = 1, \ldots, k, j = 2, \ldots, t$ for the calculation of the following feature vector. With $t = f \cdot f_u^{-1}$, only the averages $(v)_{ij}, i = 1, \ldots, k, j = t$ have to be updated. Coming back to the example of Figure 7.6, we set the update frequency to 30, which results in a moving average window of $r = 6.000 \cdot 30^{-1} = 200$ samples. With this, we can reuse $v_{1,2}, v_{1,3}, v_{1,4}, v_{1,5}$ of the first feature vector. Thereby, the elements are relabeled to $v_{1,1}, v_{1,2}, v_{1,3}, v_{1,4}$ and for $v_{1,5}$ only the sum of raw signal elements with indices $(1201, \ldots, 1400)$ need to be computed. $v_{1,5}$ is then the sum of the partial results $\sum_{l=1.001}^{1.200} |d_{1l}|$, already computed for the first feature vector, and $\sum_{l=1.201}^{1.400} |d_{1l}|$ divided by $rs = 200 \cdot 2$.

In our experiments we set the update frequency to $f(r(s + t - 1))^{-1}$: thus, the feature vectors are computed on disjoint data. If further feature normalization is applied by the classification algorithm, the channels are treated independently. For the "Day1–3," "2of3," and "121" experiments, the feature vectors are computed by a $(300, 2, 5)$ and $(100, 2, 5)$ scheme, respectively. Thus, the feature vectors consist of 20 values and the corresponding label. Both feature extraction schemes use the data of roughly one-third of a second, which is a realistic assumption for a prosthesis control.

7.1.4   The Embedded Cartesian Genetic Programming Classification Architecture

Creating our ECGP based classifier, we orient ourselves with the FUR ensemble classifier structure previously presented in Section 3.2.6. A generalized FUR architecture is shown in Figure 7.7. The architecture decomposes into *category detection modules* (CDM) computing how likely it is that an input vector corresponds to a certain category. Each module splits into single detectors, so-called *category classifiers* (CC), indicating by a 1 and a 0, whether the input vector matches or not the trained category. All category classifiers in a module detect the same category. The number of "activated" category classifiers expresses the likelihood that an input vector belongs to a certain category.

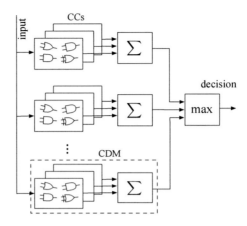

Figure 7.7: High level structure of the FUR and ECGP based EHW classifier architectures.

The generalized classification architecture in Figure 7.7 becomes specific with the implementation of the category classifiers. In the case of the functional unit row (FUR) architecture, a CC is implemented as a set of comparator elements contributing to an AND gate. For the ECGP based classification architecture, each category classifier is a general Boolean circuit with a single output, evolved to compute a "1" for an input vector corresponding to the trained category and a "0" otherwise.

Our EHW based classifier relies on a variant of the embedded Cartesian genetic programming model presented in Sections 3.4.4 and 5.2. We employ age based module creation as this particular method demonstrated higher convergence rates in our experiments. To configure the complete architecture, we define a multi-chromosome genotype, storing for each CC a complete ECGP model. The architecture's fitness is defined as a candidate solution's classification accuracy on the training dataset. More precisely, for the set of labeled training feature vectors $X = (x, l)$, the fitness f of an evolved classifier circuit c is defined as:

$$f(c) = |X|^{-1} \sum_{(x,l) \in X} \begin{cases} 1 & : \quad \text{if } c(x) = l, \\ 0 & : \quad \text{else.} \end{cases}$$

The evolution is implemented as $1 + 1$ ES, presented in Section 3.4.1. The complete set of ECGP model parameters is summarized in Table 7.1. The

Table 7.1: ECGP-based architecture parametrization.

n_i / n_o / n_r / n_c	10.000 / 1 / 1 / 1000–1500
n_n / F	4 / $\mathbb{B}^4$
mutation prob.	1.0
mutation rate	0.03
one point mutation prob.	0.6
compress / expand prob.	0.1 / 0.2
module point mutation prob.	0.04
add / remove module input prob.	0.01 / 0.02
add / remove module output prob.	0.01 / 0.02
maximum module size	3

population is initialized randomly with a length of 1000 logic blocks. Depending on the modules created, the chromosome is allowed to grow up to 1500 blocks. The architecture is configured to evolve 24 ECGP classifier circuits per category for "Day1–3" and "2of3," and 20 ECGP classifier circuits per category for "121.". Each of the 20 values in a feature vector is linearly quantized to a 9-bit representation and input to a 1-out-of-500 encoder. The resulting 20×500 bits are then fed to a classifier circuit.

7.1.4.1 Comparison of the ECGP classifier with the FUR classifier

We compare our approach with the FUR EHW architecture of Glette et al. [127], presented in Section 3.2.6. The architecture is specifically tailored to classification tasks and online evolution, and possesses register based reconfiguration capabilities. This offers very fast reconfiguration times.

The common elements of the ECGP and FUR architectures are, apart from their identical general structure, the abstraction levels of the functional elements. Both approaches employ or try to employ high level building blocks. While the ECGP approach extracts the building blocks automatically, and thus is a very general approach, the FUR architecture uses knowledge, in the form of predefined building blocks found to be good for classification.

The differences between the architectures lie in the ways they are evolved and in the ways a classification decision is taken. The complete ECGP based architecture is encoded by a multi-chromosome genotype, which is subject to evolution. The evolution of the FUR architecture decomposes into separate evolutionary runs, one for each category. The genotype describing a category decision module is further partitioned by the category classifiers. FUR's evolution considers at any point of time only a portion of CDM's genotype, describing a single CC. With this, FUR requires fewer fitness evaluations to evolve a complete architecture than the ECGP based architecture requires.

FUR's principle for making its classification decisions follows the general approach of decision trees (DT). The FUR approach compares the signal values with constants. Thus, similar to DTs, it realizes a decision boundary with sections of straight lines that must be parallel to the axes of the input space spanned by all attributes. In contrast, the decision boundary of an ECGP based classifier is implemented as a Boolean combination of signal values and constants. Therefore, similar to kNN, the decision boundaries are a composition of straight lines.

7.1.5 Conventional Classifiers

For a realistic perspective, we compare our method to conventional state of the art methods. For the comparison, we select kth nearest neighbor, decision trees, support vector machines, and neural networks, covering different kinds of decision boundaries between classes. To establish fair conditions, we employ grid search to find good algorithm parametrizations.

A kth nearest neighbor (kNN) classifier is a very simple, data based classification approach [103], i.e., it does not require any training phase. From an analysis of the very general "bias/variance dilemma" for classification tasks [100, 123], which states that variance dominates bias, it can be concluded that classifiers with a low complexity—roughly corresponding to the number of free parameters—perform well in many classification tasks. With this property in mind, we select, as a baseline method, a kNN having only one parameter, k. We consider kNN as a reference method that is expected to be outperformed by other kinds of classifiers. However, kNN classifiers require storing of and iteration through all of the sample vectors of the training dataset during the operational phase, thus they are hardly suitable for many real applications, which require a compact and fast implementation. In a kNN classifier, the form of the decision boundary between two classes is defined locally by the k nearest (using a Euclidean distance measure) samples in the training set. Therefore, the decision boundary is composed of sections of straight lines. In our experiments, the number of neighbors is set to $k = 7$.

Decision trees can be used for the classification of numerical as well as categorical data [103]. A DT realizes a set of human interpretable "if–then" rules. In a tree structure, each leaf node represents a classification decision, each non-leaf node evaluates an attribute associated with that node. An input sample vector is classified by successive tests from the root of a DT down to a leaf. Our motivation for including DT in our comparison is the possibility of extracting human-interpretable rules. Moreover, DT can be regarded as a state of the art technique for solving classification problems. DTs realize a decision boundary with sections of straight lines that must be parallel to the axes of the input space spanned by all attributes. This restriction basically enables the interpretability of the training results in the form of "if–then–else" rules. This is one reason why DTs are used for many practical applications.

In our experiments, we use the C4.5 algorithm [278] to build a DT. C4.5 selects the next attribute (based on a greedy principle) according to an information gain measure. Pruning techniques such as subtree raising are applied to reduce overfitting of the classifier to the training dataset. The confidence threshold for pruning is set to 0.25 and the minimum number of instances per leaf is 2.

Support vector machines use a hyperplane to separate any two classes [56, 148]. For problems that cannot be linearly separated in the input space, SVMs find a solution using a nonlinear transformation of the original input space into a high-dimensional so-called feature space, where an optimal separating hyperplane is determined. Those hyperplanes having a maximal margin are called optimal, where margin means the minimal distance from the separating hyperplane to the closest (mapped) data points (the so-called *support vectors*). The transformation is usually realized by nonlinear kernel functions, e.g., Gaussian kernels. C-SVMs, which are used here, introduce slack variables, being subject to minimization as well, to allow a certain degree of misclassification. With the aid of nonlinear kernel functions, SVMs are able to realize arbitrary nonlinear decision boundaries in the input space. The key advantage of SVMs is that they are based on the principle of structural risk minimization, which typically leads to a very good generalization performance. Thus, one could expect SVMs to yield very good results in our comparison.

In our experiments, we use a C-SVM with a Gaussian (radial basis function, i.e., RBF) kernel. For "Day1–3" and "2of3," we set $C = 0.5$ and $\gamma = 0.175$. The parameters for "121" are $C = 3$ and $\gamma = 1$.

Multilayer perceptrons (MLP), also known as backpropagation networks, are neural networks that are biologically inspired [46, 286]. They aim at being discriminative, but they lack a built-in mechanism for structural risk minimization like SVMs. Thus, good generalization properties must be assured by means of comprehensive cross-validation or bootstrapping tests. Like SVMs, MLP are able to realize nonlinear decision boundaries. A major difference from SVMs is that the structure of the classifier (e.g., the number of hidden neurons) must be fine tuned by hand. We have chosen MLP for our comparison because of their use as a reference classifier in related work on EHW.

In our experiments, we use an MLP with 20 input neurons (for the 20 input features), 8 and 11 output neurons (for the 8 and 11 classes), and one hidden layer consisting of 32 neurons. The MLP are trained using the backpropagation algorithm with an additional momentum term. The learning rate is set to 0.3, the momentum rate to 0.2, and the number of training epochs is 500.

7.1.6 Evaluation

Our first experiment is based on the stationary EMG measurement system and uses cross-validation for evaluation. Cross-validation is a partitioning scheme splitting the data into similar sized chunks, selecting one chunk for performance testing, and the remaining chunks for training. This scheme is repeated until all chunks have served for testing. The classifiers are trained anew for each test chunk. The data of the first experiment is used to define two benchmarks: in the first benchmark, referred to as the "Day1–3" benchmark, we investigate the asymptotic classifier accuracy by merging and shuffling all data from a single individual and evaluating the proposed classifiers with 10-fold cross validation. In the second benchmark, referred to as the "2of3" benchmark, we aim at investigating the classifier's generalization capabilities. To this end, we use a 3-fold cross validation defining the data partitioning by the recorded day. Thus, the data from two days is used for training and the data from the remaining day is used for testing.

The second experiment, referred to as the "121" benchmark, investigates longer term effects on the performance of classifying EMG signals. The main question is whether and how much the classification accuracy degrades over time if the classifiers are not being trained continuously. Assuming the EMG signal changes over time, one needs to study the nature of the change, the way it can be measured, and the effects on the classification accuracy. To design practical prosthesis controllers, one then has to devise appropriate feature extraction schemes compensating for such variations in the EMG signal, and also look at the interdependency of a recurrently trained controller and the amputee interacting with the prosthesis controller. Furthermore, one also has to analyze technical issues such as the amount of training data required for reaching high accuracy rates, the selection of the most stable feature extraction, dimensionality reduction, classification algorithm combination, and incremental learning.

In this work, we address a subset of these issues, in particular the amount of data required to reliably reach high accuracies and the fundamental question of the accuracy degradation for an initially trained classifier. Using 121 data trials, we define three validation schemes. For a test trial i, $i \geq 2$, we configure the training set to consist of

1. $1, \ldots, i - 1$,

2. $1, \ldots, \min(s, i - 1)$, and

3. $\max(i - s, 1), \ldots, i - 1$

trials. Here, s denotes the number of trials sufficient for all algorithms to reach high accuracy rates. Over all classifiers, we found five trials or the data collected during a single day to be sufficient. The first validation scheme determines the accuracy using all available data for training. It is unclear whether this results in the best possible performance since, in general, aged data might lower the classification accuracy. Moreover, a permanently growing training dataset also permanently increases the computational load for retraining. The goal of the second scheme is to check whether the accuracy degrades if a classifier is trained with data from the first day only. Finally, the third validation scheme investigates the evolution of the accuracy when using only recent data for training and thus tries to answer the question: Can the classification accuracy be improved by stripping aged data?

Experiments using kNN, DT, MLP, and SVMs are conducted with the data mining framework RapidMiner [248]. RapidMiner uses the LIBSVM [63] implementation for SVMs and the WEKA [146] implementation for DTs and MLPs. In the case of SVMs, multi-class datasets are handled by LIBSVM using the one-against-one method [170].

7.1.6.1 The "Day1–3" Experiment

As a metric for comparing the classification performance of the different approaches, we use the classification accuracy expressed by the error rate. Table 7.2 summarizes the error rates, arranged by the particular individual. The test error rates show the classifiers' generalization abilities, and the error rates obtained for the training datasets point to the classifiers' approximation abilities. Bold numbers symbolize the best error rates.

Table 7.2: The "Day1–3" experiment: Approximation and generalization errors in %. Bold numbers represent the best error rates.

	user 1		user 2		user 3	
	training	test	training	test	training	test
kNN	3.14	**3.96**	12.94	**17.29**	3.64	**4.75**
DT	1.42	8.68	4.51	25.85	1.72	8.95
MLP	3.09	4.45	23.73	25.44	4.31	5.67
SVM	5.53	5.63	32.22	32.30	6.59	6.68
ECGP	7.50	8.86	38.00	39.57	8.81	8.30
FUR [127]	9.59	10.02	45.67	46.08	11.03	11.40

The first major observation is that we achieve high training and test error rates for user 2. Since we carefully configured and adjusted the EMG sensor positions and ran tests before starting the data experiments, we can dismiss the experimental setup as being a reason for the high differences in the error rates. The daily analysis of user 2's data reveals similar bad recognition rates, separately for each day. Thus, we assume that the results are due to either a lax tension when performing the contraction phases or the physiological properties of the subject. The second observation, and this comes as a surprise, is the excellent performance of the kNN classifier. This could be explained by the "bias/variance dilemma," mentioned in Section 7.1.5, which states that even a simple classifier can achieve high accuracy rates, as low model complexity corresponds to low variance. MLPs come second, followed by SVMs. The small gaps between training and test accuracy rates imply correct parametrizations and negligible effects of overfitting. In contrast to this, and as a third observation, the DTs show a larger distance between training and test accuracies despite using pruning techniques to prevent overfitting. The EHW based classifiers close the comparison, being near to the DTs. Our architecture demonstrates a gap from the best performing algorithm of 4.9%, 22.3%, and 3.6% for users 1, 2, and 3, respectively. The FUR architecture follows, with 6.1%, 28.8% and 6.7%. High and compactly distributed accuracy rates for the user 1 and 2 experiments among all algorithms let us assume that the task of EMG signal classification using mean average features tends not to be too complex.

7.1.6.2 The "2of3" Experiment

In this experiment we focus on the real world situation in which the data of a past time period is used to train the classifiers, and the performance of a prosthesis is measured over a later time period. To this end, we define, as described in Section 7.1.6, a 3-fold cross validation scheme partitioning the data of each fold by the recording day. Since the EHW classifiers are evolved from random genotypes, each evolved classifier has a different structure and the classification rates vary slightly. The EHW experiments generate only three classifiers when computing the 3-fold cross validation scheme. To achieve reliable accuracy rates, we have evolved 10×3 classifiers and averaged the results.

Table 7.3: The "2of3" experiment: Approximation and generalization errors in %. Bold numbers represent the best error rates.

	user 1		user 2		user 3	
	training	test	training	test	training	test
kNN	2.70	12.38	12.62	**40.46**	3.02	18.25
DT	2.28	17.95	7.68	48.28	2.82	23.19
MLP	2.43	14.49	20.93	44.94	2.97	19.25
SVM	4.88	**12.10**	32.14	45,53	5.64	**17.04**
ECGP	2.90	19.63	6,88	48.43	1.49	18.05
FUR [127]	8.75	14.55	42.69	54.13	9.26	20.07

Characteristic of the "2of3" experiments are the higher error rates and larger

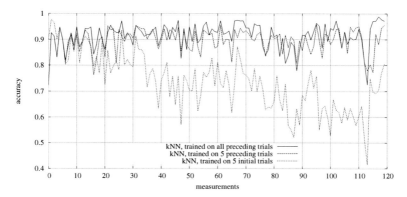

Figure 7.8: The "121" experiment: Test accuracy for the kNN algorithm trained on the first five, last five, and all preceding trials.

distances between training and test rates compared to the "Day1–3" experiment (see Table 7.3). This can be explained by an insufficient amount of data for prediction model creation and by a smaller portion of training and larger portion of test data used in the 3-fold cross validation. Additionally, data used for testing have been recorded on a different day than the data used for training. With these differences in mind, no algorithm consistently dominates according to this benchmark. While SVM and kNN still perform well, being among the three best algorithms and always taking first place, MLPs take second for user 2 and our architecture for user 3. Analogous to the "Day1–3" experiment, DTs again demonstrate some overfitting. Additionally, our architecture shows larger overfitting effects, indicating the necessity for pruning techniques. The ranges for test errors over all algorithms are roughly the same as in the previous benchmark, lying around 7% for user 1 and user 3, and around 14% for user 2.

While the observed performance behaviors in the "2of3" experiment can be explained by the same reasons mentioned when analyzing the "Day1–3" experiment, the results suggest two additional conclusions. The closer distances between SVMs, MLPs, and the EHW approaches, raise the question whether the higher decision boundary flexibility of SVMs and MLPs is really necessary. Additionally, the results support the idea that periodic retraining may be useful to maintain high classification rates.

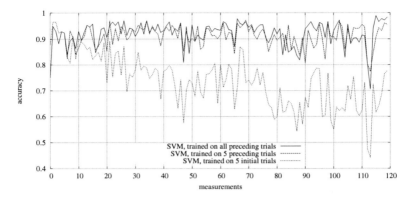

Figure 7.9: The "121" experiment: Test accuracy for the SVM algorithm trained on the first five, last five, and all preceding trials.

Table 7.4: The "121" experiment: Averaged errors in % (generalization), when trained on first five trials (roughly data recorded on a single day), five recent trials, and on all preceding trials.

	first five	preceding five	all preceding
kNN	26.19	10.45	7.86
SVM	26.23	9.00	8.66

7.1.6.3 The "121" Experiment

Figures 7.8 and 7.9 plot the accuracy results for the best performing conventional classifiers in the "121" experiment: kNN and SVM. As described in subsection 7.1.6, we evaluate three validation schemes in this experiment: employing all the preceding, the preceding five, and the initial five trials for training and the following trials for testing. While using for trial i all or five previous trials for training yields similarly good accuracy rates of roughly about 90%, training kNN and SVMs with the first five trials degrades the accuracy. This accuracy loss became visible after two to three days of omitted re-training. The averaged error rates are summarized in Table 7.4. Interestingly, there is no significant indication for negative influence of "old" data used for training. For both algorithms, the error rates improve from the second to the third column of Table 7.4. While the improvement is small for SVM, kNN improves its error rate by 2.59%. However, fading out old training data for potential accuracy improvement might make sense considering the real world prosthesis use periods.

Table 7.5: The "121" experiment: Averaged errors in % (generalization), when trained on five recent trials (roughly data recorded on a single day). Bold numbers represents the best error rate.

	error rate
kNN	10.45
DT	17.91
MLP	10.44
SVM	**9.00**
ECGP	16.48
FUR [127]	13.72

We limit the evaluation for the remaining classification algorithms to the "preceding five trials" scheme, as training became costly with increasing data sizes. We chose this scheme as it is relevant to the prosthesis controller application. The results are summarized in Table 7.5. Similar to the previous experiments, kNN and SVMs perform best followed by MLPs. EHW approaches lie between this group and the DTs. The error rates spread in a 9% interval bounded by SVMs at 9.0% and DTs at 17.91%. The values are similar to the user 1 and 3 results of the "2of3" experiment. The peak classification rates are slightly better while being somewhat broadly distributed. The similarities of the "2of3" and "121" experiments are not surprising. Both evaluation schemes use data from disjoint recording sessions for training and testing. The slightly better results of the "121" experiment can be explained by the larger data portion used for training. This is also probably an explanation for the broader accuracy distribution. All algorithms are able to improve their classification accuracies using more training data in the "121" experiment (cf. Table 7.3, user 1 test column and Table 7.5). While for some algorithms the improvements are rather small (cf. DT with a 0.04%), other algorithms manage to get roughly 3% to 4% improvements, such as, our architecture, the SVMs, and the MLPs.

7.1.6.4 Discussion

From the experimental results, we can make the following observations:

- Among the conventional classifiers, kNN yields surprisingly good results. While this approach is likely to be inapplicable to a real PHC, as all the data have to be stored and evaluated for the classification decision, it shows that the classification problems posed by our experiments can be solved with very simple classifiers. DT, despite the pruning techniques which were applied, were prone to overfitting in this application, in particular in experiment "2of3." Amongst the conventional classifiers, kNN and SVM yield the best results. However, similar to kNN, SVM might be susceptible to a growing training dataset.

- Our ECGP based architecture together with the FUR architecture— and this is the main result of our experiments—also yield a good classification performance. While the "Day1–3" experiment turned out to be tough for both approaches (both architectures clearly rank at the bottom), the "2of3" experiment shows a more compact distribution of accuracies with the EHW approaches deviating by 2%, 8%, and 1% from the best performing classifier. In the "121" experiment, the distances from the best performing algorithms amount to 4.7% and 7.5%.

- We observe that the task of EMG signal classification using mean average features needs online learning. The classification rates fall by 8%, 23%, and 12% from the "Day1–3" experiment, where 10-fold validation was applied on the shuffled dataset, to the "2of3" experiment, where the data of two days was used to classify the data of the third day. This is an indication that data of only a few days is insufficient to evolve a highly predictive model. In an additional experiment, we observed that the classification rates degrade when retraining is not continuous.

The classification rates achieved, except the results for the second user in the "2of3" experiment, are high enough for a PHC: a PHC relies only partly on the accuracy of the utilized classifier. In recent work, a more holistic approach has been introduced by Englehart et al. [154] and Shenoy et al. [316], accounting for the success and execution time of complex and real world hand movements. This kind of metric implicitly rate the classification accuracy. The authors state that: "Perhaps most importantly, these results [154] support clinical observations that training data which includes transient MES [myoelectric signal] information can lead to more robust usability and performance while yielding a seemingly 'worse' classifier. The authors [Englehart et al.] therefore suggest caution in accepting classification error as the sole measure of a system's usability and performance" [154]. Englehart et al. found that accuracy rates below 85% start to affect the performance of complex movement executions.

The accuracy rates in our experiments can certainly be improved. The goal of our work is not to reach the highest classification rates possible, but to have a fair comparison of pattern matching algorithms. To this end, we have spent roughly the same amount of time finding configurations with good performance for the different classifiers. We used grid search for conventional and our expert knowledge for EHW approaches. Additionally, the experiments were executed by subjects not familiar with EMG controlled prostheses. An amputee usually spends months of training before being able to reliably create pronounced muscular tensions, and also learns how and which muscles to activate to achieve the desired response from the prosthesis. Higher recognition rates can be approached by a model view of the prosthesis's mechanics. A prosthesis cannot respond to very short misclassifications of some milliseconds. Elimination of misclassification glitches by a low-pass filter, while slowing down prosthesis latency, increases the overall accuracy rate. In our experiments we observed improvements of 3% to 7%. Furthermore, complex hand movements decompose into basic hand actions. Each action has a typical duration and some follow-up actions, specified by their probabilities. Capturing the action space of a prosthesis by a Markov chain model helps reduce misclassification during a single action and select a correct follow-up action more quickly and reliably. The accuracy can also be improved by using additional feature extraction schemes. Their efficiency, however, needs to fit the computational complexity of an embedded system.

All of the classification approaches are able to provide a differentiated output of the certainty of the match to a given class (movement). This implies that implementation details are key to the selection of a classifier for prosthesis control. A PHC's primary requirements are a secure operation mode with guaranteed functional and temporal aspects, as well as energy efficiency. This gives hardware approaches an advantage over software methods for the following reasons: the exclusive use of a computational resource often allows giving hardware approaches precise execution time estimations and response time guarantees. Hardware solutions also have a somewhat simpler function verification. While some modern microcontrollers have low energy consumption [348], they lack larger memories and floating point units. Together with limited computational power, often only simplified classification algorithms can be realized there. Evolving and retraining classifiers, storing larger data models and datasets, and acquiring dynamic data is seldom possible on such small systems. Hardware approaches, on the other hand, while also offering energy efficiency and compactness, are much more capable of solving computationally extensive tasks and can be designed to efficiently interface with large memories.

Generally, we can state that our ECGP as well as the FUR architecture do not have peak accuracy rates as high as today's best pattern matching algorithms on EMG signal classification, but can compete with well known approaches such as DTs. The observed classification accuracies are close to each other, suggesting that implementation details become dominant when selecting a classifier for a prosthetic control system. Additionally, the requirement of dynamic learning makes a run-time adaptable EHW system one of the most promising candidates for application in prosthesis control.

7.2 Classifier Adaptation to Resource Fluctuations

Adaptation in Evolvable Hardware is typically considered regarding two kinds of stimuli. The predominant research effort has been put into the investigation of function adaption to environmental changes. The second line of research examines adaptation techniques to defects within reconfigurable hardware fabrics. Extending these scenarios by our idea introduced in Section 1.1, we study the capability of Evolvable Hardware to adapt to run-time fluctuations in the available resources, i.e., the chip area, in this section. Therefore, we investigate in this section the adaptation behavior of an Evolvable Hardware classifier during resource changes. In our analysis we add and remove the category classifiers of a continuously evolved system. The observed recovery rates can be seen as lower bounds for the adaptation speed. In the context of a multi-objective adaptation mechanism for EHW, where gradual and radical changes are compensated by continuous evolution and the selection of a most suitable Pareto solution, our experiments give insights into the adaptation and evolution speeds of a Pareto individual that has been instantiated after a change in the resources.

The ability to deal with fluctuating resources can be used to support the optimization process by assigning more resources when the speed of adaptation is crucial. Additionally, when energy considerations or new tasks reduce the available amount of resources, replacing EHW functions by alternatives with smaller circuit sizes, while probably decreasing the performance, allows for retaining the functionality.

To demonstrate our approach, we leverage the FUR architecture presented in Section 3.2.6. We apply the FUR classifier to two medical benchmarks, the Pima and Thyroid datasets from the UCI Machine Learning Repository. While these benchmarks do not benefit from fast processing times, resource efficient implementations, or run-time adaptation of Evolvable Hardware, we consider them as model applications because they demonstrate FUR's properties, such as fast recovery time, the ability to reach high accuracy rates using compact configurations, and stable accuracy behavior under a wide range of parameters. We first investigate FUR's general performance for these benchmarks before examining its classification behavior during architectural reconfigurations. To minimize the impact of architecture scaling, we introduce two reconfiguration techniques. The reconfiguration techniques gather statistical data during the training phases and use it to select the basic pattern matching elements to duplicate or remove when changing the architecture size.

7.2.1 The Reconfigurable Functional Unit Row Architecture

During design time, FUR's architecture can be parametrized along three dimensions: the number of

- categories,

- CCs in a category, and

- FUs in a CC.

The authors of the FUR architecture show, in [366], that the partial reconfiguration capabilities of FPGAs can be used to change the architecture's size dynamically. For our experiments, we decided to vary the number of CCs in a CDM for the following reasons: the number of categories is typically known *a priori* and is fixed. When comparing the classification principles of the FUR architecture and decision trees, the number of FUs in a CC can be seen as similar to the depth of a decision tree, which roughly represents the dimensionality of the decision space. The dimensionality of the decision space is highly application specific. Reducing the amount of FUs per CC without increasing the number of CCs in a CDM would be likely to create systems unable to reach the high classification rates of a properly configured architecture.

An additional motivation for changing the number of CCs in a CDM is that the FUR architecture is fully operational with only one CC per CDM. The number of CCs in a CDM can be seen as the CDM's resolution. While with one or few CCs in a CDM, the FUR architecture shows basic discrimination abilities, with a rising number of CCs, the accuracy rate reaches higher regions.

Reconfiguration of the FUR architecture is sketched in Figure 7.10. For a sequence $I = \{i_1, i_2, \ldots, i_k\}$, we evolve a FUR architecture having i_1 FUs per CDM, then switching to i_2 FUs per CDM and re-evolving the architecture without flushing the configuration evolved so far.

In our experiments we want to examine the the sensitivity of the classification accuracy to the changes described above, and how fast the evolutionary algorithm is able to reestablish pre-reconfiguration accuracy rates. Furthermore, we would like to investigate whether our non-randomized strategies for replacing and duplicating CCs minimize the impact of architectural reconfigurations compared to the baseline randomized method.

7.2.2 Evaluation

For our investigations we rely on the UCI machine learning repository [33] and, more specifically, on the Pima and the Thyroid benchmarks. Pima,

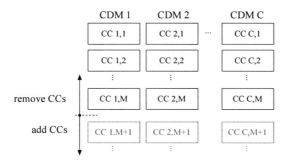

Figure 7.10: Reconfigurable FUR architecture: The FUR architecture is parametrized by the number of categories, category classifiers, and functional units (FU) per CC. While the number of categories is fixed and the number of FUs is largely application dependent, we scale the FUR architecture by changing the number of category classifiers in a category detection module.

or the Pima Indians Diabetes dataset, was collected by the John Hopkins University in Baltimore, MD, USA, and consists of 768 samples with eight feature values each, divided into a class of 500 samples representing negative tested individuals and a class of 268 samples representing positive tested individuals.

The data of the Thyroid benchmark represents samples of regular individuals and individuals suffering hypo- and hyper-thyroidism. Thus, the samples are divided into 6,666, 166, and 368 samples, representing regular, subnormal, and hyper-functional individuals. A sample consists of 22 feature values.

Neither benchmark relies on high classification speeds or run-time adaptation of EHW hardware classifiers. However, these benchmarks were selected because of their pronounced effects in the run-time reconfiguration experiments presented in the next section.

7.2.2.1 Methodology

We implement FUR's parameter analysis by a grid search over the number of CCs and number of FUs. For a single (i, j)-tuple, where i denotes the number of CCs and j the number of FUs, we evolve a FUR classifier by running $1 + 4$ evolutionary strategies for 100,000 generations. In contrast to the original work on the FUR architecture in [131] and experiments in Section 7.1, we do not use incremental evolution evolving CDMs separately, but evolve the complete FUR architecture in a single ES run. Thereby we use a mutation

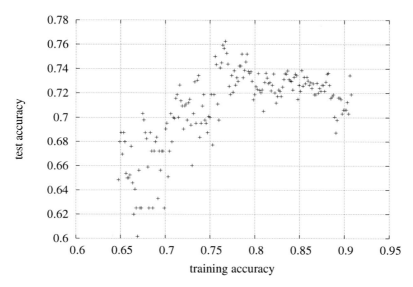

Figure 7.11: Overfitting analysis for the Pima dataset and FUR architecture having 8 FUs per CC and 30 CCs per CDM. In this example, the termination training accuracy is around 0.76, before the test accuracy begins to decline, indicating overfitting.

operator modifying three genes in every CC. As we employ a 12-fold cross validation scheme, the evolution is repeated 12 times while alternating the training and test datasets. During the evolution, we log for every increase in the training accuracy FUR's performance on the test dataset. The test accuracies are not used while the evolution runs. To detect the tipping point where FUR starts to overfit, i.e., where FUR learns to match each training vector instead of learning the general model, we average the test accuracies logged during the evolutionary runs and select the termination training accuracy according to the highest average test accuracy. This is shown in Figure 7.11 for the Pima benchmark and the $(30, 8)$ configuration. The average test accuracy, drawn along the y-axis, rises in relation to the average training accuracy, drawn along the x-axis, until the training accuracy reaches 0.76. After this point the test accuracy degrades gradually. Consequently, we note 0.76 and 0.76 as the best combination of test and termination training accuracies.

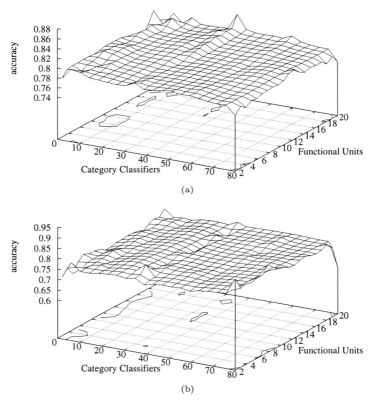

Figure 7.12: Pima overfitting analysis: Best generalization (a) and the corresponding termination training (b) accuracies for the Pima benchmark.

7.2.2.2 FUR's General Performance for the Pima and Thyroid Benchmarks

To examine the general FUR performance for the Pima and Thyroid datasets, we configure and evaluate the FUR architecture for all combinations of $2, 4, 6, \ldots, 20$ FUs per CC and for 2, 4, 6, 8, 10, 14, 16, 20, 25, 30, 35, 40, 50, 60, 70, and 80 CCs. Figures 7.12 and 7.13 display the results. Along the horizontal level, the diagrams span the parameter area of the CCs and FUs. The accuracy for each parameter tuple is drawn along the z-axis with a projection of equipotential accuracy lines on the horizontal level. While the test accuracies for the Pima benchmark, presented in Figure 7.12(a) are

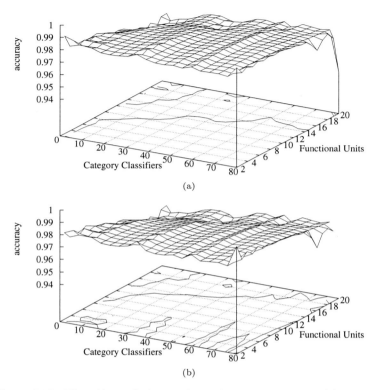

Figure 7.13: Thyroid overfitting analysis: Best generalization (a) and the corresponding termination training (b) accuracies for the Thyroidbenchmark.

largely independent of the number of FUs and CCs, with small islands of improved behavior around the $(8, 8 - 10)$ configurations, the Thyroid benchmark presented in Figure 7.13(a) has a performance loss in regions with a large number of FUs and few CCs.

Tables 7.6 and 7.7 compare FUR's results for the Pima and the Thyroid benchmarks to related work. We also use the data mining tool Rapid-Miner [248] to create the numbers for the standard and state of the art algorithms and their modern implementations. To this end, we evaluate with a 12-fold cross validation the algorithms DT, kNN, MLPs, LDA, SVMs, and classification and regression trees (CART). For the Pima benchmark, the FUR architecture outperforms any other method. It forms, together

Table 7.6: Pima benchmark: Error rates and standard deviation in %. We use the data mining toolbox RapidMiner [248] to evaluate the algorithms marked by "*." Preliminarily, we identify algorithm parameters with good performance by a grid search. The remaining results are taken from [388].

	Error Rate	SD
FUR	**21.35**	
SVM*	22.79	4.84
LDA*	23.18	4.64
Shared Kernel Models [358]	23.27	2.56
kNN*	23.56	3.07
GP with OS, |pop|=1.000 [388]	24.47	3.69
CART*	25.00	3.61
DT*	25.13	4.30
GP with OS, |pop|=100 [388]	25.13	4.95
MLP*	25.26	4.50
Enhanced GP [105]	25.80–24.20	
Simple GP [105]	26.30	
ANN [52, 92]	26.41–22.59	1.91–2.26
EP / kNN [281]	27.10	
Enhanced GP [105]	27.70–25.90	
GP [52]	27.85–23.09	1.29–1.49
GA / kNN [281]	29.60	
GP [92]	30.36–24.84	0.29–1.30
Bayes [281]	33.40	

with the SVMs, LDA, the shared kernel models, and kNN, a group of best performing algorithms within a 3% margin. The accuracy range of the Thyroid benchmark is much smaller because of the disproportional category data sizes and a single dominant category amounting to 92.5% of the data. In this benchmark, the FUR architecture lies 0.66% behind the best algorithm.

7.2.3 Functional Unit Row Architecture Reconfiguration Schemes

In our second experiment we investigate FUR's run-time adaptation capabilities to gradual and radical changes in resource sizes. To this end, we configure FUR with 4 FUs per CC and change the number of CCs every 50,000 generations. We split the dataset into disjoint training and test sets similar to the previously used 12-fold cross validation scheme and start the training with 10 CCs. Then, we gradually change the number of CCs to 9, 8, ..., 1, and then back to 2, 3, ..., and 10, executing altogether 10^6 generations. In the second experiment we investigate larger changes, switching from 10 to 4 to 2 to 5 and back to 10 CCs. For sound results, we repeat the first experiment 96 times, and the second experiment 32 times.

Table 7.7: Thyroid benchmark: Error rates and standard deviation in %. We use the data mining toolbox RapidMiner [248] to evaluate the algorithms marked by "*." First, we identify algorithm parameters with good performance by a grid search. Remaining results are taken from [388].

	Error Rate	SD
DT*	0.29	0.18
CART*	0.42	0.27
CART [386]	0.64	
PVM [386]	0.67	
Logical Rules [102]	0.70	
FUR	**1.03**	
GP with OS [388]	1.24	
GP [52]	1.44 – 0.89	
BP + local adapt. rates [293]	1.50	
ANN [294]	1.52	
BP + genetic opt. [293]	1.60	
GP [125]	1.60–0.73	
Quickprop [293]	1.70	
RPROP [293]	2.00	
GP [37]	2.29–1.36	
SVM*	2.35	0.51
MLP*	2.38	0.62
ANN [52]	2.38–1.81	
PGPC [225]	2.74	
GP [234]	5.10–1.80	
kNN*	5.96	0.44

Our basic implementation of FUR's reconfiguration reduces and increases the amount of CCs in a CDM by removing randomly selected and adding randomly initialized CCs to a CDM. In order to improve adaptation times during the architectural reconfigurations, we define two additional schemes to change the amount of CCs in a CDM by removing "worst" and duplicating "best" CCs. To quantify the quality of a CC, we define for every CC a penalty counter that is increased by the number of wrongly activated CCs in the same CDM for some input vector. A specific CC's counter is only increased when the CC itself decides incorrectly. The rationale behind this is that FUR's global decision is taken at the CDM level. Thus, a CDM with, for instance, 4 wrongly decided CCs is more likely to cause an incorrect global decision than a CDM with only 2 wrongly decided CCs. In the first case, every CC in the particular CDM with an incorrect decision adds a 4 to its penalty counter while in the second case, a 2 is added. Consequently, a CC is considered "bad" when having a higher penalty counter and "good" otherwise.

7.2.4 Evaluation

Table 7.8: Averaged accuracy drops in % over 96 algorithm runs. $1 + 4$ ES is executed for 50,000 generations between the reconfigurations. During a reconfiguration, randomly selected "best" CCs are removed and "worst" CCS are duplicated. Bold numbers indicate the best performing replacement strategy.

		delete rows $10 \to 9 \to \cdots \to 1$		insert rows $1 \to 2 \to \cdots \to 10$	
		training	test	training	test
Pima	random	10.87	5.70	8.33	5.70
	best	13.57	7.90	7.18	**5.15**
	worst	9.39	**4.23**	8.90	6.11
Thyroid	random	23.94	23.77	15.91	**15.74**
	best	40.87	40.73	16.13	16.03
	worst	12.21	**12.00**	20.60	20.53

Figure 7.14 and Figure 7.15 compare accuracy drop magnitudes during architectural reconfiguration using "random," "best," and "worst" schemes for the Pima and the Thyroid benchmarks, respectively. The top two diagram lines show the training and test behavior when randomly removing a CC and adding a randomly initialized CC to the FUR architecture, respectively. The diagrams in the next two pairs of lines illustrate the test accuracy behavior for the "best" and "worst" reconfiguration schemes. The diagrams in the bottom line display the development of the available resources, expressed by the number of CCs in a CDM. Additionally, Table 7.8 summarizes the training and test accuracy drops during the reconfigurations.

An obvious conclusion is that removing the "worst" CCs result in the smallest accuracy drops. Analogously, duplicating the "best" CCs helps minimizing accuracy drops when adding resources to the FUR architecture. Generally, we observe, for the Pima benchmark, the following:

- The training and test accuracies drop for any reconfiguration scheme for almost any positive and negative changes in the number of CCs, and subsequently recover. The drops are slightly larger for configurations with few CCs. The average accuracy drops, as summarized in Table 7.8, are minimized when removing the "worst" and duplicating the "best" CCs during the FUR reconfiguration. Randomly removing and initializing new CCs comes second, while removing the "best" and duplicating the "worst" CCs result in the largest accuracy losses. Altogether, the differences between the reconfiguration schemes are rather small, amounting to roughly 3.5% for removing and 1% for adding CCs.

- We observed the maximal training accuracies to be somewhat lower when using fewer CCs, while the test accuracies tend to stay at the same levels. Only for configurations with one and sometimes two CCs per CDM, the accuracy rates did not reach the pre-switch levels. The gaps, however, are small, roughly amounting for up to 5%.

- Test accuracies are recovered quickly for most schemes and FUR configurations. However, the strategy of removing the "worst" and "random" CCs maintains a fast recovery speed also when going below five CCs per CDM, whereas removing the "best" leads to significantly longer times before the asymptotic test accuracies are recovered.

- The test accuracies are mostly located between 0.72 and 0.76, independently of the changes in the number of CCs. Thus, and this is the main observation, the FUR architecture shows to a large extent a robust test accuracy behavior under reconfiguration for the Pima benchmark.

For the Thyroid benchmark, we can draw the following conclusions:

- The test accuracies drop significantly when changing the number of CCs. The drops are roughly three to five times larger, reaching up to 40%. Reducing FUR size, the accuracy drops became the smallest when removing the "worst" CCs during reconfigurations, followed by schemes selecting random and "best" CCs. When increasing the number of CCs, the smallest accuracy drops are obtained from the random CC duplication scheme, followed by schemes duplicating the "best" and the "worst" CCs. The difference between the random and "best" duplication scheme is, however, small, accounting for 0.69%.

- As anticipated by previous results shown in Fig. 7.13 (a), the test accuracy degrades for FUR architecture configurations with very few CCs. For instance, a FUR configuration with only one CC has an error rate of 7%. This is considerably low, as the baseline recognition rate lies at 92.5%, which corresponds to an error rate of 7.5% due to a single category's amounting to 6,666 out of 7,200 vectors.

- The main result is that given enough resources, reconfigurations are quickly compensated. The limitation in the case of the Thyroid benchmark is the minimum amount of CCs required to achieve high recognition rates.

Adaptation Behavior to Radical Changes

The challenges for an autonomous and adaptable embedded system are manifold. It may for instance have to react to aperiodic events where the solution may benefit from additional resources. With its typically restricted energy, an embedded system sometimes also faces the challenge of balancing resources

Table 7.9: Averaged accuracy drops in % over 32 algorithm runs. $1 + 4$ ES is executed for 50,000 generations between the reconfigurations. During a reconfiguration randomly selected, "best," or "worst" CCs are removed or duplicated. Bold numbers indicate the best performing replacement strategy.

		$10 \to 4$		$4 \to 2$	
		training	test	training	test
Pima	random	21.90	13.76	17.75	9.91
	best	21.59	10.93	19.94	11.52
	worst	16.65	**10.30**	10.57	**5.61**
Thyroid	random	60.00	59.37	45.96	45.55
	best	54.50	54.28	54.75	54.72
	worst	34.27	**33.91**	35.71	**35.89**

		$2 \to 5$		$5 \to 10$	
		training	test	training	test
Pima	random	13.46	11.86	18.27	15.42
	best	8.98	**6.34**	16.52	**9.32**
	worst	14.66	11.91	21.71	16.35
Thyroid	random	30.29	30.27	44.13	44.00
	best	30.14	29.88	34.90	**34.93**
	worst	18.65	**18.30**	71.84	72.16

between multiple applications. We anticipate resource assignment changes in such situations being of a more radical nature. To investigate FUR's behavior in such situations, we define a second reconfiguration sequence, switching form 10 to 4 to 2 to 5 and back to 10 CCs. In each reconfiguration step, we nearly halve or double the FUR's size. The results are summarized in Table 7.9. Almost all observations and conclusions made in the previous experiment hold also for the current experiment. The important differences are:

- The accuracy drops are now mostly two to three times as large compared to the gradual FUR size changes. Despite the dramatic numbers, accuracies recover similarly fast.

- Similar to the previous experiment, removing the "worst" CCs and duplicating the "best" CCs reduces the accuracy drops for Pima and Thyroid benchmarks. There is, however, one exception. The lowest test accuracy drops when switching from 2 to 5 CCs in the Thyroid benchmark are achieved by duplicating the "worst" CC three times.

In summary, for all the experiments in this section, we can conclude that the FUR architecture is exceptionally fast in recovering from architectural reconfigurations, provided that enough resources are available for learning.

Still, the proposed schemes of removing the "worst" and adding the "best" CCs help to reduce the impact on the classification rate after reconfiguration of the dimensions of the architecture. This is both in terms of lower magnitudes of instantaneous accuracy drops, as well as a shortened recovery time before pre-reconfiguration test accuracies are regained.

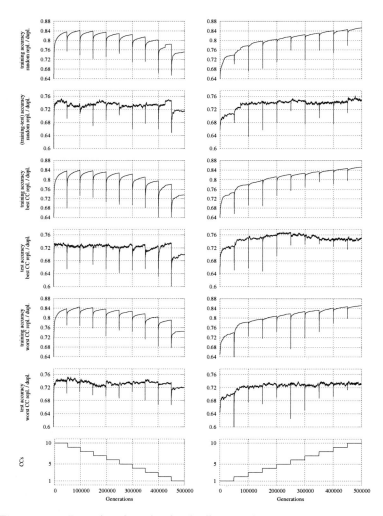

Figure 7.14: Pima benchmark: Gradually reconfiguring the FUR architecture. The left column presents FUR's averaged classification behavior in % when reducing and the right column when increasing the number of CCs. The diagrams on the bottom show the number of CCs in the system. Two diagram lines on the top show examples of the training and test behavior for the randomized reconfiguration scheme. Diagrams in the second and third pair of lines show training and test behavior for the "best" and "worst" FUR reconfiguration schemes, respectively.

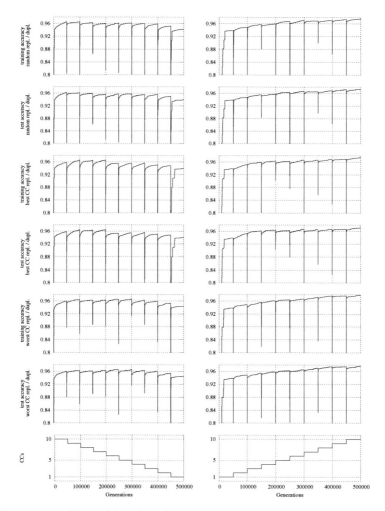

Figure 7.15: Thyroid benchmark: Gradually reconfiguring the FUR architecture. The left column presents FUR's averaged classification behavior in % when reducing and the right column when increasing the number of CCs. The diagrams on the bottom show the number of CCs in the system. Two diagram lines on the top show examples of the training and test behavior for the randomized reconfiguration scheme. Diagrams in the second and third pair of lines show training and test behavior for the "best" and "worst" FUR reconfiguration schemes, respectively.

189

7.3 Adaptation of Cache Mappings

The Evolvable Hardware principle is perceived and presented in the original work [163] as an adaptation methodology for autonomous embedded systems. The EHW principle is, though, not limited to this application domain. In this section, we present *EvoCaches*, an approach for implementing application specific caches. The key innovation of EvoCaches is to make the function that maps memory addresses from the CPU address space to cache indices programmable. To this end, we support arbitrary Boolean mapping functions that are implemented within a small reconfigurable logic fabric. For the evolution of suitable cache mapping functions, we rely on the regular EHW methods and models presented earlier in this thesis.

7.3.1 The Concept of EvoCaches

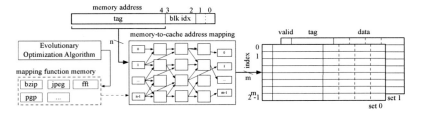

Figure 7.16: The evolvable cache ("EvoCaches") architecture provides a configurable mapping from CPU memory addresses to cache indices. The optimization process evolves the configuration of node functions and wiring between them. The nodes implement Boolean functions with four inputs and one output. The figure shows an example of a two way set associative cache.

The key idea of the EvoCaches approach is presented in Figure 7.16. A very small reconfigurable logic fabric implements a hashing function that maps a part of a memory address to a cache line index. The hashing function is encoded by a Cartesian genetic program and optimized to achieve a low overall execution time for a specific application. For optimization, we employ evolutionary strategies. Our architecture provides a mapping function memory that can store several configurations for the reconfigurable logic fabric, which allows quickly switching to different memory-to-cache address mappings. To prevent storing several potentially dirty copies of the same physical address at different indices in the cache, we flush the cache when a new mapping is activated.

The EvoCaches approach is orthogonal to other work trying to select and/or reconfigure the cache organization in an application specific way, e.g., [24, 280,

412]. While Figure 7.16 displays an address mapping for a byte-addressable architecture to a 2-way associative cache with a block size of four words, the EvoCaches principle is applicable to all possible configurations and levels of caches. Compared to classical modulo mappings or mappings based on bit permutations [329] and XOR functions [375, 376], EvoCaches utilizes more complex hashing functions, allowing them to reduce an application's overall execution time and energy requirements.

Including EvoCaches in a processor architecture will also increase the logic area, the hit time, and the overall number of memory cells for the cache. The increase in logic area is due to the reconfigurable fabric itself which is assumed to be small, as the fabric comprises only a handful of look-up tables (LUTs). Additionally, we require a mapping function memory to store the configurations for the logic fabric. The size of a configuration is dependent on the architecture. The architecture used for the case study comes with a configuration size of 151 bytes.

The increase of the cache size is due to the fact that the flexibility in the hashing function requires us to store the full address excluding block and byte offsets as tags in the cache. The additional overhead incurred depends on the actual cache configuration. For example, a conventional 4-way set associative cache of 16 KByte data with block size of two words for a byte-addressable architecture with 32 bit addresses comes with an overhead of 25.56%, where the overhead includes for each cache block the valid bit and the tag. Switching to an EvoCaches of the same data size and organization increases the overhead to 34.88%. We think this overhead is bearable since today most processor designs are not restricted by the silicon area but by performance and performance per energy. The increase in hit time is more critical. The additional delay depends strongly on the depth of the LUT network. This depth can be restricted in the optimization process to satisfy timing constraints. Moreover, for many embedded processors with clock frequencies well below 1 GHz, the pressure on the timing is moderate. High performance processors, on the other hand, have several levels of cache, and only the first level is optimized for hit time. Here, the EvoCaches approach can still be applied to the second and third level caches.

We focus on a single process system without an OS. Extending the EvoCaches approach to a multi-application platform, we need to cope with the multi-processing of several and different applications running concurrently. Here, we envision a canonical solution by evolving general cache mappings covering complete application domains and avoiding the need for different concurrent cache mappings. A more sophisticated solution could allow separate cache mappings for concurrent applications. However, this would introduce redundant cache blocks and could reduce the usage. Additionally, the evolution needs to consider the multi-application situation to minimize the potentially negative interaction effects of different cache mappings.

7.3.2 Algorithms, Representation Models, and Metrics

We model the reconfigurable cache mapping function by a single row CGP with $n_c = 32$ nodes. Each node implements a 4-input LUT and restrictions are imposed on its functional set. The circuit's inputs are fed from $n_i = 27$ primary inputs taken from the memory address. The $n_o = 15$ bit outputs of the circuit encode the cache line index. The levels-back parameter is set to ∞. The circuit depth is an important parameter for EvoCaches as it is proportional to the delay of the resulting hashing function which adds to the cache hit time. While constraining the circuit depth during optimization can be easily done, the experiments in this paper have been conducted with unconstrained circuit depth. Instead, in Section 7.3.3.2, we report on the depths and sizes of the evolved circuits. For optimization, a $1 + 4$ ES scheme, presented in Algorithm 3 has been employed. The mutation operator modifies a single gene during child creation, i.e., the function of a single logic node or the wiring of one of its inputs is affected.

For the experiments, we leverage our MOVES EHW toolbox, presented in Chapter 4. The tool setup is presented in Figure 7.17. The MOVES toolbox includes the CGP model and the ES. Whenever a new candidate circuit is generated, it is passed to the processor simulator SimpleScalar [35] for fitness evaluation. SimpleScalar reads the description of the circuit and simulates the execution of a specified benchmark and input data on a processor with given cache configuration in a cycle-accurate manner. We have chosen SimpleScalar for system simulation as it is easily extended and it models a variant of the widely used MIPS instruction set architecture. Two modifications to the original SimpleScalar tool have been necessary. First, its command line interface was extended to include the activation and specification of up to four mapping functions. These circuit specifications are read in and stored in a data structure. Second, for the actual mapping between the addresses and the cache line index, SimpleScalar needs to determine the logic result for the mapping function. To this end, the circuit evaluation routine already available in the MOVES toolbox has been extracted into a library and linked with SimpleScalar. In each simulation run, SimpleScalar determines an application's overall runtime and feeds it back to the evolutionary optimizer as the fitness value.

Besides the cycle-accurate runtime, SimpleScalar determines the miss rates for the different levels of caches. Our interest in the miss rate is motivated by the fact that related work has used miss rates to measure the fitness of a specific cache configuration. However, for more sophisticated processor architectures, metrics solely based on miss rates might be less conclusive than execution time. The downside of using the cycle-accurate execution time as the main metric is the long simulation time. We have constrained the simulation time to three to five minutes for a single fitness evaluation, which results in a overall runtime of roughly one week for a single and complete

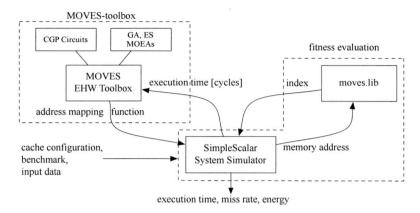

Figure 7.17: EvoCaches tools setup: SimpleScalar is invoked by the MOVES toolbox and returns the overall execution time in clock cycles as a fitness measure.

ES run. These constraints on the simulation time resulted in limiting the input data size for the benchmarked applications to some 100 KBytes, which puts sufficient pressure on the cache architecture of an embedded processor as modeled in our work. However, a modern general purpose processor's cache architecture would not be stressed sufficiently and thus might require the simulation of application runs on larger data sizes.

As energy estimate, we use a variant of the energy model presented in [412] which splits the energy demand into two parts: static and dynamic. We model an embedded processor with up to two levels of cache and an external memory. For each of the caches, i.e., split level one caches L1:I and L1:D and unified level two cache L2:U, as well as for the external memory, the static or standby energy per cycle is given by $E_{L1:I,s}, E_{L1:D,s}, E_{L2:U,s}$, and $E_{M,s}$. With c as the number of clock cycles required for program execution, the static energy is

$$E_{static} = c \cdot (E_{L1:I,s} + E_{L1:D,s} + E_{L2:U,s} + E_{M,s}).$$

The dynamic energies per access are given by $E_{L1:I,d}, E_{L1:D,d}, E_{L2:U,d}$, and $E_{M,d}$; the number of accesses is $a_{L1:I}, a_{L1:D}, a_{L2:U}$, and a_M. Thus, the dynamic energy turns out to be

$$\begin{aligned} E_{dynamic} = \ & a_{L1:I} \cdot E_{L1:I,d} + a_{L1:D} \cdot E_{L1:D,d} + \\ & a_{L2:U} \cdot E_{L2:U,d} + a_M \cdot E_{M,d}. \end{aligned}$$

The actual values in $[nJ]$ for the static energy per cycle and dynamic energy per access are derived from the CACTI cache model [318] for a 90 nm technology node. For the external memory, these values have been derived from the data sheet of a standard V58C2256 DDR SDRAM module. The overall number of clock cycles and the number of accesses are determined by the SimpleScalar simulator. Finally, the CPU energy E_{cpu} is computed by assuming a CPU with an average power consumption of 0.45 mW per MHz at a clock frequency of 200 MHz implemented in 90 nm technology [31]. The overall energy for an application run thus adds up to

$$E = E_{cpu} + E_{static} + E_{dynamic}.$$

7.3.3 Evaluation

To evaluate the EvoCaches concept, we configured a processor and its memory hierarchy in a configuration similar to those of current ARM processors [31]. The configuration is shown in Figure 7.18 and includes a split first level cache and a unified second level cache. The L1 caches are 2-way associative with a hit latency of one cycle, 64 sets, and a block size of 16 bytes. The L2 cache has an associativity of four ways with a hit latency of 6 cycles, 128 sets, and a block size of 32 bytes. The memory bus between the L2 cache and the external memory is 8 bytes wide. The external memory shows an access time of 18 cycles and a 2-cycle delay for consecutive data transfers in burst mode. Hence, the miss penalty for the L2 cache amounts to 24 cycles. Using this configuration, a conventional cache system for a byte-addressable architecture with 32 bit addresses has a 22 bit tag and a 6 bit index for the L1 caches and a 20 bit tag and 7 bit index for the L2 cache. For EvoCaches, the original tags and indices merge into a single tag of 28 and 27 bits for the L1 and L2 caches, respectively. We have evolved mapping functions for two optimization scenarios. In the first optimization scenario, only the first level caches (LI:I and L1:D) are EvoCaches with evolved mapping functions; in the second scenario, all three caches receive evolved mapping functions. Thus, a single chromosome describing the system's mapping functions consists of two CGP chromosomes in the first optimization scenario and of three CGP chromosomes in the second optimization scenario.

For evaluation, we simulated the execution of two benchmarks, BZIP2 (version 1.0.4) and JPEG (version 6a), each with different sets of input data. BZIP2 is a recent data compressor based on the Burrows–Wheeler transformation [314] and has been reported to cause a large amount of cache misses. The picture encoding application JPEG [384] is a commonly used benchmark for performance analysis.

For each combination of benchmark and optimization scenario, we proceeded as follows. First, we evolved a mapping function for a given input dataset, referred to as the training data. This optimization step was repeated 16 times.

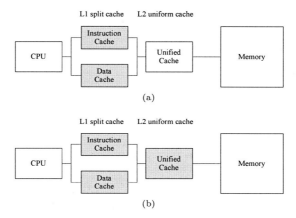

Figure 7.18: Two memory hierarchy configurations are considered for optimization. In the first case, the mapping functions of L1 instruction and data caches are optimized (Figure (a)), while in the second case additionally the mapping function of the uniform L2 cache is considered (Figure (b)).

To study the potential of EvoCaches, we analyzed the fitness development of the best and the worst individual in each generation as well as the average over all 16 runs over two reference systems. These are a cacheless system with a one cycle memory access time which, as such, is unrealistic but serves as a point of reference, and a two-level cache with classical modulo address mapping functions.

Second, we determined the generalization behavior by evaluating the best evolved mapping functions on different sets of input data, referred to as the test data. These results are actually more important than the results achieved for the training data, as they reflect the practical use case of EvoCaches. We used random mapping functions to initialize the evolutionary optimizer for both benchmarks, but also experimented with modulo mappings as the initial individuals for BZIP2.

For BZIP2, the training dataset consists of the HyperText Markup Language (HTML) code from Wikipedia's page, "Genetic Programming" [81]. The test data consists of 30 datasets partitioned into HTML data, Linux binaries, and human readable text files. For JPEG, the training dataset originates from the standard picture contained in the JPEG source code distribution. As test data, we use ten datasets from [373] and [166].

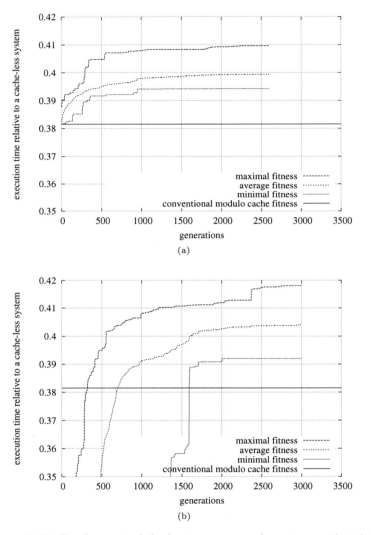

Figure 7.19: Development of the best, average, and worst execution time over 16 runs for the BZIP2 benchmark and the simultaneous optimization of split L1 and unified L2 caches. Execution time is expressed relative to a cacheless system including one-cycle access memory. In (a), the evolutionary optimizer has been initialized with the classic modulo mapping function, in (b) a random initialization was chosen.

7.3.3.1 Training EvoCaches

Figure 7.19 presents the results for BZIP2 and optimization scenario two, i.e., evolving address mapping functions for L1:I, L1:D, and L2:U simultaneously. In Figure 7.19(a), the evolutionary strategy started with classical modulo mapping functions, whereas Figure 7.19(b) shows the fitness development for the randomly initialized evolutionary search. The four curves in each graph are plotted against the number of generations and picture the fitness which is defined as the reciprocal of the overall execution time relative to the cacheless reference system with a one-cycle access time. That is, since for BZIP2 to execute the training data on the cacheless reference system requires 13'131'325 cycles, and on the classical modulo cache 34'417'080 cycles (2.62X slowdown), the modulo cache is indicated by a straight line at 0.3815.

The remaining curves in Figure 7.19 show the maximal, minimal, and averaged execution time for the evolved mapping functions. The main result is that it is easy to evolve mapping functions that outperform the modulo cache. Comparing Figures 7.19(a) and 7.19(b), we can observe that starting evolution from the classical modulo functions is not beneficial. Starting from the random mapping functions, we obviously need more generations to beat the modulo cache mapping but the resulting fitness values are overall better and more varied.

Optimization scenario one, i.e., evolving mapping functions for first level caches only, reveals similar behavior. Table 7.10 lists the performance gains over the classical modulo cache mappings for both experiments. The table shows the best and average individuals of the 16 runs. The fitness is indicated in columns three and five. For example, the best fitness achieved in the 16 runs for evolving mapping functions for the level one cache (L1:I, L1:D) was 0.39996, which results in a 4.7% improvement in execution time over the classical modulo mapping function.

Table 7.11 summarizes the training results for the JPEG benchmark. Here, we report only experiments with randomly initialized individuals. We can observe that the average performance achieved for optimizing both cache levels is actually higher than the performance achieved for optimizing only level one caches. The best individual, with a 17.1% improvement in runtime, is found, however, by optimizing only level one caches.

7.3.3.2 Testing EvoCaches

To verify the generalization performance of EvoCaches, we evaluated the execution times, miss rates, and energy requirements for BZIP2 and JPEG and the different optimization settings. For BZIP2, we selected the four best training individuals according to both optimization and the individual initialization settings. The test data for BZIP2 comprise ten datasets taken from Linux

Table 7.10: Training execution times for the BZIP2 benchmark after 2500 generations. The numbers are expressed relative to a cacheless system including one-cycle access memory and as performance gains to a standard system with identical cache parameters (size, associativity, block size, access times, and way prediction).

initialized:		by modulo function		randomly	
relative to:		cacheless	mod cache	cacheless	mod cache
L1	avg	0.3952	3.6%	0.4038	5.8%
	best	0.3996	4.7%	0.4086	7.1%
L1, L2	avg	0.3994	4.6%	0.4037	5.8%
	best	0.4096	7.3%	0.4174	9.4%

Table 7.11: Training execution times for the JPEG benchmark after 1400 generations. The numbers are expressed relative to a cacheless system including one-cycle access memory and as performance gains to a standard system with identical cache parameters (size, associativity, block size, access times, and way prediction).

initialized:		randomly	
relative to:		cacheless	mod cache
L1	avg	0.6623	11.2%
	best	0.6975	17.1%
L1, L2	avg	0.6718	12.8%
	best	0.6962	16.9%

binaries (ELF benchmark), ten datasets taken from HTML dumps of popular web sites (HTML benchmark), and ten datasets taken from RFCs (TXT benchmark). The detailed results are shown in Table 7.12. The numbers for a single benchmark are averaged over the ten datasets and measured relative to the performance of a conventional system with modulo address mappings. That is, positive percentages indicate an improvement in execution time, a reduction in miss rate, and a reduction in energy. The miss rates of all caches have been added to achieve the miss rate metric.

On analyzing the results in Table 7.12, the following observations can be made for the BZIP2 benchmark.

- EvoCaches generalizes well and delivers for all test data substantial performance improvements. The improvements in execution time are up to 10.98% and the reductions in energy are up to 10.70%.

- Having EvoCaches in both levels of cache (L1:I, L1:D and L2:U) leads to higher performance gains than having EvoCaches only in level one.

- The advantage of cache mapping functions evolved from random map-

Table 7.12: EvoCaches generalization performance gains in % relative to a
standard system with identical cache parameters (size, associativity, block
size, access times, and way prediction) for the BZIP2 benchmark trained
on the Wikipedia "Genetic Programming" HTML page. The test data are
partitioned into compressed Linux binaries in ELF format (bash, cpio, dbus-
daemon, awk, sh, gawk, tar, tcsh, vim, zsh), web pages in HTML format
(Ancient Egypt [W], Ancient Greece [W], Ancient Rome [W], Germany [W],
heise.de, Andrey Kolmogorov [W], sailinganarchy.com, spiegel.de, wired.com,
slashdot.org), and text files (rfc 2068, 2246, 845, 1000, 1001, 1002, 1005,
1008, 1009, 2658). Data sets marked with [W] have been collected from
wikipedia.org.

optimized:		ELF benchmark				HTML benchmark			
		L1		L1, L2		L1		L1, L2	
initialized:		mod	rnd	mod	rnd	mod	rnd	mod	rnd
exe.	best	1.40	4.92	3.94	5.90	4.00	5.31	4.18	6.98
time	avg	0.74	4.36	3.38	5.60	2.74	3.86	3.32	4.94
	worst	0.14	3.36	2.36	4.87	1.75	2.47	2.06	3.46
miss	best	-0.01	6.11	5.55	9.00	3.76	5.94	5.24	8.92
rate	avg	-0.49	5.59	5.02	8.51	2.55	4.15	3.55	6.41
	worst	-1.40	4.13	3.52	7.94	1.08	1.64	1.92	4.88
energy	best	1.64	4.64	3.55	5.49	4.58	5.61	5.09	7.31
req.	avg	1.08	4.13	3.06	5.23	3.55	4.53	3.87	5.29
	worst	0.59	3.27	2.17	4.57	2.34	3.21	2.60	3.77

optimized:		TXT benchmark			
		L1		L1, L2	
initialized:		mod	rnd	mod	rnd
exe.	best	5.22	7.30	7.03	10.98
time	avg	2.34	4.49	4.08	6.66
	worst	-5.72	-4.15	-5.56	1.95
miss	best	4.27	8.45	7.27	11.38
rate	avg	1.48	4.82	4.20	8.26
	worst	-11.00	-9.31	-11.18	2.63
energy	best	4.71	6.88	6.07	10.70
req.	avg	3.06	4.93	4.33	6.98
	worst	-4.53	-2.83	-4.33	2.16

Table 7.13: EvoCaches generalization performance gains relative to a standard system with identical cache parameters (size, associativity, block size, access times, and way prediction) for the JPEG encoder benchmark trained on the sample image from the jpeg6a source code distribution.

initialized:		randomly	
optimized:		L1	L1, L2
execution	best	14.31%	12.96%
time	avg	12.73%	10.78%
	worst	11.48%	9.12%
miss	best	41.25%	40.35%
rate	avg	37.40%	37.19%
	worst	31.64%	30.46%
energy	best	16.43%	14.46%
requirement	avg	14.19%	11.93%
	worst	12.53%	10.49%

ping functions over mappings evolved from modulo functions can be also observed when evaluating the cache with test data and is even more pronounced as in the training phase.

For testing EvoCaches on JPEG, we selected ten test images from [373] and [166]. The detailed results are shown in Table 7.13 and can be summarized as follows:

- EvoCaches again generalizes well with even larger improvements in execution time (up to 14.31%) and reductions in energy (up to 16.43%).

- The average performance when optimizing only the L1 caches is about 2% higher than when optimizing both cache levels. This corresponds with the observation made when training EvoCaches for JPEG where the best training performance was reached by optimizing only the L1 caches. Consequently, the individual with best test performance gains better test performance, even if not being further optimized for the L2 cache too.

- While the reductions in the miss rates are rather high, the reductions in execution times are lower. This demonstrates that for multiple levels of cache, the total miss rate is not necessarily a suitable and precise metric correlating with the real performance improvement of a system.

The results of our experiments are summarized in Figure 7.20, which shows for both benchmarks, BZIP2 and JPEG, and optimization setups, the relative improvement by EvoCaches in execution time, miss rate, and energy requirements over a modulo address mapping function.

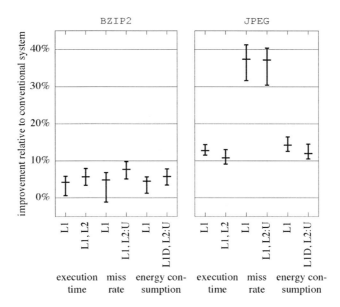

Figure 7.20: Summary of the EvoCaches generalization performance gains for the BZIP2 and JPEG benchmarks compared to a regular system with identically parametrized cache architecture. The data is for randomly initialized mapping functions. The best, worst, and average values are indicated for every optimization setting and metric.

The area (number of 4-LUTs) and the delay (depth of the circuit) parameters for the resulting reconfigurable logic circuits are presented in Table 7.14. Besides the average and maximal values, the values for the fittest circuit used for testing is also listed. These circuits show depths between three and six LUTs. It has to be noted that the circuits were the result of an evolutionary design process and thus have been optimized for neither area nor delay nor combinatorial reduction. Delay minimization could possibly further reduce the circuits' propagation times and thus the cache hit times. Altogether, the best solutions evolved during the experiments have the longest path, of up to 6, and a size of up to 19 LUTs.

7.4 Chapter Conclusion

In this chapter we have presented some of our work on EHW applications. We have selected the contributions to demonstrate following:

Table 7.14: Delays and areas of the evolved reconfigurable address mapping functions. Delays are measured by the number of wires in the longest path, and areas, by the number of 4-input LUTs.

		BZIP2				JPEG	
		delay	size	delay	size	delay	size
initialized:		by mod function		randomly		randomly	
L1	avg	4.10	13.50	4.63	16.94	4.38	15.13
	max	6	19	7	22	7	22
	best	5	18	4	18	6	19
L1, L2	avg	4.06	14.00	4.19	15.81	4.44	15.44
	max	6	20	8	24	6	22
	best	5	16	3	14	4	17

Continuous multi-objective optimization can help avoiding functional drops during the adaptation to radical changes. As shown in Section 7.2, adaptation to radical resource requirement changes can lead to large degradation of the classification accuracy. Continuously evolving alternative solutions with diverse architecture sizes helps switching immediately to a best suited and fully functional solution. If the new solution does not employ all assigned resources, evolution can search for a functionally better alternative using all assigned resources in parallel.

If an Evolvable Hardware approach is on par with conventional methods, secondary properties such as the execution time, simplicity of an adaptive mode, learning effort, energy and compactness become pivotal for the selection of an appropriate method. For the application of electromyographic signal classification, presented in Section 7.1, an Evolvable Hardware solution offers a lot of properties required by a prosthesis control and can therefore be the better solution compared to conventional methods.

The Evolvable Hardware paradigm can create intriguing use cases for applications, not have been targeted by conventional adaptation techniques yet. We have demonstrated this for the adaptation of processor caches in Section 7.3, where the execution time of an application could be significantly improved by the introduction of evolved memory-to-cache address mapping functions. Additionally, today's global networking infrastructure together with a large amount of computing nodes allows us to extend the evolvable caches idea to a true Evolvable Hardware system. CPUs with EvoCaches engines can thereby be seen as local nodes of an island EA (cf. Section 2.3). In a distributed manner, nodes may evolve and exchange their solutions, establishing a library of application- and data-specific EvoCaches.

Chapter 8

Summary and Outlook

8.1 Contributions

Evolvable hardware has been investigated in related work mostly regarding either its adaptation performance to variations in the distribution of the input data or to effects due to degradation of the computational resources. Little attention, however, has been paid to a holistic approach, employing the very same adaptation principle for compensating both gradual and radical as well as environmental and systemic changes.

With this thesis, we have made the following fundamentally new contributions to the area of Evolvable Hardware:

1. We have introduced a meaningful recombination operator for Cartesian genetic programming [6]. This is a prerequisite for the employment of Pareto based multi-objective evolutionary algorithms as a uniform Evolvable Hardware adaptation engine. Typically, modern MOEAs rely on information drift among individuals by means of a recombination operator. The implicit coding of non-functional elements within the CGP model makes the implementation of a meaningful recombination operator complex. With our realization of a recombination operator that transfers functionally coherent genotype substructures, we have created a uniform EHW adaptation mechanism able to master both gradual and radical changes.

2. We have significantly improved the scalability of circuit evolution in Cartesian genetic programming using the following measures:

   a) We have established an automatic cone-based subfunction extraction and reuse [6]. Similar to conventional engineering's encapsulating half- and full-adder circuits in unique functions, the automatic identification and reuse of frequently appearing circuit patterns enables evolutionary algorithms for hierarchical designs. Especially, applications from the arithmetic domain comprising repetitive substructures profit from this technique.

b) We have created an automatic age based subfunction identification and reuse [6]. This method is inspired by Nature's way of building organs from structures that persist unchanged in the genotype for a long period of time and therefore contribute implicitly to the genotype's success. Our technique encapsulates genes that have not been touched by the mutation operator for some period of time. This technique has been proven highly beneficial for applications with irregular and randomized structures, such as pattern matching kernels [7, 9, 10, 12, 17, 20].

c) We have found an efficient objective weighting scheme for multi-objective Cartesian genetic programming [1, 4, 8]. While single-objective and local search style evolutionary algorithms excel in Cartesian genetic programming, Pareto based multi-objective EAs need to be tailored for CGP. We have analyzed the dependencies of objective functions such as functional quality, area, and delay, and have identified a weighting scheme enabling algorithms such as SPEA2 to converge quickly in the dimension of functional quality while preserving the diversity of the evolved nondominated set. Objective weighting can even outperform single-objective EAs in functional quality for more complex functions and evolve better nondominated sets than state of the art MOEAS for positively correlated objectives.

d) We have introduced a systematic approach for blending properties and convergence rates of population based evolutionary algorithms [13]. Our method executes a sequence of algorithms rotationally, propagating candidate solutions through each of the sequence' algorithms. We additionally have created Evolutionary Strategies able to respect the nondomination and diversity principles of a population created by a Pareto based MOEA. With this, we have improved substantially the multi-objective evolution of CGP circuits.

3. We verified these methods, showing the feasibility of the Evolvable Hardware approach for the following applications:

a) We created an Evolvable Hardware ensemble pattern matching architecture and compared it to state of the art classifiers, such as support vector machines, multilayer perceptrons, C4.5 decision trees, and other algorithms [7, 9, 10, 12, 15, 16, 18, 20]. Our method was verified as being on a par with conventional data mining techniques, and we investigated the benefits of an EHW classifier for prosthesis control.

b) We introduced reconfiguration schemes for an Evolvable Hardware classifier, significantly reducing the negative impact of architectural reconfigurations on the classification accuracy [14, 17, 19]. By adding additional resources to the architecture, we were also able to maintain a high accuracy recovery rate.

c) We optimized embedded processor caches using Evolvable Hardware [11, 15]. Introducing a small reconfigurable fabric to a CPU for translating memory to cache addresses, we subjected the fabric's configuration to evolutionary optimization. The goal of the evolution was to find a CGP mapping function that reduces the cycle-accurate execution time for a test application and its data set. Once such a mapping function was found, we observed excellent generalization capabilities for unknown data, improving the execution time and energy consumption for the BZIP2 and JPEG functions by more than 10%.

4. We implemented a versatile framework for digital circuit evolution [2]. The framework offers a graphical interface for algorithm testing as well as a command line interface for compute-cluster based experiment execution. For the efficient implementation of new methods, the framework comprises a flexible software architecture separating the representation models, algorithms, and evolutionary operators. Using our framework, we implemented genetic algorithms; evolutionary strategies and genetic programming; state of the art multi-objective evolutionary optimizers such as SPEA2, NSGAII, IBEA, and OMOEAII; and the Cartesian as well as Embedded Cartesian genetic programming representation models. Any evolved circuit in our framework can be exported via the EDIF hardware description format and synthesized via the Xilinx FPGA tools.

With our methods for efficient multi-objective evolution of digital circuits, we have enabled Evolvable Hardware for the compensation of both gradual and radical changes, facilitating a unified adaptation method for autonomous systems. The benefits of our approach have been verified on a set of applications including challenging real world tasks of prosthesis control and processor optimization.

8.2 Conclusions and Lessons Learned

During our work on Evolvable Hardware systems we gained the following insights:

Although we have demonstrated how it can be tackled for CGP circuits, scalability remains one of the central challenges in Evolvable Hardware. The reason for this lies in the very nature of the evolutionary algorithms and is indicated by the No Free Lunch theorem. An adequate convergence of the adaptation mechanism has to be ensured for every new and different hardware encoding model, reconfigurable hardware platform, and application domain. In the Introduction, we outlined the different algorithmic facets of an Evolvable Hardware system and showed how they can be approached for the domain of Boolean gates. From our work, we have gained the insight that when building an Evolvable Hardware system one should start by analyzing and understanding the inner structure of the application to identify the representational and reconfigurable granularities. With this in hand, an appropriate hardware encoding can be determined, which is a key for fast design space exploration. Additionally, application specific as well as general knowledge can then be embedded into the evolutionary operators.

The compensation of radical changes by the evolution of alternative solutions relies upon a tight correlation between the fluctuating objective function and its impact on the remaining objectives. For instance, one would assume that evolution can find asymptotically better solutions when able to explore larger design spaces. For the area of Boolean gates, this means that one would expect that giving evolution a larger reconfigurable area for circuit encoding solutions would result in higher functional qualities. While this is the case for some configurations of the Evolvable Hardware classifier (cf. Section 7.2), we have typically observed evolution finding very compact Boolean circuits with the highest functional qualities. Changing the available resource a solution may use seems to barely affect the highest evolvable functional qualities. The ability to change the available resources during the evolution, however, has turned out to be very beneficial for the adaptation performance. Whenever the change rate exceeds the adaptation rate for, e.g., a hardware classifier, the classifier architecture can be scaled up, allowing for faster adaptation. The available resources can then be reduced gradually until no more reduction is possible, without affecting the best functional quality and the adaptation rate. Hence, the proposed principle for the compensation of radical changes can serendipitously be used for the improvement of the adaptation time.

Non-deterministic adaptation for autonomous systems is not yet in the standard engineering toolbox. This is mainly due to the missing guarantees of the adaptation times. While some applications require these guarantees, for many applications, safety considerations play a negligible role. Especially for the family of applications without a correctness measure, such as in the evolvable caches example, adaptation time is of minor interest. Continuous adaptation allows these cases to engineer innovative and powerful solutions, creating true alternatives to conventional ones. Moreover, the Evolvable Hardware paradigm can open completely new perspectives on improving and adapting systems, not yet being considered or even able to be considered by conventional engineering.

The understanding of adaptation principles and their relevance for autonomous systems as well as the inspiration for new ideas comes, to a significant extent, from the evaluation of applications. For instance, we have observed the utmost importance of efficient multi-objective circuit evolution and the potential of distributed and collaborative evolution for the application of evolvable caches. The benefit of additional resources for the adaptation performance came to us during the experiments on classifier reconfiguration. While mostly EHW applications currently come from the digital domain, our impression is that *"Thinking in Evolvable Hardware"* may spread to other areas, emphasizing continuous run-time optimization in classic engineering and revealing novel adaptation mechanisms.

Efficient hardware reconfiguration, especially for systems with constrained computational power, is of utmost importance. Efficient reconfiguration allows relocating complex operations directly to hardware for adaptation performance unmatched by simulative approaches. Additionally, energy consumption has become an essential benefit, serving autonomous operation. An example of the potential advantages of efficient hardware reconfiguration is our experiment on the evolution of CGP based pattern matching architectures. While we used a simulation based approach, efficiently reconfigurable architecture for Boolean gate circuits would evaluate the accuracy of a candidate solutions many orders of magnitude faster. We therefore argue that efficient reconfiguration, even if needing a greater implementation effort and incurring overhead in chip resources, is a prerequisite for many Evolvable Hardware systems.

8.3 Future Directions

Based on the work presented in this thesis, the following lines of research can be identified:

On the general scale, evolutionary algorithms' scalability is paramount and requires fundamentally new approaches. Biological cells and organisms demonstrate incredibly complex physical structures and chemical regulatory networks with extraordinarily well-balanced metabolisms. The evolution of such systems using today's methods of artificial intelligence appears to be practically impossible. We have often observed artificial evolution evolving compact yet complicated solutions instead of large and complex solutions. Complicated solutions are built mostly without a visible hierarchical structure while complex solutions comprise a hierarchical design and employ repetitive functional patterns. The methods of Artificial Intelligence seem to be struggling with the evolution and use of implicitly given rules of hierarchical design. A hierarchical design can be seen as a symmetry function, reducing the representation size by reusing structures and partial solutions. A biological cell or organism demonstrates a vast number of symmetries. On the molecular level, symmetric patterns appear in the structure of cell membranes, in the way a protein folds, and in the way a DNA molecule twists into a chromosome. On the cellular level, tissues are highly symmetric; and on the organ level, redundant systems and symmetric shapes arise. Symmetry appears at many locations and on different levels. Additionally, the kind of symmetry and the way it is expressed are also subject to evolution. In AI, the principles of symmetry began with the automatic acquisition and reuse of subfunctions by Koza and Lindenmayer's generative L-systems. Today, Miller's Developmental Cartesian Genetic Programming is an example of automatic symmetry discovery. We feel that the key to complex design and scalability in AI lies in the evolution of nested computational models and the implicated expression functions.

In our investigations we have concentrated on Evolvable Hardware for Boolean logic circuits. However, Evolvable Hardware applied to more coarsely grained hardware encoding models may be even more promising, for several reasons. The implementation of efficiently reconfigurable coarse grained architectures typically incurs a much smaller overhead than is the case for fine grained architectures. Additionally, the main FPGA manufacturers have incorporated coarse-grained functional blocks, such as arithmetical–logical units, reducing even further the overhead incurred by the implementation and reconfiguration. But the main reason is that a coarse-grained hardware model is able to encode numbers, busses, and complex mathematical functions, and is therefore much better suited for capturing solutions for a wide set of real world applications, such as those from, for instance, the signal processing and control domain. Especially for the latter case, where mathematical tools for convergence analysis often exist, the comparison with the non-deterministic Evolvable Hardware approach in terms of adaptation performance and the compensation of events not covered by the conventional controller might be of the utmost interest.

The evolvable cache application has demonstrated that distributed and island evolution may become relevant for systems with negligible communication limitations. Similar to the raw parallelism of the organic world, this helps distribute the computational effort among a set of nodes, reducing the load on a single node. More importantly, distributed Evolvable Hardware may offer new ways of capturing and defining adaptation cases and preventatively propagating solutions to other nodes. Altogether, with the increasing number of connected and reconfigurable systems, distributed and island evolutionary adaptation has become an even more relevant research area.

The evolvable caches application has emerged as a highly promising one. For further investigation, however, the challenges of efficient and realistic system simulation and of cache reconfiguration for the multi-application and the multi-threaded use cases have to be solved. The former challenge can be approached by heuristic methods and by a synthesizable and cycle-accurate CPU model comprising a custom cache with a reconfigurable memory-to-cache address translation function. For the latter challenge, new cache flushing and reordering strategies, universal cache mappings, and other ideas need to be investigated.

Author's Publications

[1] P. Kaufmann and M. Platzner. Multi-objective Intrinsic Hardware Evolution. In *Intl. Conf. Military Applications of Programmable Logic Devices (MAPLD)*, 2006.

[2] P. Kaufmann and M. Platzner. MOVES: A Modular Framework for Hardware Evolution. In *Adaptive Hardware and Systems (AHS)*, pages 447–454. IEEE, 2007. **Awarded best paper in the 'Evolvable Hardware' category.**

[3] T. Schumacher, E. Lübbers, P. Kaufmann, and M. Platzner. Accelerating the Cube Cut Problem with an FPGA-Augmented Compute Cluster. In *Parallel Computing: Architectures, Algorithms and Applications (PARCO)*, volume 15 of *Advances in Parallel Computing*, pages 749–756. IOS Press, 2007.

[4] P. Kaufmann and M. Platzner. Toward Self-adaptive Embedded Systems: Multi-objective Hardware Evolution. In *Architecture of Computing Systems (ARCS)*, volume 4415 of *LNCS*, pages 199–208. Springer, 2007.

[5] T. Schumacher, R. Meiche, P. Kaufmann, E. Lübbers, C. Plessl, and M. Platzner. A Hardware Accelerator for k-th Nearest Neighbor Thinning. In *Proc. Intl. Conf. on Engineering of Reconfigurable Systems & Algorithms (ERSA)*, pages 245–251. CSREA Press, 2008.

[6] P. Kaufmann and M. Platzner. Advanced Techniques for the Creation and Propagation of Modules in Cartesian Genetic Programming. In *Genetic and Evolutionary Computation (GECCO)*, pages 1219 – 1226. ACM Press, 2008.

[7] K. Glette, T. Gruber, P. Kaufmann, J. Torresen, B. Sick, and M. Platzner. Comparing Evolvable Hardware to Conventional Classifiers for Electromyographic Prosthetic Hand Control. In *Adaptive Hardware*

and Systems (AHS), pages 32–39. IEEE, 2008. **Awarded best paper in the 'Evolvable Hardware' category.**

[8] T. Knieper, B. Defo, P. Kaufmann, and M. Platzner. On Robust Evolution of Digital Hardware. In *Biologically Inspired Collaborative Computing (BICC)*, volume 268 of *IFIP International Federation for Information Processing*, pages 2313–222. Springer, 2008.

[9] K. Glette, J. Torresen, P. Kaufmann, and M. Platzner. A Comparison of Evolvable Hardware Architectures for Classification Tasks. In *Intl. Conf. on Evolvable Systems (ICES)*, volume 5216 of *LNCS*, pages 22–33. Springer, 2008.

[10] A. Boschmann, P. Kaufmann, M. Platzner, and M. Winkler. Towards Multi-movement Hand Prostheses: Combining Adaptive Classification with High Precision Sockets. In *Technically Assisted Rehabilitation (TAR)*, 2009.

[11] P. Kaufmann, C. Plessl, and M. Platzner. EvoCaches: Application-specific Adaptation of Cache Mappings. In *Adaptive Hardware and Systems (AHS)*, pages 11–18. IEEE CS, 2009.

[12] P. Kaufmann, K. Englehart, and M. Platzner. Fluctuating EMG Signals: Investigating Long-term Effects of Pattern Matching Algorithms. In *32nd Intl. Conf. of the IEEE Engineering in Medicine and Biology Society (EMBC)*, pages 6357–6360. IEEE, 2010.

[13] P. Kaufmann, T. Knieper, and M. Platzner. A Novel Hybrid Evolutionary Strategy and its Periodization with Multi-objective Genetic Optimizers. In *IEEE World Congress on Computational Intelligence (WCCI), Congress on Evolutionary Computation (CEC)*, pages 541–548. IEEE, 2010.

[14] T. Knieper, P. Kaufmann, K. Glette, M. Platzner, and J. Torresen. Coping with Resource Fluctuations: The Run-time Reconfigurable Functional Unit Row Classifier Architecture. In *Intl. Conf. on Evolvable Systems (ICES)*, volume 6274 of *LNCS*, pages 250–261. Springer, 2010. **Awarded best student paper.**

[15] L. Sekanina, J. A. Walker, P. Kaufmann, C. Plessl, and M. Platzner. Evolution of Electronic Circuits. In *Cartesian Genetic Programming*, Natural Computing Series, pages 125–179. Springer Berlin Heidelberg, 2011.

[16] J. A. Walker, J. F. Miller, P. Kaufmann, and M. Platzner. Problem Decomposition in Cartesian Genetic Programming. In *Cartesian Genetic Programming*, Natural Computing Series, pages 35–99. Springer Berlin Heidelberg, 2011.

[17] P. Kaufmann and M. Platzner. Multi-objective Intrinsic Evolution of Embedded Systems. In C. Müller-Schloer, H. Schmeck, and T. Ungerer, editors, *Organic Computing — A Paradigm Shift for Complex Systems*, volume 1 of *Autonomic Systems*, pages 193–206. Springer Basel, 2011.

[18] A. Boschmann, P. Kaufmann, and M. Platzner. Accurate Gait Phase Detection using Surface Electromyographic Signals and Support Vector Machines. In *Intl. Conf. Bioinformatics and Biomedical Technology (ICBBT)*. IEEE, 2011.

[19] P. Kaufmann, K. Glette, M. Platzner, and J. Torresen. Compensating Resource Fluctuations by Means of Evolvable Hardware: The Run-Time Reconfigurable Functional Unit Row Classifier Architecture. *Intl. J. Adaptive, Resilient and Autonomic Systems (IJARAS)*, 3(4):17–31, 2012.

[20] P. Kaufmann, K. Glette, T. Gruber, M. Platzner, J. Torresen, and B. Sick. Classification of electromyographic signals: Comparing evolvable hardware to conventional classifiers. *IEEE Trans. Evolutionary Computation*, 17(1):46 –63, 2013.

Bibliography

[21] Advanced Linear Devices Inc. *Electrically Programmable Analog Devices (EPAD)*. Advanced Linear Devices Inc., Sunnyvale California, USA, 1998.

[22] F. J. Aherne, N. A. Thacker, and P. I. Rockett. Optimising Object Recognition Parameters using a Parallel Multiobjective Genetic Algorithm. In *Proceedings of the 2nd IEE/IEEE International Conference on Genetic Algorithms in Engineering Systems: Innovations and Applications (GALESIA '97)*, pages 1–6, Glasgow, Scotland, 1997. IEE.

[23] E. Alba and B. Dorronsoro. *Cellular Genetic Algorithms*. Springer, 2008.

[24] D. H. Albonesi. Selective Cache Ways: On-demand Cache Resource Allocation. In *Proc. ACM/IEEE Intl. Symp. on Microarchitecture*, pages 248–259. IEEE, 1999.

[25] Algotronics, Ltd. *CAL1024 Datasheet*, 1990.

[26] B. Ali, A. E. A. Almaini, and T. Kalganova. Evolutionary Algorithms and Theirs Use in the Design of Sequential Logic Circuits. In *Genetic Programming and Evolvable Machines*, volume 5, pages 11–29. Kluwer Academic Publishers, 2004.

[27] L. Altenberg. The Schema Theorem and Price's Theorem. In *Foundations of Genetic Algorithms 3*, pages 23–49, Estes Park, Colorado, USA, 1994. Morgan Kaufmann. 1995.

[28] Anadigm Inc. *Application Note: Dynamically Reconfiguring the FPAA*. Anadigm Inc., Mesa, Arizona, USA, 2002.

[29] Analog Devices Inc. *Zero-Drift, Digitally Programmable Sensor Signal Amplifier AD8555*. Analog Devices Inc., Norwood, Massachusetts, USA, 2004.

[30] V. Arkov, C. Evans, P. J. Fleming, D. C. Hill, J. P. Norton, I. Pratt, D. Rees, and K. Rodriguez-Vazquez. System Identification Strategies Applied to Aircraft Gas Turbine Engines. *Annual Reviews in Control*, 24(1):67–81, 2000.

[31] ARM. ARM10E Processor Family. http://www.arm.com/products/CPUs/families/ARM10EFamily.html, 2010.

[32] V. G. Asouti and K. C. Giannakoglou. Aerodynamic optimization using a parallel asynchronous evolutionary algorithm controlled by strongly interacting demes. *Engineering Optimization*, 41(3):241–257, 2009.

[33] A. Asuncion and D. Newman. UCI Machine Learning Repository. University of California, Irvine, School of Information and Computer Sciences, 2007.

[34] Atmel, Inc. *AT94KAL Series Field Programmable System Level Integrated Circuit*. Atmel, Inc., San Jose, 2008.

[35] T. Austin, E. Larson, and D. Ernst. SimpleScalar: An Infrastructure for Computer System Modeling. In *IEEE Computer*, volume 35(2), pages 59–67. IEEE, 2002.

[36] T. Bäck, D. B. Fogel, and Z. Michalewicz. *Handbook of Evolutionary Computation*. IOS Publishing Ltd., 1997.

[37] W. Banzhaf and C. Lasarczyk. Genetic Programming of an Algorithmic Chemistry. In *Genetic Programming - Theory and Applications*, pages 175–190. O'Reilly, 2004.

[38] N. A. Barricelli. Esempi Numerici di Processi di Evoluzione. In *Methodos*, pages 45–68, 1954.

[39] J. Becker and Y. Manoli. A Continuous-Time Field Programmable Analog Array (FPAA) Consisting of Digitally Reconfigurable Gm-C Cells. In *IEEE Intl. Symposium on Circuits and Systems (ISCAS)*, pages 1092–1095. IEEE, 2004.

[40] P. Bellows and B. Hutchings. JHDL - An HDL for Reconfigurable Systems. In *IEEE Symposium on FPGAs for Custom Computing Machines*, pages 175–184. IEEE, 1998.

[41] S. Bender. Programmierbar und Trotzdem Analog: Analog Silicon Breadboard – Signalverarbeitung mit FPADs. In *Elektronik*, volume 46, pages 81–85, 1997.

[42] S. Bhattacharyya and K. Mehta. Evolutionary Induction of Trading Models. In S.-H. Chen, editor, *Evolutionary Computation in Economics and Finance*, volume 100 of *Studies in Fuzziness and Soft Computing*, chapter 17, pages 311–332. Physica Verlag, 2002.

[43] S. Bhattacharyya, O. Pictet, and G. Zumbach. Representational Semantics for Genetic Programming Based Learning in High-Frequency Financial Data. In *Genetic Programming 1998: Proceedings of the Third Annual Conference*, pages 11–16, University of Wisconsin, Madison, Wisconsin, USA, 1998. Morgan Kaufmann.

[44] S. Bhattacharyya, O. V. Pictet, and G. Zumbach. Knowledge-intensive genetic discovery in foreign exchange markets. *IEEE Transactions on Evolutionary Computation*, 6(2):169–181, 2002.

[45] Biovision. EMG Amplifier. www.biovison.eu.

[46] C. M. Bishop. *Neural Networks for Pattern Recognition*. Clarendon Press, 1995.

[47] S. Bitzer and P. van der Smagt. Learning EMG Control of a Robotic Hand: Towards Active Prostheses. In *Intl. Conf. on Robotics and Automation*, pages 2819–2823, 2006.

[48] S. Bleuler, M. Brack, L. Thiele, and E. Zitzler. Multiobjective Genetic Programming: Reducing Bloat Using SPEA2. In *Proceedings of the Congress on Evolutionary Computation 2001 (CEC'2001)*, volume 1, pages 536–543, Piscataway, New Jersey, 2001. IEEE Service Center.

[49] S. Bleuler, M. Laumanns, L. Thiele, and E. Zitzler. PISA — A Platform and Programming Language Independent Interface for Search Algorithms. In *Intl. Conf. on Evolutionary Multi-Criterion Optimization (EMO)*, LNCS, pages 494–508. Springer, 2003.

[50] A. Boschmann. Aufbau und experimentelle Bewertung eines Systems zur Langzeitklassifikation von EMG-Signalen. Term thesis, University of Paderborn, 2008.

[51] G. E. P. Box. Evolutionary Operation: A Method for Increasing Industrial Productivity. In *J. Royal Statistical Society. Series C (Applied Statistics)*, volume 6, pages 81–101. Blackwell Publishing for the Royal Statistical Society, 1955.

[52] M. Brameier and W. Banzhaf. A Comparison of Linear Genetic Programming and Neural Networks in Medical Data Mining. In *IEEE Trans. Evolutionary Computation*, volume 5, pages 17–26. IEEE Press, 2001.

[53] A. Bratt and I. Macbeth. DPAD2—A Field Programmable Analog Array. In *Analog Integrated Circuits and Signal Processing*, volume 17, pages 67–89. Springer Netherlands, 1998.

[54] A. M. Brintrup, H. Takagi, and J. Ramsden. Evaluation of Sequential, Multi-objective, and Parallel Interactive Genetic Algorithms for Multi-objective Floor Plan Optimisation. In *Applications of Evolutionary Computing. EvoWorkshops 2006: EvoBIO, EvoCOMNET, EvoHOT, EvoIASP, EvoINTERACTION, EvoMUSART, and EvoSTOC*, pages 586–598, Budapest, Hungary, 2006. Springer, LNCS Vol. 3907.

[55] W. M. Brown, A. P. Thompson, and P. A. Schultz. Efficient hybrid evolutionary optimization of interatomic potential models. *Journal of Chemical Physics*, 132(2):024108, 2010.

[56] C. J. C. Burges. A Tutorial on Support Vector Machines for Pattern Recognition. *Data Mining and Knowledge Discovery*, 2(2):121–167, 1998.

[57] X. Cai, S. L. Smith, and A. M. Tyrrell. Positional Independence and Recombination in Cartesian Genetic Programming. In *European Conf. on Genetic Programming (EuroGP)*, volume 3905 of *LNCS*, pages 351–360. Springer, 2006.

[58] F. Castellani and G. Franceschini. Use of Genetic Algorithms as an Innovative Tool for Race Car Design. In *SAE World Congress & Exhibition Technical Papers*. SAE Intl., 2003.

[59] L. N. d. Castro. *Fundamentals of Natural Computing (Chapman & Hall/CRC Computer and Information Sciences)*. Chapman & Hall/CRC, 2006.

[60] V. Cerny. A Thermodynamical Approach to the Travelling Salesman Problem: an Efficient Simulation Algorithm. In *Journal of Optimization Theory and Applications*, volume 45, pages 45–51. Plenum Publishing Corp., 1985.

[61] A. Chan and K. Englehart. Continuous Myoelectric Control for Powered Prostheses Using Hidden Markov Models. In *Biomedical Engineering*, volume 52(1), pages 121–124. IEEE Press, 2005.

[62] F. Chan, Y.-S. Yang, F. Lam, Y.-T. Zhang, and P. Parker. Fuzzy EMG Classification for Prosthesis Control. In *Rehabilitation Engineering*, volume 8(3), pages 305–311. IEEE, 2000.

[63] C.-C. Chang and C.-J. Lin. *LIBSVM: a library for support vector machines*, 2001.

[64] S. Chang, B. Hayes-Gill, and C. Paull. Implementation of a Multi-Function Signal Detection Block for a Field- Programmable Analogue Array. In *Fifth Eurochip Workshop on VLSI Design Training*, pages 226–231, 1994.

[65] D. A. Childress. A Myoelectric Three State Controller Using Rate Sensitivity. In *8th ICMBE*, volume S4–5, 1969.

[66] D. S. Childress. An Approach of Powered Grasp. In *4th Intl. Symposium on External Control of Human Extremities.*, 1973.

[67] D. S. Childress and M. V. Podlusky. Letter To The Editor. In *Medical and Biological Engineering and Computing*, volume 7, page 345. Springer, 1969.

[68] P. Chongstitvatana and C. Aporntewan. Improving Correctness of Finite-State Machine Synthesis from Multiple Partial Input/Output Sequences. *NASA/DoD Conference on Evolvable Hardware*, page 262, 1999.

[69] P. Chow and P. G. Gulak. A Field-Programmable Mixed-Analog-Digital Array. *Intl. ACM Symposium on Field-Programmable Gate Arrays*, pages 104–109, 1995.

[70] J.-U. Chu, I. Moon, Y.-J. Lee, S.-K. Kim, and M.-S. Mun. A Supervised Feature-Projection-Based Real-Time EMG Pattern Recognition for Multifunction Myoelectric Hand Control. *Transactions on Mechatronics, IEEE/ASME*, 12(3):282–290, 2007.

[71] S. Churcer, T. Kean, and B. Wilke. XC6200 FASTMAP processor interface. In *Proc. Intl. Workshop on Field-programmable Logic and Applications (FPL)*, 1995.

[72] J. Clegg, J. A. Walker, and J. F. Miller. A New Crossover Technique for Cartesian Genetic Programming. In *Genetic and Evolutionary Computation (GECCO)*, pages 158–1587. ACM, 2007.

[73] C. A. C. Coello, A. H. Aguirre, and B. P. Buckles. Evolutionary Multiobjective Design of Combinational Logic Circuits. In *Evolvable Hardware*, pages 161–171. IEEE CS, 2000.

[74] C. A. Coello Coello. Treating Constraints as Objectives for Single-Objective Evolutionary Optimization. In *Engineering Optimization*, volume 32(2), pages 275–308. Taylor and Francis, 2000.

[75] C. A. Coello Coello. A Short Tutorial on Evolutionary Multiobjective Optimization. In *First International Conference on Evolutionary Multi-Criterion Optimization*, pages 21–40. Springer-Verlag. LNCS No. 1993, 2001.

[76] C. A. Coello Coello. Constraint-handling Techniques Used with Evolutionary Algorithms. In *Genetic and Evolutionary Computation (GECCO)*, pages 2445–2466. ACM, 2008.

[77] C. A. Coello Coello and A. H. Aguirre. Design of Combinational Logic Circuits through an Evolutionary Multiobjective Optimization Approach. In *Artificial Intelligence for Engineering Design, Analysis and Manufacturing*, volume 16(1), pages 39–53. Cambridge University Press, 2002.

[78] C. A. Coello Coello and G. T. Pulido. A Micro-Genetic Algorithm for Multiobjective Optimization. In *Intl. Conf. on Evolutionary Multi-Criterion Optimization (EMO)*, volume 1993 of *LNCS*, pages 126–140. Springer, 2001.

[79] R. C. Cofer and B. F. Harding. *Rapid System Prototyping - Accelerating the Design Process*. Elsevier Science Publishers B. V., 2006.

[80] J. Cohoon, S. Hegde, W. Martin, and D. Richards. Punctuated Equilibria a Parallel Genetic Algorithm. In *Proc. Intl. Conf. on Genetic Algorithms*, pages 148–154. Lawrence Erlbaum Associates, 1987.

[81] W. Commons. Genetic Programming. http://en.wikipedia.org/wiki/Genetic_programming.

[82] J. Cong and Y. Ding. Combinational Logic Synthesis for LUT Based Field Programmable Gate Arrays. *ACM Transactions in Design Automation of Electronic Systems*, 1(2):145–204, 1996.

[83] W. Conover. *Practical Nonparametric Statistics (Third ed.)*. John Wiley and Sons, 1999.

[84] O. Cordon, F. Moya, and C. Zarco. A new evolutionary algorithm combining simulated annealing and genetic programming for relevance feedback in fuzzy information retrieval systems. *Soft Computing - A Fusion of Foundations, Methodologies and Applications*, 6(5):308–319, 2002.

[85] N. L. Cramer. A representation for the Adaptive Generation of Simple Sequential Programs. In *Proceedings of an International Conference on Genetic Algorithms and the Applications*, pages 183–187, Carnegie-Mellon University, Pittsburgh, PA, USA, 1985.

[86] Cypress Semiconductors. *PSoC Mixed Signal Array*. Cypress Semiconductors, San Jose, Califonia, USA, 2002.

[87] E. Damiani, V. Liberali, and A. Tettamanzi. Evolutionary Design of Hashing Function Circuits Using an FPGA. In *Intl. Conf. on Evolvable Systems (ICES)*, pages 36–46. Springer, 1998.

[88] C. Darwin. *On the Origin of Species by Means of Natural Selection*. John Murray, United Kingdom, 1859.

[89] L. Davis. Adapting Operator Probabilities in Genetic Algorithms. In *Proc. Intl. Conf. on Genetic Algorithms*, pages 61–69. Morgan Kaufmann, 1989.

[90] T. Davis and J. C. Principe. A Simulated Annealing Like Convergence Theory for Simple Genetic Algorithm. In *Proc. Intl. Conf. on Genetic Algorithms (ICGA)*, pages 174–181. Morgan Kaufmann, 1991.

[91] T. E. Davis and J. C. Principe. A Markov Chain Framework for the Simple Genetic Algorithm. *J. Evolutionary Computation*, 1:269–288, 1993.

[92] I. De Falco, A. Della Cioppa, and E. Tarantino. Discovering Interesting Classification Rules with Genetic Programming. *Applied Soft Computing*, 1(4):257–269, 2001.

[93] H. de Garis. Evolvable Hardware: Genetic Programming of a Darwin Machine. In *Intl. Conf. on Artificial Neural Nets and Genetic Algorithms*, pages 441–449. Springer, 1993.

[94] H. de Garis. CAM-BRAIN: The Evolutionary Engineering of a Billion Neuron Artificial Brain by 2001 Which Grows/Evolves at Electronic Speeds Inside a Cellular Automata Machine (CAM). In *Intl. Conf. on Evolvable Systems (ICES)*, volume 1062 of *LNCS*, pages 76–98. Springer, 1995.

[95] K. De Jong. On Using Genetic Algorithms to Search Program Spaces. In *Genetic Algorithms and their Applications: Proceedings of the second international conference on Genetic Algorithms*, pages 210–216, MIT, Cambridge, MA, USA, 1987. Lawrence Erlbaum Associates.

[96] O. L. De Weck. Multiobjective Optimization : History and Promise. In *The Third China-Japan-Korea Joint Symposium on Optimization of Structural and Mechanical Systems*, 2004.

[97] K. Deb and R. Agrawal. Simulated Binary Crossover for Continuous Search Space. In *Complex Systems*, volume 9, pages 115–148, 1995.

[98] K. Deb, S. Agrawal, A. Pratap, and T. Meyarivan. A Fast Elitist Nondominated Sorting Genetic Algorithm for Multi-Objective Optimisation: NSGA-II. In *Parallel Problem Solving from Nature (PPSN'00)*, pages 849–858. Springer, 2000.

[99] R. D'Mello and P. Gulak. Design Approaches to Field-Programmable Analog Integrated Circuits. In *Analog Integrated Circuits and Signal Processing*, volume 17, pages 7–34. Springer Netherlands, 1998.

[100] P. Domingos. A Unified Bias-Variance Decomposition for Zero-One and Squared Loss. In *Artificial Intelligence and Innovative Applications of Artificial Intelligence*, pages 564–569, 2000.

[101] D. S. Dorcas and R. N. Scott. A Three-state Myoelectric Control. In *Medical & Biological Engineering*, volume 4, pages 367–370, 1966.

[102] W. Duch, R. Adamczak, and K. Grabczewski. A New Methodology of Extraction, Optimization and Application of Crisp and Fuzzy Logical Rules. In *IEEE Trans. Neural Netw*, volume 12, pages 277–306. IEEE Press, 2001.

[103] R. O. Duda, P. E. Hart, and D. G. Stork. *Pattern Classification*. John Wiley & Sons, Chichester, New York, 2001.

[104] F. Y. Edgeworth. *Mathematical Psychics*. P. Keagan, London, UK, 1881.

[105] J. Eggermont, J. N. Kok, and W. A. Kosters. Genetic Programming for Data Classification: Partitioning the Search Space. In *ACM Symposium on Applied Computing (SAC'04)*, pages 1001–1005, New York, NY, USA, 2004. ACM.

[106] A. Eiben, E. Aarts, and K. Van Hee. Global Convergence of Genetic Algorithms: A Markov Chain Analysis. In *Parallel Problem Solving from Nature (PPSN)*, volume 496 of *LNCS*, pages 3–12. Springer, 1991.

[107] A. E. Eiben and J. Smith. *Introduction to Evolutionary Computing*. Springer, 2003.

[108] S. Embabi, X. Quan, N. Oki, A. Manjrekar, and E. Sanchez-Sinencio. A Field Programmable Analog Signal Processing Array. In *IEEE Midwest Symposium on Circuits and Systems*, volume 1, pages 151–154. IEEE, 1996.

[109] K. Englehart and B. Hudgins. A Robust, Real-time Control Scheme for Multifunction Myoelectric Control. In *IEEE Transactions on Biomedical Engineering*, volume 50(7), pages 848–854. IEEE Press, 2003.

[110] K. Englehart, B. Hudgins, and P. A. Parker. Time-Frequency Based Classification of the Myoelectric Signal: Static vs. Dynamic Contractions. In *Engineering in Medicine and Biology Society (EMBS)*. IEEE, 2000.

[111] K. Englehart, B. Hudgins, and P. A. Parker. A Wavelet Based Continuous Classification Scheme for Multifunction Myoelectric Control. In *Biomedical Engineering*, volume 48(3), pages 302–331. IEEE Press, 2001.

[112] K. Englehart, B. Hudgins, P. A. Parker, and M. Stevenson. Improving Myoelectric Signal Classification Using Wavelet Packets and Principal Components Analysis. In *21st Intl. Conf. of the IEEE Engineering in Medicine and Biology Society*. IEEE Press, 1999.

[113] D. H. J. Epema, M. Livny, R. van Dantzig, X. Evers, and J. Pruyne. A Worldwide Flock of Condors: Load Sharing Among Workstation Clusters. In *Future Gener. Comput. Syst.*, volume 12(1), pages 53–65. Elsevier Science Publishers B. V., 1996.

[114] C. Evans, P. J. Fleming, D. C. Hill, J. P. Norton, I. Pratt, D. Rees, and K. Rodriguez-Vazquez. Application of system identification techniques to aircraft gas turbine engines. *Control Engineering Practice*, 9(2):135–148, 2001.

[115] I. V. Evstigneev, T. Hens, and K. R. Schenk-Hoppe. Evolutionary Finance. In *Handbook of Financial Markets: Dynamics and Evolution*, pages 507–566. North-Holland, San Diego, 2009.

[116] O. O. Fares. *Configurable Analogue Building Blocks For Field-Programmable Analogue Arrays*. PhD thesis, King Fahd University of Petroleum & Minerals, Saudi Arabia, 2004.

[117] K. A. Farry and I. D. Walker. Myoelectric Teleoperation of a Complex Robotic Hand. In *IEEE Intl. Conf. on Robotics and Automation (ICRA)*, volume 3, pages 502–509. IEEE, 1993.

[118] J. Faura, C. Horton, P. van Duong, J. Madrenas, M. Aguirre, and J. Inserser. A Novel Mixed Signal Programmable Device with On-chip Microprocessor. In *IEEE Proc. of Custom Integrated Circuits Conference*, pages 103–106. IEEE, 1997.

[119] R. R. Finley and R. W. Wirta. Myocoder Studies of Multiple Myocoder Response. In *Arch Phys Med Rehabil*, volume 48, page 598, 1967.

[120] R. A. Fisher. On the Interpretation of χ^2 from Contingency Tables, and the Calculation of P. *Journal of the Royal Statistical Society*, 85(1):87–94, 1922.

[121] L. J. Fogel, A. J. Owens, and M. J. Walsh. *Artificial Intelligence Through Simulated Evolution*. Wiley & Sons, Inc., New York, 1966.

[122] C. M. Fonseca and P. J. Fleming. Genetic Algorithms for Multi-objective Optimization: Formulation, Discussion and Generalization. In *Proceedings of the Fifth International Conference on Genetic Algorithms*, pages 416–423, San Mateo, California, 1993. University of Illinois at Urbana-Champaign, Morgan Kauffman Publishers.

[123] J. H. Friedman. On Bias, Variance, 0/1-Loss, and the Curse-of-Dimensionality. *Data Mining and Knowledge Discovery*, 1(1):55–77, 1997.

[124] Z. Gajda and L. Sekanina. Reducing the Number of Transistors in Digital Circuits Using Gate-Level Evolutionary Design. In *Genetic and Evolutionary Computation Conf.*, pages 245–252. ACM, 2007.

[125] C. Gathercole and P. Ross. Dynamic Training Subset Selection for Supervised Learning in Genetic Programming. In *Parallel Problem Solving from Nature (PPSN'94)*, volume 866 of *LNCS*, pages 312–321, London, UK, 1994. Springer-Verlag.

[126] C. Giraud-Carrier. A Note on the Utility of Incremental Learning. *AI Communications*, 13(4):215 – 223, 2000.

[127] K. Glette and J. Torresen. A Flexible On-Chip Evolution System Implemented on a Xilinx Virtex-II Pro Device. In *Intl. Conf. on Evolvable Systems (ICES)*, volume 3637 of *LNCS*, pages 66–75. Springer, 2005.

[128] K. Glette, J. Torresen, and M. Yasunaga. An Online EHW Pattern Recognition System Applied to Face Image Recognition. In *Applications of Evolutionary Computing (EvoWorkshops)*, volume 4448 of *LNCS*, pages 271–280. Springer, 2007.

[129] K. Glette, J. Torresen, and M. Yasunaga. An Online EHW Pattern Recognition System Applied to Sonar Spectrum Classification. In *Intl. Conf. on Evolvable Systems (ICES)*, volume 4684 of *LNCS*, pages 1–12. Springer, 2007.

[130] K. Glette, J. Torresen, and M. Yasunaga. Online Evolution for a High-Speed Image Recognition System Implemented On a Virtex-II Pro FPGA. In *Adaptive Hardware and Systems (AHS)*, pages 463–470. IEEE, 2007.

[131] K. Glette, J. Torresen, M. Yasunaga, and Y. Yamaguchi. On-Chip Evolution Using a Soft Processor Core Applied to Image Recognition. In *Adaptive Hardware and Systems (AHS)*, pages 373–380. IEEE, 2006.

[132] F. Glover. Future Paths for Integer Programming and Links to Artificial Intelligence. *Computers and Operations Research*, 13:533–549, 1986.

[133] D. Goldberg. *Genetic Algorithms in search, optimization, and machine learning*. Addison–Wesley, 1989.

[134] L. González, E. Whitney, K. Srinivas, K. Wong, and J. Périaux. Multidisciplinary Aircraft Conceptual Design Optimisation Using a Hierarchical Asynchronous Parallel Evolutionary Algorithm (HAPEA). In *Adaptive Computing in Design and Manufacture VI*, pages 273–284, London, 2004. Springer.

[135] F. Goodenough. Voltage-Tunable Linear Filters Move onto a Chip. In *Electronic Design*, 1990.

[136] T. Gordon and P. Bentley. Development Brings Scalability to Hardware Evolution, 2004.

[137] T. G. W. Gordon and P. J. Bentley. On Evolvable Hardware. In *Soft Computing in Industrial Electronics*, pages 279–323. Physica-Verlag, 2002.

[138] J. Graupe and K. Cline. Functional Separation of EMG Signals Via ARMA Identification Methods for Prosthesis Control Purposes. In *IEEE Transactions on Systems, Man, and Cybernetics*, volume 5, pages 252–259. IEEE Press, 1975.

[139] H. Gray. *Anatomy of the Human Body.* Lea & Febiger, Philadelphia, 1918.

[140] G. W. Greenwood, D. Hunter, and E. Ramsden. Fault Recovery in Linear Systems via Intrinsic Evolution. *NASA/DoD Conference on Evolvable Hardware*, pages 115–122, 2004.

[141] G. W. Greenwood and A. M. Tyrrell. *Introduction to Evolvable Hardware: A Practical Guide for Designing Self-Adaptive Systems.* IEEE Press Series on Computational Intelligence. Wiley-IEEE Press, 2006.

[142] J. J. Grefenstette. Deception Considered Harmful. In *Proc. Workshop on Foundations of Genetic Algorithms (FOGA)*, pages 75–91. Morgan Kaufmann, 1992.

[143] J. J. Grefenstette and J. E. Baker. How Genetic Algorithms Work: A Critical Look at Implicit Parallelism. In *Proc. Intl. Conf. on Genetic Algorithms (ICGA)*, pages 20–27. Morgan Kaufmann, 1989.

[144] J. Grimbleby. Automatic Analogue Network Synthesis Using Genetic Algorithms. In *Genetic Algorithms in Engineering Systems: Innovations and Applications (GALESIA)*, pages 53 –58. IEEE, 1995.

[145] A. Guillén, I. Rojas, J. González, H. Pomares, L. J. Herrera, and B. Paechter. Improving the Performance of Multi-objective Genetic Algorithm for Function Approximation Through Parallel Islands Specialisation. In *AI 2006: Advances in Artificial Intelligence, 19th Australian Joint Conference on Artificial Intelligence*, pages 1127–1132, Hobart, Australia, 2006. Springer. LNCS. Volume 4304.

[146] M. Hall, E. Frank, G. Holmes, B. Pfahringer, P. Reutemann, and I. H. Witten. The WEKA Data Mining Software: An Update. In *SIGKDD Explor. Newsl.*, volume 11(1), pages 10–18. ACM, 2009.

[147] T. S. Hall. *Field-Programmable Analog Arrays: A Floating-Gate Approach.* PhD thesis, Georgia Institute of Technology, 2004.

[148] L. Hamel. *Knowledge Discovery With Support Vector Machines.* John Wiley & Sons, 2009.

[149] M. P. Hansen and A. Jaszkiewicz. Evaluating the Quality of Approximations to the Non-Dominated Set. Technical report, Technical University of Denmark, Poznan University of Technology, 1998.

[150] S. Harding, J. Miller, and W. Banzhaf. Developments in Cartesian Genetic Programming: self-modifying CGP. *Genetic Programming and Evolvable Machines*, 11(3):397–439–439, 2010.

[151] S. Harding and J. F. Miller. Evolution of Robot Controller Using Cartesian Genetic Programming. In *EuroGP*, volume 3447 of *LNCS*, pages 62–73. Springer, 2005.

[152] S. Harding, J. F. Miller, and W. Banzhaf. Self-modifying cartesian genetic programming. In *GECCO*, pages 1021–1028. ACM, 2007.

[153] S. Harding, J. F. Miller, and W. Banzhaf. Self modifying cartesian genetic programming: finding algorithms that calculate pi and e to arbitrary precision. In *GECCO*, pages 579–586. ACM, 2010.

[154] L. Hargrove, Y. Losier, B. Lock, K. Englehart, and B. Hudgins. A Real-Time Pattern Recognition Based Myoelectric Control Usability Study Implemented in a Virtual Environment. In *Engineering in Medicine and Biology Society (EMBS)*, pages 4842–4845. IEEE, 2007.

[155] M. Hartmann, P. Haddow, and F. Eskelund. Evolving Robust Digital Designs. *Evolvable Hardware (EH)*, 0:36, 2002.

[156] S. Hauck and A. DeHon. *Reconfigurable Computing: The Theory and Practice of FPGA-Based Computation*. Morgan Kaufmann Publishers Inc., San Francisco, CA, USA, 2007.

[157] H. Hemmi, J. Mizoguchi, and K. Shimohara. Development and Evolution of Hardware Behaviors. In *Artificial Life IV: Proc. 4th Int. Workshop Synthesis Simulation Living Syst.*, pages 371–376. MIT Press, 1994.

[158] P. Herberts. Myoelectric Signals in Control of Prostheses. In *Acta Orth. Scand.*, volume 40, page 124, 1969.

[159] T. Higuchi. Industrial Applications of Evolvable Hardware. In *Knowledge-Based Intelligent Information and Engineering Systems*, volume 3213 of *LNCS*, pages 6–7. Springer, 2004.

[160] T. Higuchi, M. Iwata, I. Kajitani, H. Iba, Y. Hirao, B. Manderick, and T. Furuya. Evolvable Hardware and its Applications to Pattern Recognition and Fault-Tolerant Systems. In *Towards Evolvable Hardware: The evolutionary Engineering Approach*, volume 1062 of *LNCS*, pages 118–135. Springer, 1996.

[161] T. Higuchi, M. Iwata, I. Kajitani, H. Yamada, B. Manderick, Y. Hirao, M. Murakawa, S. Yoshizawa, and T. Furuya. Evolvable Hardware with Genetic Learning. In *Intl. Sym. Circuits and Systems (ISCAS)*, volume 4, pages 29 –32 vol.4. IEEE, 1996.

[162] T. Higuchi, T. Niwa, H. I. T. Tanaka, and T. Furuya. A Parallel Architecture for Genetic Based Evolvable Hardware. In *Proc. Intl. Conf. Artificial Intelligence (IJCAI)*, pages 46–52, 1993.

[163] T. Higuchi, T. Niwa, T. Tanaka, H. Iba, H. de Garis, and T. Furuya. Evolving Hardware with Genetic Learning: a First Step Towards Building a Darwin Machine. In *From Animals to Animats*, pages 417–424. MIT Press, 1993.

[164] A. Hiraiwa, N. Uchida, N. Sonehara, and K. Shimohara. EMG Pattern Rcognition by Neural Networks for Prosthetic Fingers Control - Cyber Finger. In *Measurement and control in Robotics*, pages 535–542, 1992.

[165] A. J. Hirst. Notes on the Evolution of Adaptive Hardware. In *Proc. Adaptive Computing in Engineering Design and Control (ACEDC)*, pages 212–219. University of Plymouth, 1996.

[166] hlevkin.com. Classis Test Still Images. http://hlevkin.com.

[167] J. H. Holland. Adaptation in Natural and Artificial Systems. Ann Arbor MI, USA: University of Michigan Press, 1975.

[168] J. Horn and N. Nafpliotis. Multiobjective Optimization using the Niched Pareto Genetic Algorithm. Technical Report IlliGAl Report 93005, University of Illinois at Urbana-Champaign, Urbana, Illinois, USA, 1993.

[169] J.-L. Hou. *Constructing Static and Dynamic Investment Strategy Portfolios by Genetic Programming*. Doctoral dissertation, Information Management, National Central University, Taiwan, 2008.

[170] C.-W. Hsu and C.-J. Lin. A Comparison of Methods for Multi-class Support Vector Machines. *IEEE Transactions on Neural Networks*, 13(2):415–425, 2002.

[171] H.-P. Huang, Y.-H. Liu, L.-W. Liu, and C.-S. Wong. EMG Classification for Prehensile Postures Using Cascaded Architecture of Neural Networks With Self-organizing Maps. In *Robotics and Automation (ICRA)*, volume 1, pages 1497–1502. IEEE, 2003.

[172] Y. Huang, K. Englehart, B. Hudgins, and A. Chan. Optimized Gaussian Mixture Models for Upper limb Motion Classification. In *Engineering in Medicine and Biology Society (IMBS)*, volume 1, pages 72–75. IEEE Press, 2004.

[173] B. Hudgins, P. Parker, and R. Scott. A New Strategy for Multifunction Myoelectric Control. In *Biomedical Engineering*, volume 40(1), pages 82–94. IEEE, 1993.

[174] J. S. Huxley and T. H. Huxley. *Evolution and Ethics: 1893-1943*. The Pilot Press, 1947.

[175] D. Ierardi. 2d-Bubblesorting in Average Time O(sqrt N lg N)*. In *Symposium on Parallel Algorithms and Architectures (SPAA '94)*, pages 36–45. ACM Press, 1994.

[176] IMP Inc. *IMP50E10 and IMP50E30 Data Sheet: Programmable Analog Signal Conditioning Circuit*. IMP Inc., 1994.

[177] K.-S. Jeong, D.-K. Kim, P. Whigham, and G.-J. Joo. Modelling Microcystis aeruginosa bloom dynamics in the Nakdong River by means of evolutionary computation and statistical approach. *Ecological Modelling*, 161(1-2):67–78, 2003.

[178] Q. Ji, Y. Wang, M. Xie, and J. Cui. Research on Fault-tolerance of Analog Circuits Based on Evolvable Hardware. In *Intl. Conf. on Evolvable Systems (ICES)*, number 4684 in LNCS, pages 100–108. Springer, 2007.

[179] M. Jiang and A. H. Wright. A Hierarchical Genetic System for Symbolic Function Identification. In *Proceedings of the 24th Symposium on the Interface: Computing Science and Statistics, College Station, Texas*, 1992.

[180] B. R. Jones, W. A. Crossley, and A. S. Lyrintzis. Aerodynamic and Aeroacoustic Optimization of Airfoils via a Parallel Genetic Algorithm. In *Proceedings of the 7th AIAA/USAF/NASA/ISSMO Symposium on Multidisciplinary Analysis and Optimization, AIAA-98-4811*. AIAA, 1998.

[181] I. Kajitani, T. Hoshino, D. Nishikawa, H. Yokoi, S. Nakaya, T. Yamauchi, T. Inuo, N. Kajihara, M. Iwata, D. Keymeulen, and T. Higuchi. A Gate-Level EHW Chip: Implementing GA Operations and Reconfigurable Hardware on a Single LSI. In *Intl. Conf. on Evolvable Systems (ICES)*, volume 1478 of *LNCS*, pages 1–12. Springer, 1998.

[182] I. Kajitani, M. Murakawa, D. Nishikawa, H. Yokoi, N. Kajihara, M. Iwata, D. Keymeulen, H. Sakanashi, and T. Higuchi. An Evolvable Hardware Chip for Prosthetic Hand Controller. *microneuro*, 0:179, 1999.

[183] I. Kajitani, I. Sekita, N. Otsu, and T. Higuchi. Improvements to the Action Decision Rate for a Multi-Function Prosthetic Hand. In *Measurement, Analysis and Modeling of Human Functions (ISHF)*, pages 84–89, 2001.

[184] T. Kalganova and J. Miller. Evolving More Efficient Digital Circuits by Allowing Circuit Layout Evolution and Multi-Objective Fitness. In *NASA/DoD Workshop on Evolvable Hardware (EH)*, pages 54–63. IEEE, 1999.

[185] B. Karlik, M. Osman Tokhi, and M. Alci. A Fuzzy Clustering Neural Network Architecture for Multifunction Upper-limb Prosthesis. In *Biomedical Engineering*, volume 50(11), pages 1255–1261. IEEE, 2003.

[186] S. Karlsson, J. Yu, and M. Akay. Time-frequency Analysis of Myoelectric Signals During Dynamic Contractions: a Comparative Study. In *Biomedical Engineering*, volume 47(2), pages 228–238. IEEE, 2000.

[187] P. Kaufmann. Experimentelle Auswertung Kurzperiodischer, Insbesondere 2-dimensionaler Sortierverfahren. Master's thesis, University of Paderborn, Paderborn, Germany, 2002.

[188] T. A. Kean. *Configurable Logic: A Dynamically Programmable Cellular Architecture and its VLSI Implementation.* PhD thesis, University of Edinburgh, 1989.

[189] D. Keymeulen, M. Durantez, K. Konaka, Y. Kuniyoshi, and T. Higuchi. An Evolutionary Robot Navigation System Using a Gate-Level Evolvable Hardware. In *Intl. Conf. on Evolvable Systems (ICES)*, pages 195–209, 1996.

[190] D. Keymeulen, M. Iwata, Y. Kuniyoshi, and T. Higuchi. Online Evolution for a Self-Adapting Robotic Navigation System Using Evolvable Hardware. *Artif. Life*, 4(4):359–393, 1998.

[191] S. Kirkpatrick, J. Gelatt, C. D., and M. P. Vecchi. Optimization by Simulated Annealing. *Science*, 220(4598):671–680, 1983.

[192] J. Knowles, L. Thiele, and E. Zitzler. A Tutorial on the Performance Assessment of Stochastic Multiobjective Optimizers. Technical report, Computer Engineering and Networks Laboratory (TIK), ETH Zurich, Switzerland, 2006.

[193] J. D. Knowles and D. W. Corne. The Pareto Archived Evolution Strategy: A New Baseline Algorithm for Multiobjective Optimisation. In *1999 Congress on Evolutionary Computation*, pages 98–105, Washington, D.C., 1999. IEEE Service Center.

[194] J. D. Knowles and D. W. Corne. Approximating the Nondominated Front Using the Pareto Archived Evolution Strategy. In *Evolutionary Computation*, volume 8(2), pages 149–172. MIT Press, 2000.

[195] A. E. Kobrinski, S. V. Bolkovitin, D. M. Voskoboinikova, L. M. Ioffe, E. P. Polyan, B. P. Popov, Y. L. Slavutski, Y. A. Sysin, and Y. S.

Yakobson. Problems of Bioelectric Control. In *Automatic and Remote Control*, volume 2, pages 619–629, 1960.

[196] A. Kolmogorov. Sulla Determinazione Empirica di una Legge di Distribuzione. *G. Inst. Ital. Attuari*, 4:83, 1933.

[197] A. Koopmann. Hardware-Friendly Genetic Regulatory Networks in POEtic tissue. Master's thesis, Institute for Information and Computing Sciences, Utrecht University, 2004.

[198] J. Koza. *Genetic Programming: On the Programming of Computers by Means of Natural Selection*. MIT Press, 1992.

[199] J. R. Koza. *Genetic Programming II: Automatic Discovery of Reusable Programs*. MIT Press, 1994.

[200] J. R. Koza, F. H. Bennett, D. Andre, and M. A. Keane. Automated Design of Both the Topology and Sizing of Analog Electrical Circuits Using Genetic Programming. In *Arlificial Inlelligence in Design*. Kluwer Academic Publishers, 1996.

[201] J. R. Koza, F. H. Bennett, III, V. Scholar, J. L. Hutchings, S. L. Bade, M. A. Keane, and D. Andre. Evolving Sorting Networks using Genetic Programming and Rapidly Reconfigurable Field-Programmable Gate Arrays. In *Intl. Conf. Artificial Intelligence*, pages 27–32. IEEE Press, 1997.

[202] W. H. Kruskal and W. A. Wallis. Use of Ranks in One-Criterion Variance Analysis. *Journal of the American Statistical Association*, 47(260):583–621, 1952.

[203] I. Kuscu and C. Thornton. Design of artificial neural networks using genetic algorithms: review and prospect. Cognitive Science Research Paper 319, School of Cognitive and Computing Sciences, University of Sussex, Falmer, Brighton, Sussex, UK, 1994.

[204] H. Kutuk and S.-M. Kang. A Field-programmable Analog Array (FPAA) using Switched-capacitor Techniques. In *IEEE International Symposium on Circuits and Systems (ICAS)*, volume 4, pages 41–44. IEEE, 1996.

[205] T. Kuyucu. *Evolution of Circuits in Hardware and The Evolvability of Artificial Development*. PhD thesis, University of York, UK, 2010.

[206] S. kyu Kim, K. Ito, D. Yoshihara, and T. Wakisaka. Application of a Genetic Algorithm to the Optimization of Rate Constants in Chemical Kinetic Models for Combustion Simulation of HCCI Engines. *JSME Intl. J. Fluids and Thermal Engineering*, 48(4):717–724, 2005.

[207] S. K. Lakshmanan. *Towards Dynamically Reconfigurable Mixed-signal Electronics for Embedded and Intelligent Sensors Systems*. PhD thesis, TU Kaiserslautern, 2008.

[208] S. K. Lakshmanan and A. Konig. Reconfigurable Amplifier Circuits for Adaptive Sensor Systems Employing Bio-Inspiration. In *Intl. Conf. on Hybrid Intelligent Systems (HIS)*, pages 38–43. IEEE Computer Society, 2004.

[209] S. K. Lakshmanana and A. König. Towards a Generic Sensor Electronics Front-End Chip Employing Reconfigurable CMOS Analog Arrays. In *Dresdner Arbeitstagung Schaltungs- und Systementwurf (DASS)*. Fraunhofer-Gesellschaft, 2008.

[210] J. Langeheine, J. Becker, S. Foiling, K. Meier, and J. Schemmel. A CMOS FPTA Chip For Intrinsic Hardware Evolution of Analog Electronic Circuits. In *Adaptive Hardware and Systems (AHS)*, pages 172 – 175. IEEE, 2001.

[211] J. Langeheine, J. Becker, S. Fölling, K. Meier, and J. Schemmel. Initial Studies of a New VLSI Field Programmable Transistor Array. In *Intl. Conf. on Evolvable Systems (ICES)*, volume 2210 of *LNCS*, pages 62–73. Springer, 2001.

[212] J. Langeheine, K. Meier, and J. Schemmel. Intrinsic Evolution of Quasi DC Solutions for Transistor Level Analog Electronic Circuits Using a CMOS FPTA Chip. In *Proc. NASA/DoD Conf. on Evolvable Hardware (EH)*, page 75. IEEE Computer Society, 2002.

[213] J. Langeheine, K. Meier, and J. Schemmel. Intrinsic Evolution of Analog Electronic Circuits Using a CMOS FPTA Chip. In *Intl. Congress on Evolutionary Methods for Design, Optimization and Control with Applications to Industrial Problems (EUROGEN)*, Barcelona, 2003. CIMNE.

[214] J. Langeheine, K. Meier, J. Schemmel, and M. Trefzer. Intrinsic Evolution of Digital-to-analog Converters Using a CMOS FPTA Chip. In *Adaptive Hardware and Systems (AHS)*, pages 18 – 25. IEEE, 2004.

[215] P. Laskov, C. Gehl, S. Krüger, and K.-R. Müller. Incremental Support Vector Learning: Analysis, Implementation and Applications. *Journal of Machine Learning Research*, 7:1909 – 1936, 2006.

[216] Lattice Semiconductor Corporation. *In-System Programmable Analog Circuits- ispPAC*. Lattice Semiconductor Corporation, Hillsboro, Oregon, USA, 1999.

[217] Lattice Semiconductor Corporation. *ispPAC-10 In-System Programmable Analog Circuit*. Lattice Semiconductor Corporation, Hillsboro, Oregon, USA, 2000.

[218] P. Layzell. The Evolvable Motherboard – A Test Platform for the Research of Intrinsic Hardware Evolution. Technical report, University of Sussex, UK, 1998.

[219] E. Lee and P. G. Gulak. Prototype Design of a Field-programmable Analog Array. In *Proc. of Canadian Conf. on Very Large Scale Integration (CCVLSI)*, Ottawa, Canada, 1990.

[220] E. K. F. Lee and P. G. Gulak. Field Programmable Analogue Array Based On MOSFET Transconductors. *Electronics Letters*, 28:28–29, 1992.

[221] J. Lee and P. Hajela. Parallel Genetic Algorithm Implementation in Multidisciplinary Rotor Blade Design. *Journal of Aircraft*, 33(5):962–969, 1996.

[222] C. León, G. Miranda, and C. Segura. Parallel Hyperheuristic: A Self-Adaptive Island-Based Model for Multi-Objective Optimization. In *2008 Genetic and Evolutionary Computation Conference (GECCO'2008)*, pages 757–758, Atlanta, USA, 2008. ACM Press. ISBN 978-1-60558-131-6.

[223] G. H. Lewes. *Problems of Life and Mind*. Trübner, & Co, London, 1874.

[224] L. Li, C. Weinberg, T. Darden, and L. Pedersen. Gene Selection for Sample classification Based on Gene Expression Data Study of Sensitivity to Choice of Parameters of the GA KNN Method. In *Bioinformatics*, volume 17, pages 1131–1142. Oxford University Press, 2001.

[225] P. Lichodzijewski and M. I. Heywood. Pareto-coevolutionary Genetic Programming for Problem Decomposition in Multi-class Classification. In *Genetic and Evolutionary Computation (GECCO'07)*, pages 464–471, New York, NY, USA, 2007. ACM.

[226] P.-C. Lin and J.-S. Chen. FuzzyTree crossover for multi-valued stock valuation. *Information Sciences*, 177(5):1193–1203, 2007. Including: The 3rd International Workshop on Computational Intelligence in Economics and Finance (CIEF'2003).

[227] H. Liu, J. Miller, and A. Tyrrell. Intrinsic Evolvable Hardware Implementation of a Robust Biological Development Model for Digital Systems. In *NASA/DoD Conf. Evolvable Hardware*, pages 87 – 92, 2005.

[228] W. Liu, M. Murakawa, and T. Higuchi. ATM Cell Scheduling by Function Level Evolvable Hardware. In *Intl. Conf. on Evolvable Systems (ICES)*, volume 1259 of *LNCS*, pages 180–192. Springer, 1996.

[229] W. Liu and B. Schmidt. Mapping of Hierarchical Parallel Genetic Algorithms for Protein Folding onto Computational Grids. *Transactions on Information and Systems (IEICE)*, E89-D(2):589–596, 2006.

[230] J. Lohn. Evolvable Systems Evolvable Systems Evolvable Systems for Space Applications. Technical report, Evolvable Systems Group, Mountain View, CA USA, 2003.

[231] J. Lohn, G. Hornby, and D. Linden. Evolutionary Antenna Design for a NASA Spacecraft. In *Genetic Programming Theory and Practice II*, chapter 18, pages 301–315. Springer, 2004.

[232] M. Lones. *Enzyme Genetic Programming*. PhD thesis, University of York, 2003.

[233] M. A. Lones and A. M. Tyrrell. Biomimetic Representation with Genetic Programming Enzyme. *Genetic Programming and Evolvable Machines*, 3(2):193–217, 2002.

[234] T. Loveard and V. Ciesielski. Representing Classification Problems in Genetic Programming. In *Evolutionary Computation*, volume 2, pages 1070–1077. IEEE Press, 2001.

[235] P. Lysaght, B. Blodget, J. Mason, J. Young, and B. Bridgford. Enhanced Architectures, Design Methodologies and CAD Tools for Dynamic Reconfiguration of Xilinx FPGAs. In *Intl. Conf. on Field-programmable Logic and Applications (FPL)*, pages 1–6. IEEE, 2006.

[236] H. Mann and D. Whitney. On a test of whether one of two random variables is stochastically larger than the other. *Ann. Math. Stat.*, 18:50–60, 1947.

[237] C. Manovit, C. Aporntewan, and P. Chongstitvatana. Synthesis of Synchronous Sequential Logic Circuits from Partial Input/Output Sequences. In *Intl. Conf. on Evolvable Systems (ICES)*, volume 1478 of *LNCS*, pages 98–105. Springer, 1998.

[238] P. Marchal, C. Piguet, D. Mange, A. Stauffer, and S. Durand. Embryological Development on Silicon. In *Artificial Life*, volume 5, pages 365–370. MIT Press, 1994.

[239] S. Martello and P. Toth. *Knapsack problems: algorithms and computer implementations*. John Wiley & Sons, Inc., 1990.

[240] T. Martínek and L. Sekanina. An Evolvable Image Filter: Experimental Evaluation of a Complete Hardware Implementation in FPGA. In *Intl. Conf. on Evolvable Systems (ICES)*, pages 76–85, 2005.

[241] I. Matlab. Global Optimization Toolbox 3.1. In *Matlab Inc.*, 2010.

[242] MAZeT GmbH. *Multi-Channel Programmable Gain Transimpedance Amplifier – MTI04Bx-BF*. MAZeT GmbH, Jena, Germany, 2006.

[243] A. Megacz. A Library and Platform for FPGA Bitstream Manipulation. In *Proc. IEEE Symposium on Field-Programmable Custom Computing Machines (FCCM)*, pages 45–54, Washington, DC, USA, 2007. IEEE Computer Society.

[244] Melexis Microelectronic Systems. *Programmable Sensor Interface MLX90308*. Melexis Microelectronic Systems, Ieper, Belgium, 2004.

[245] G. Mendel. Versuche über Pflanzenhybriden. *Verhandlungen des Naturforschenden Vereines in Brünn*, Band 4:3–47, 1866.

[246] N. Metropolis, A. W. Rosenbluth, M. N. Rosenbluth, A. H. Teller, and E. Teller. Equation of State Calculations by Fast Computing Machines. In *The Journal of Chemical Physics*, volume 21, pages 1087–1092. AIP, 1953.

[247] S. Micera, A. M. Sabatini, P. Dario, and B. Rossi. A Hybrid Approach to EMG Pattern Analysis for Classification of Arm Movements Using Statistical and Fuzzy Techniques. In *Medical engineering & physics*, volume 21(1350–4533), pages 303–311. Butterworth-Heinemann, 1999.

[248] I. Mierswa, M. Wurst, R. Klinkenberg, M. Scholz, and T. Euler. YALE: Rapid Prototyping for Complex Data Mining Tasks. In *Intl. Conf. on Knowledge Discovery and Data Mining (KDD)*, pages 935 – 940, 2006.

[249] J. S. Mill. *A System of Logic Ratiocinative and Inductive*. John W. Parker and Son, London, 1872.

[250] J. Miller. What Bloat? Cartesian Genetic Programming on Boolean Problems. In *Genetic and Evolutionary Computation (GECCO)*, pages 295–302. Morgan Kaufmann, 2001.

[251] J. Miller and M. Hartmann. Untidy Evolution: Evolving Messy Gates for Fault Tolerance. In *Intl. Conf. on Evolvable Systems (ICES)*, volume 2210 of *LNCS*, pages 14–25. Springer, 2001.

[252] J. Miller and P. Thomson. Cartesian Genetic Programming. In *European Conf. on Genetic Programming (EuroGP)*, pages 121–132. Springer, 2000.

[253] J. F. Miller. An Empirical Study of the Efficiency of Learning Boolean Functions Using a Cartesian Genetic Programming Approach. In *Genetic and Evolutionary Computation (GECCO)*, volume 2, pages 1135–1142. Morgan Kaufmann, 1999.

[254] J. F. Miller, D. Job, and V. K. Vassilev. Principles in the Evolutionary Design of Digital Circuits—Part I. In *Genetic Programming and Evolvable Machines (GPEM)*, volume 1, pages 7–35. Springer, 2000.

[255] J. F. Miller, D. Job, and V. K. Vassilev. Principles in the Evolutionary Design of Digital Circuits—Part II. In *Genetic Programming and Evolvable Machines (GPEM)*, volume 1, pages 259–288. Springer, 2000.

[256] J. F. Miller and P. Thomson. Evolving Digital Electronic Circuits for Real-Valued Function Generation using a Genetic Algorithm. In *Genetic Programming 1998: Proceedings of the Third Annual Conference*, pages 863–868, University of Wisconsin, Madison, Wisconsin, USA, 1998. Morgan Kaufmann.

[257] J. F. Miller, P. Thomson, and T. Fogarty. Designing Electronic Circuits Using Evolutionary Algorithms. Arithmetic Circuits: A Case Study. In *Genetic Algorithms and Evolution Strategy in Engineering and Computer Science*, pages 105–131. John Wiley and Sons, 1998.

[258] MindMedia. Nexus 10. `www.mindmedia.nl`.

[259] M. Murakawa, S. Yoshizawa, T. Adachi, S. Suzuki, K. Takasuka, M. Iwata, and T. Higuchi. Analogue EHW Chip for Intermediate Frequency Filters. In *Intl. Conf. on Evolvable Systems (ICES)*, volume 1478 of *LNCS*, pages 134–143. Springer, 1998.

[260] M. Murakawa, S. Yoshizawa, I. Kajitani, T. Furuya, M. Iwata, and T. Higuchi. Hardware Evolution at Function Level. In *Parallel Problem Solving from Nature (PPSN)*, volume 1141 of *LNCS*, pages 62–71. Springer, 1996.

[261] National Instruments. USB-6009. `www.ni.com`.

[262] B. Naujoks, L. Willmes, T. Bäck, and W. Haase. Evaluating Multicriteria Evolutionary Algorithms for Airfoil Optimization. In *Parallel Problem Solving from Nature—PPSN VII*, pages 841–850, Granada, Spain, 2002. Springer-Verlag. LNCS No. 2439.

[263] D. Nishikawa, W. Yu, H. Yokoi, and Y. Kakazu. EMG Prosthetic Hand Controller Discriminating Ten Motions Using Real-time Learning Method. In *Intelligent Robots and Systems (IROS)*, volume 3, pages 1592–1597. IEEE, 1999.

[264] A. E. Nix and M. D. Vose. Modeling Genetic Algorithms With Markov Chains. In *Annals of Mathematics and Artificial Intelligence*, volume 5, pages 79–88. Springe, 1992.

[265] B. Pankiewicz, M. Wojcikowski, S. Szczepanski, and Y. Sun. A Field Programmable Analog Array for CMOS Continuous-time OTA-C Filter

Applications. In *IEEE Journal of Solid-State Circuits*, volume 37, pages 125 –136. IEEE, 2002.

[266] K. Papathanasio. *Palmo: A Novel Pulsed Based Signal Processing Technique for Programmable Mixed-signal VLSI.* PhD thesis, Dept. Elect. Eng., Univ. Edinburgh, UK, 1998.

[267] V. Pareto. *Manuale di Economia Politica.* Societa Editrice Libraria, Milano, Italy, 1906.

[268] S. Park and S. P. Lee. EMG Pattern Recognition Based on Artificial Intelligence Techniques. In *IEEE Transactions on Rehabilitation Engineering*, volume 6, pages 400–405. IEEE Press, 1998.

[269] P. A. Parker, K. B. Englehart, and B. S. Hudgins. *Electromyography : Physiology, Engineering, and Non-Invasive Applications*, chapter Control of Powered Upper Limb Prostheses. IEEE Press Series on Biomedical Engineering. IEEE, 2004.

[270] C. M. N. A. Pereira and C. M. F. Lapa. Parallel Island Genetic Algorithm Applied to a Nuclear Power Plant Auxiliary Feedwater System Surveillance Tests Policy Optimization. *Annals of Nuclear Energy*, 30(16):1665 – 1675, 2003.

[271] S. Perkins, R. B. Porter, and N. R. Harvey. Everything on the Chip: A Hardware-Based Self-Contained Spatially-Structured Genetic Algorithm for Signal Processing. In *Intl. Conf. on Evolvable Systems (ICES)*, pages 165–174. Springer, 2000.

[272] E. Pierzchala, M. A. Perkowski, P. V. Halen, and R. Schaumann. Current-Mode Amplifier-Integrator for a Field-programmable Analog Array. In *IEEE Intl. Conf. on Solid State Circuits*, pages 196–197. IEEE, 1995.

[273] R. Polikar, L. Upda, S. S. Upda, and V. Honavar. Learn++: an incremental learning algorithm for supervised neural networks. *IEEE Transactions on Systems, Man, and Cybernetics, Part C: Applications and Reviews*, 31(4):497 – 508, 2001.

[274] C. Poloni, M. Fearon, and D. Ng. Parallelisation of Genetic Algorithms for Aerodynamic Design Optimisation. In *Proceedings of the Second International Conference on Adaptive Computing in Engineering Design and Control*, pages 59–64, Plymouth, UK, 1996. University of Plymouth.

[275] Precision Monolithics Inc. *Analog Signal Processing Subsystem: GAP-01.* Precision Monolithics Inc., 1982.

[276] C. Premont, R. Grisel, N. Abouchi, and J.-P. Chante. Current-conveyor Based Field Programmable Analog Array. In *Midwest Symposium on Circuits and Systems*, volume 17, pages 105–124. Springer, 1996.

[277] G. T. Pulido and C. A. C. Coello. The Micro Genetic Algorithm 2: Towards Online Adaptation in Evolutionary Multiobjective Optimization. In *Evolutionary Multi-Criterion Optimization*, LNCS, pages 252–266. Springer, 2003.

[278] J. R. Quinlan. *C4.5 Programs for Machine Learning*. Morgan Kaufmann Publishers, San Mateo, California, 1993.

[279] G. R. Raidl. Heuristische Optimierungsverfahren. Vorlesungsskript, Technische Universität Wien, 2004.

[280] P. Ranganathan, S. Adve, and N. P. Jouppi. Reconfigurable Caches and their Application to Media Processing. In *SIGARCH Comput. Archit. News*, volume 28, pages 214–224. ACM, 2000.

[281] M. L. Raymer, L. A. Kuhn, and W. F. Punch. Knowledge Discovery in Biological Datasets Using a Hybrid Bayes Classifier/Evolutionary Algorithm. In *Symposium on Bioinformatics and Bioengineering (BIBE'01)*, page 236, Washington, DC, USA, 2001. IEEE Computer Society.

[282] I. Rechenberg. *Evolutionsstrategie: Optimierung technischer Systeme nach Prinzipien der biologischen Evolution*. Frommann-Holzboog, 1973.

[283] P. G. K. Reiser. *Evolutionary Algorithms for Learning Formulae in first-order Logic*. PhD thesis, Computer Science, Aberystwyth, University of Wales, 1999.

[284] R. Reiter. Eine neue Elektrokunsthand. In *Grenzgebiete der Medizin*, volume 4, pages 133–135, 1948.

[285] D. Roggen. *Multi-Cellular Reconfigurable Circuits: Evolution, Morphogenesis and Learning*. PhD thesis, Ecole Polytechnique Fédérale de Lausanne, 2005.

[286] R. Rojas. *Neural Networks – A Systematic Introduction*. Springer, 1996.

[287] A. E. Ruano, P. J. Fleming, C. Teixeira, K. Rodriguez-Vazquez, and C. M. Fonseca. Nonlinear identification of aircraft gas-turbine dynamics. *Neurocomputing*, 55(3-4):551–579, 2003.

[288] G. Rudolph. Convergence of Non-Elitist Strategies. In *Proc. IEEE Intl. Conf. Evolutionary Computation*, pages 63–66. IEEE Press, 1994.

[289] M. Salami, M. Murakawa, and T. Higuchi. Data Compression Based on Evolvabel Hardware. In *Intl. Conf. on Evolvable Systems (ICES)*, volume 1259, pages 169–179. Springer, 1996.

[290] S. Salcedo-Sanz, Y. Xu, and X. Yao. Meta-Heuristic Algorithms for FPGA Segmented Channel Routing Problems with Non-standard Cost Functions. *Genetic Programming and Evolvable Machines*, 6(4):359–379, 2005.

[291] E. Sanchez and M. Tomassini. *Towards Evolvable Hardware: The Evolutionary Engineering Approach*, volume 1062 of *LNCS*. Springer, 1996.

[292] J. D. Schaffer. *Multiple Objective Optimization with Vector Evaluated Genetic Algorithms*. PhD thesis, Vanderbilt University, 1984.

[293] W. Schiffmann, M. Joost, and R. Werner. Comparison of Optimized Backpropagation Algorithms. In *European Symposium on Artificial Neural Networks (ESANN'93)*, pages 97–104, 1993.

[294] W. Schiffmann, M. Joost, and R. Werner. Optimization of the Backpropagation Algorithm for Training Multilayer Perceptrons. Tech. Rep. 15, University of Koblenz, Institute of Physics, 1994.

[295] T. Schnier, X. Yao, R. Beale, B. Hendley, and W. Byrne. Nature Inspired Creative Design - Bringing Together Ideas from Nature, Computer Science, Engineering, Art, Design. In *Designing for the 21st Century: Questions and Issues*, pages 192–204. Gower Ashgate, 2007.

[296] M. Schoenauer and Z. Michalewiczy. Evolutionary Computation. In *Control and Cybernetics*, volume 26, pages 307–338, 1997.

[297] H.-P. Schwefel. *Numerical Optimization of Computer Models*. John Wiley & Sons, 1981.

[298] U. Schwiegelshohn. A Short Periodic Two-dimensional Systolic Sorting Algorithm. In *Intl. Conf. on Systolic Arrays*, pages 257–264. Computer Society Press, 1988.

[299] L. Sekanina. Image Filter Design with Evolvable Hardware. In *Proceedings of the Applications of Evolutionary Computing on EvoWorkshops 2002*, pages 255–266, London, UK, UK, 2002. Springer-Verlag.

[300] L. Sekanina. Virtual Reconfigurable Circuits for Real-World Applications of Evolvable Hardware. In *Intl. Conf. on Evolvable Systems (ICES)*, pages 186–197. Springer, 2003.

[301] L. Sekanina. Evolutionary Design Space Exploration for Median Circuits. In *Applications of Evolutionary Computing*, volume 3005 of *LNCS*, pages 240–249. Springer, 2004.

[302] L. Sekanina. *Evolvable Components: From Theory to Hardware Implementations*. Springer, 2004.

[303] L. Sekanina. Evolving Constructors for Infinitely Growing Sorting Networks and Medians. In *SOFSEM*, pages 314–323, 2004.

[304] L. Sekanina. Evolutionary Design of Gate-Level Polymorphic Digital Circuits. In *EvoWorkshops*, volume 3449 of *LNCS*, pages 185–194. Springer, 2005.

[305] L. Sekanina and M. Bidlo. Evolutionary Design of Arbitrarily Large Sorting Networks Using Development. *Genetic Programming and Evolvable Machines*, 6(3):319–347, 2005.

[306] L. Sekanina and V. Drabek. Automatic Design of Image Operators Using Evolvable Hardware. In *Design and Diagnostics of Electronic Circuits and Systems*, pages 132–139. IEEE, 2002.

[307] L. Sekanina and S. Friedl. An Evolvable Combinational Unit for FPGAs. *Computers and Artificial Intelligence*, 23(5):461–486, 2004.

[308] L. Sekanina and S. Friedl. On Routine Implementation of Virtual Evolvable Devices Using COMBO6. In *Evolvable Hardware*, pages 63–70, 2004.

[309] L. Sekanina and R. Ruzicka. Design of the Special Fast Reconfigurable Chip Using Common FPGA. In *Design and Diagnostics of Electronic Circuits and Systems (DDECS)*, pages 161–168, 2000.

[310] L. Sekanina and R. Ruzicka. Easily Testable Image Operators: The Class of Circuits Where Evolution Beats Engineers. In *Evolvable Hardware*, pages 135–144, 2003.

[311] L. Sekanina, R. Ruzicka, and Z. Gajda. Polymorphic FIR Filters with Backup Mode Enabling Power Savings. In *AHS '09: Proceedings of the 2009 NASA/ESA Conference on Adaptive Hardware and Systems*, pages 43–50, Washington, DC, USA, 2009. IEEE Computer Society.

[312] L. Sekanina and Z. Vasícek. On the Practical Limits of the Evolutionary Digital Filter Design at the Gate Level. In *EvoWorkshops*, pages 344–355, 2006.

[313] L. Sekanina and R. S. Zebulum. Intrinsic Evolution of Controllable Oscillators in FPTA-2. In *Intl. Conf. on Evolvable Systems (ICES)*, volume 3637 of *LNCS*, pages 98–107. Springer, 2005.

[314] J. Seward. bzip2: A Freely Available, Patent Free, High-quality Data Compressor. http://www.bzip.org, 2009.

[315] K. J. Shaw, A. L. Nortcliffe, M. Thompson, J. Love, C. M. Fonseca, and P. J. Fleming. Assessing the Performance of Multiobjective Genetic Algorithms for Optimization of a Batch Process Scheduling Problem. In *Evolutionary Computation*, pages 37–45. IEEE, 1999.

[316] P. Shenoy, K. Miller, B. Crawford, and R. Rao. Online Electromyographic Control of a Robotic Prosthesis. *IEEE Transactions on Biomedical Engineering*, 2008.

[317] A. Shilton, M. Palaniswami, D. Ralph, and A. C. Tsoi. Incremental Training of Support Vector Machines. *IEEE Transactions on Neural Networks*, 16(1):114 – 131, 2005.

[318] P. Shivakumar and N. P. Jouppi. CACTI 3.0: An Integrated Cache Timing, Power, and Area Model. Technical report, COMPAQ Western Research Lab, Palo Alto, California 94301 USA, 1999.

[319] M. Sipper. *Evolution of Parallel Cellular Machines: The Cellular Programming Approach.* Springer, 1997.

[320] M. Sipper, E. Sanchez, D. Mange, M. Tomassini, A. Perez-Uribe, and A. Stauffer. A Phylogenetic, Ontogenetic, and Epigenetic View of Bioinspired Hardware Systems. *IEEE Trans. Evolutionary Computation*, 1(1):83 –97, 1997.

[321] M. A. Sivilotti. A Dynamically Configurable Architecture for Prototyping Analog Circuits. In *Proc. of the fifth MIT conference on Advanced research in VLSI*, pages 237–258. MIT Press, 1988.

[322] K. Slany and L. Sekanina. Fitness landscape analysis and image filter evolution using functional-level CGP. In *EuroGP'07: Proceedings of the 10th European conference on Genetic programming*, pages 311–320, Berlin, Heidelberg, 2007. Springer-Verlag.

[323] N. Smirnov. Tables for Estimating the Goodness of Fit of Empirical Distributions. *Annals of Mathematical Statistic*, 19:279, 1948.

[324] S. L. Smith, S. Leggett, and A. M. Tyrrell. An Implicit Context Representation for Evolving Image Processing Filters. In *Applications on Evolutionary Computing*, volume 3449 of *LNCS*, pages 407–416. Springer, 2005.

[325] Sonowin. USI-01 USB Isolator. www.sonowin.de.

[326] P. Sparto, M. Parnianpour, E. Barria, and J. Jagadeesh. Wavelet and Short-time Fourier Transform Analysis of Electromyography for Detection of Back Muscle Fatigue. In *Rehabilitation Engineering*, volume 8(3), pages 433–436. IEEE, 2000.

[327] W. Spears, K. De Jong, T. Bäck, D. Fogel, and H. de Garis. An Overview of Evolutionary Computation. In *Proc. European Conference on Machine Learning*, volume 667 of *LNCS*, pages 442–459. Springer, 1993.

[328] N. Srinivas and K. Deb. Comparative study of vector evaluated GA and NSGA applied to multiobjective optimization. In *Proceedings of the Symposium on Genetic Algorithms*, pages 83–90, 1995.

[329] M. Stanca, S. Vassiliadis, S. Cotofana, and H. Corporaal. Hashed Addressed Caches for Embedded Pointer Based Codes. In *Intl. Conf. on Parallel Processing (Euro-Par)*, volume 1900 of *LNCS*, pages 965–968. Springer, 2000.

[330] T. J. Stanley and T. Mudge. A Parallel Genetic Algorithm for Multiobjective Microprocessor Design. In *Proceedings of the Sixth International Conference on Genetic Algorithms*, pages 597–604, San Mateo, California, 1995. University of Pittsburgh, Morgan Kaufmann Publishers.

[331] A. Stoica. Reconfigurable Transistor Array for Evolvable Hardware. Technical report, Caltech/JPL Novel Technology Report, 1996.

[332] A. Stoica. Toward Evolvable Hardware Chips: Experiments with a Programmable Transistor Array. In *Proc. Intl. Conf. on Microelectronics for Neural, Fuzzy and Bio-Inspired Systems (MicroNeuro)*, pages 156–162, 1999.

[333] A. Stoica, D. Keymeulen, and R. Zebulum. Evolvable Hardware Solutions For Extreme Temperature Electronics. In *NASA/DoD Workshop on Evolvable Hardware (EH)*, pages 93 – 97. IEEE Computer Society, 2001.

[334] A. Stoica, D. Keymeulen, R. Zebulum, M. Mojarradi, S. Katkoori, and T. Daud. Adaptive and Evolvable Analog Electronics for Space Applications. In *Intl. Conf. on Evolvable Systems (ICES)*, volume 4684 of *LNCS*, pages 379–390. Springer, 2007.

[335] A. Stoica, X. Wang, D. Keymeulen, R. S. Zebulum, M. I. Ferguson, and X. Guo. Circuit Recovery Under Gamma Ray Radiation. In *Congress on Evolutionary Computation (CEC)*, pages 2469–2475. IEEE, 2005.

[336] A. Stoica, R. Zebulum, D. Keymeulen, R. Tawel, T. Daud, and A. Thakoor. Reconfigurable VLSI Architectures for Evolvable Hardware: From Experimental Field Programmable Transistor Arrays to Evolution-oriented Chips. In *IEEE Transactions on Very Large Scale Integration (VLSI) Systems*, volume 9, pages 227 –232. IEEE, 2001.

[337] A. Stoica, R. S. Zebulum, M. I. Ferguson, D. Keymeulen, and V. Dong. Evolving Circuits in Seconds: Experiments with a Stand-alone Board-level Evolvable System. In *NASA/DoD Workshop on Evolvable Hardware (EH)*, pages 67–74. IEEE, 2002.

[338] A. Stoica, R. S. Zebulum, D. Keymeulen, M. I. Ferguson, V. Duong, and X. Guo. Evolvable Hardware Techniques for On-chip Automated Reconfiguration of Programmable Devices. In *Soft Computing - A Fusion of Foundations, Methodologies and Applications*, volume 8, pages 354–365. Springer, 2004.

[339] K. Strohbehn. Field Programmable Analog Array for Space Applications. In *Proc. NASA Symposium on VLSI Design*, pages 5.1.1–5.1.10. NASA, 1998.

[340] J. Suzuki. A Markov Chain Analysis on A Genetic Algorithm. In *Proc. Intl. Conf. on Genetic Algorithms*, pages 146–154. Morgan Kaufmann Publishers Inc., 1993.

[341] E. Talbi and H. Meunier. Hierarchical parallel approach for GSM mobile network design. *Journal of Parallel and Distributed Computing*, 66(2):274–290, 2006.

[342] K. C. Tan, Q. Yu, C. M. Heng, and T. H. Lee. Evolutionary computing for knowledge discovery in medical diagnosis. *Artificial Intelligence in Medicine*, 27(2):129–154, 2003.

[343] M. Tanaka, H. Sakanashi, M. Salami, M. Iwata, T. Kurita, and T. Higuchi. Data compression for digital color Electrophotographic printer with evolvable hardware. In *Intl. Conf. on Evolvable Systems (ICES)*, volume 1478 of *LNCS*, pages 106–114. Springer, 1998.

[344] I. T. Tanev, T. Uozumi, and Y. Morotome. An Application Service Provider Approach For Hybrid Evolutionary Algorithm-based Real-world Flexible Job Shop Scheduling Problem. In *GECCO 2002: Proceedings of the Genetic and Evolutionary Computation Conference*, pages 1219–1226, New York, 2002. Morgan Kaufmann Publishers.

[345] G. Tempesti. Evaluation of Ontogenetic Methods in Digital Systems. Technical Report 4, Information Society Technologies Program, European Community, http://www.poetictissue.org, 2002.

[346] G. Tempesti, D. Roggen, E. Sanchez, Y. Thoma, R. Canham, and A. Tyrrell. POEtic Tissue: An Integrated Architecture for Bio-Inspired Hardware. In *Intl. Conf. on Evolvable Systems (ICES)*, volume 2606, pages 129–140. Springer, 2003.

[347] Texas Instruments Inc. *Voltage Output Programmable Sensor Conditioner- PGA309*. Texas Instruments, Dallas, Texas, USA, 2003.

[348] Texas Instruments Inc. *16-Bit Ultra-Low Power MSP430 Microcontrollers*. Texas Instruments, Dallas, Texas, USA, 2011.

[349] Y. Thoma, E. Sanchez, J.-M. Moreno, and G. Tempesti. A Dynamic Routing Algorithm for a Bio-inspired Reconfigurable Circuit. In *Field Programmable Logic and Application (FPL)*, volume 2778, pages 681–690. Springer, 2003.

[350] Y. Thoma, G. Tempesti, E. Sanchez, and J.-M. M. Arostegui. PO-Etic: An Electronic Tissue for Bio-Inspired Cellular Applications. In *Biosystems*, volume 76, pages 191–200. Elsevier, 2004.

[351] A. Thompson. Evolving Electronic Robot Controllers that Exploit Hardware Resources. In *European Conference on Artificial Life (ECAL)*, volume 929 of *LNAI*, pages 640–656. Springer, 1995.

[352] A. Thompson. Evolving Fault Tolerant Systems. In *Proc. IEE/IEEE Int. Conf. on Genetic Algorithms in Engineering Systems: Innovations and Applications (GALESIA'95)*, pages 524–529. IEE Conf. Publication No. 414, 1995.

[353] A. Thompson. Silicon Evolution. In *Proc. Conf. Genetic Programming (GP)*, pages 444–452. MIT Press, 1996.

[354] A. Thompson. An Evolved Circuit, Intrinsic in Silicon, Entwined With Physics. In *Intl. Conf. on Evolvable Systems (ICES)*, volume 1259 of *LNCS*, pages 390–405. Springer, 1997.

[355] A. Thompson and P. Layzell. Analysis of Unconventional Evolved Electronics. *Communications of the ACM*, 42(4):71–79, 1999.

[356] A. Thompson and P. Layzell. Evolution of Robustness in an Electronics Design. In *Intl. Conf. on Evolvable Systems (ICES)*, volume 1801 of *LNCS*, pages 218–228. Springer, 2000.

[357] A. Thompson, P. Layzell, and R. Zebulum. Explorations in Design Space: Unconventional Electronics Design Through Artificial Evolution. *IEEE Trans. Evolutionary Computation*, 3(3):167 –196, 1999.

[358] M. Titsias and A. Likas. Shared Kernel Models for Class Conditional Density Estimation. In *IEEE Trans. Neural Networks*, volume 12, pages 987–997, 2001.

[359] J. Torresen. Evolvable Hardware - A Short Introduction. In *Intl. Conf. On Neural Information Processing (ICONIP)*, 1997.

[360] J. Torresen. Possibilities and Limitations of Applying Evolvable Hardware to Real-World Applications. In *Field-Programmable Logic and Applications: The Roadmap to Reconfigurable Computing*, volume 1896 of *LNCS*, pages 230–239. Springer, 2000.

[361] J. Torresen. Two-Step Incremental Evolution of a Digital Logic Gate Based Prosthetic Hand Controller. In *Intl. Conf. on Evolvable Systems (ICES)*, volume 2210 of *LNCS*, pages 1–13. Springer, 2001.

[362] J. Torresen. Evolving Multiplier Circuits by Training Set and Training Vector Partitioning. In *Intl. Conf. on Evolvable Systems (ICES)*, pages 228–237. Springer, 2003.

[363] J. Torresen. An Evolvable Hardware Tutorial. In *Field Programmable Logic and Application*, volume 3203 of *LNCS*, pages 821–830. Springer, 2004.

[364] J. Torresen. Exploring Knowledge Schemes for Efficient Evolution of Hardware. In *Evolvable Hardware*, pages 209–216. IEEE, 2004.

[365] J. Torresen and J. Jakobsen. An FPGA Implemented Processor Architecture with Adaptive Resolution. In *Adaptive Hardware and Systems (AHS)*, pages 386–389. IEEE, 2006.

[366] J. Torresen, G. Senland, and K. Glette. Partial Reconfiguration Applied in an On-line Evolvable Pattern Recognition System. In *NORCHIP 2008*, pages 61–64. IEEE, 2008.

[367] M. Trefzer, J. Langeheine, K. Meier, and J. Schemmel. Operational Amplifiers: An Example for Multi-objective Optimization on an Analog Evolvable Hardware Platform. In *Intl. Conf. on Evolvable Systems (ICES)*, pages 86–97. Springer, 2005.

[368] M. Trefzer, J. Langeheine, J. Schemmel, and K. Meier. New Genetic Operators to Facilitate Understanding of Evolved Transistor Circuits. In *Adaptive Hardware and Systems (AHS)*, pages 217 – 224. IEEE, 2004.

[369] M. A. Trefzer. *Evolution of Transistor Circuits*. PhD thesis, Ruperto-Carola-University of Heidelberg, Germany, 2006.

[370] I. G. Tsoulos and I. E. Lagaris. GenMin: An enhanced genetic algorithm for global optimization. *Computer Physics Communications*, 178(11):843–851, 2008.

[371] G. Tufte and P. C. Haddow. Prototyping a GA Pipeline for Complete Hardware Evolution. In *NASA/DoD Conference on Evolvable Hardware*, page 18. IEEE CS, 1999.

[372] A. Tyrrell, E. Sanchez, D. Floreano, G. Tempesti, D. Mange, J.-M. Moreno, J. Rosenberg, and A. Villa. Ontogenetic Development and Fault Tolerance in the POEtic Tissue. In *Intl. Conf. on Evolvable Systems (ICES)*, volume 2606, pages 141–152. Springer, 2003.

[373] USC. The USC-SIPI Image Database. http://sipi.usc.edu/database.

[374] D. Vallancourt and Y. Tsividis. A Fully-programmable Analog CMOS Sampled-data Filter with Transfer Function Coefficients Determined by Timing. In *IEEE Journal of Solid-State Circuits*, volume SC–22, no. 6, pages 1022–1030. IEEE, 1987.

[375] H. Vandierendonck and K. D. Bosschere. Constructing Optimal XOR-Functions to Minimize Cache Conflict Misses. In *21st Intl. Conf. on Architecture of Computing Systems (ARCS '08)*, volume 4934 of *LNCS*, pages 261–272. Springer, 2008.

[376] H. Vandierendonck, P. Manet, and J. Legat. Application-specific Reconfigurable XOR-indexing to Eliminate Cache Conflict. In *Proc. Design, Automation and Test in Europe (DATE)*, pages 357–362, 2006.

[377] Z. Vasicek and L. Sekanina. Reducing the area on a chip using a bank of evolved filters. In *ICES'07: Proceedings of the 7th international conference on Evolvable systems*, pages 222–232, Berlin, Heidelberg, 2007. Springer-Verlag.

[378] V. K. Vassilev and J. F. Miller. Embedding Landscape Neutrality to Build a Bridge from the Conventional to a More Efficient Three-bit Multiplier Circuit. In *Genetic and Evolutionary Computation (GECCO)*, page 539. Morgan Kaufmann, 2000.

[379] K. A. Vinger and J. Torresen. Implementing Evolution of FIR-Filters Efficiently in an FPGA. In *Evolvable Hardware*, pages 26–32. IEEE, 2003.

[380] J. A. Walker and J. F. Miller. Evolution and Acquisition of Modules in Cartesian Genetic Programming. In *European Conf. on Genetic Programming (EuroGP)*, volume 3003 of *LNCS*, pages 187–197. Springer, 2004.

[381] J. A. Walker and J. F. Miller. Improving the Evolvability of Digital Multipliers Using Embedded Cartesian Genetic Programming and Product Reduction. In *Intl. Conf. on Evolvable Systems (ICES)*, volume 3637 of *LNCS*, pages 131–142. Springer, 2005.

[382] J. A. Walker and J. F. Miller. The Automatic Acquisition, Evolution and Reuse of Modules in Cartesian Genetic Programming. *IEEE Trans. Evolutionary Computation*, 12(4):397–417, 2008.

[383] J. A. Walker, J. F. Miller, and R. Cavill. A multi-chromosome approach to standard and embedded cartesian genetic programming. In *GECCO*, pages 903–910. ACM, 2006.

[384] G. K. Wallace. The JPEG Still Picture Compression Standard. *Communications of the ACM*, 34(4):30–44, 1991.

[385] S. Watanabe, T. Hiroyasu, and M. Miki. Parallel Evolutionary Multi-Criterion Optimization for Mobile Telecommunication Networks Optimization. In *Evolutionary Methods for Design, Optimization and Control with Applications to Industrial Problems. Proceedings of the EUROGEN'2001. Athens. Greece, September 19-21*, pages 167–172, Baracelona, Spain, 2001. International Center for Numerical Methods in Engineering(CIMNE).

[386] S. M. Weiss and I. Kapouleas. An Empirical Comparison of Pattern Recognition, Neural Nets, and Machine Learning Classification Methods. In *Artificial Intelligence (IJCAI'89)*, pages 781–787, San Francisco, CA, USA, 1989. Morgan Kaufmann Publishers Inc.

[387] D. Whitley. A Genetic Algorithm Tutorial. *Statistics and Computing*, 4:65–85, 1994.

[388] S. M. Winkler, M. Affenzeller, and S. Wagner. Using Enhanced Genetic Programming Techniques for Evolving Classifiers in the Context of Medical Diagnosis. In *Genetic Programming and Evolvable Machines*, volume 10(2), pages 111–140. Kluwer Academic Publishers, 2009.

[389] N. Xiao and M. P. Armstrong. A Specialized Island Model and Its Application in Multiobjective Optimization. In *Genetic and Evolutionary Computation—GECCO 2003. Proceedings, Part II*, pages 1530–1540. Springer. LNCS Vol. 2724, 2003.

[390] Xicor Inc. *Nonvolatile Digital Potentiometer: X9C102*. Xicor Inc., 1994.

[391] Xilinx, Inc. *XCX6200 Field Programmable Gate Arrays Product Description*. Xilinx, Inc., San Jose, 1997.

[392] Xilinx, Inc. *PlanAhead User Guide*. Xilinx, Inc., San Jose, 2009.

[393] Xilinx, Inc. *Virtex-6 FPGA Configurable Logic Block User Guide*. Xilinx Inc., San Jose, 2009.

[394] Xilinx, Inc. *Virtex-5 FPGA User Guide*. Xilinx Inc., San Jose, 2010.

[395] X. Yao. An Overview of Evolutionary Computation. *Chinese Journal of Advanced Software Research*, 3:12–29, 1996.

[396] X. Yao and T. Higuchi. Promises and Challenges of Evolvable Hardware. In *IEEE Transactions on Systems, Man, and Cybernetics*, volume 29, pages 87 –97. IEEE, 1999.

[397] X. Yao and Y. Xu. Recent Advances in Evolutionary Computation. In *J. Comput. Sci. Technol.*, volume 21, pages 1–18. Springer, 2006.

[398] M. Yasunaga, T. Nakamura, and I. Yoshihara. Evolvable Sonar Spectrum Discrimination Chip Designed by Genetic Algorithm. In *Systems, Man and Cybernetics*, volume 5, pages 585–590. IEEE, 1999.

[399] T. Yu and J. Miller. Neutrality and the Evolvability of Boolean Function Landscape. In *European Conf. on Genetic Programming (EuroGP)*, volume 2038 of *LNCS*, pages 204–217. Springer, 2001.

[400] T. Yu and J. F. Miller. Through the Interaction of Neutral and Adaptive Mutations, Evolutionary Search Finds a Way. *Artificial Life*, 12(4):525–551, 2006.

[401] T. Yu, D. Wilkinson, and D. Xie. A Hybrid GP-Fuzzy Approach for Reservoir Characterization. In *Genetic Programming Theory and Practise*, chapter 17, pages 271–290. Kluwer, 2003.

[402] W. Yuan, A. Odjo, N. E. Sammons, Jr., J. Caballero, and M. R. Eden. Process Structure Optimization Using a Hybrid Disjunctive-Genetic Programming Approach. In *10th International Symposium on Process Systems Engineering: Part A*, volume 27 of *Computer Aided Chemical Engineering*, pages 669–674. Elsevier, 2009.

[403] M. Zardoshti-Kermani, B. Wheeler, K. Badie, and R. Hashemi. EMG Feature Evaluation for Movement Control of Upper Extremityprostheses. In *IEEE Transactions on Rehabilitation Engineering*, volume 3(4), pages 324–333. IEEE Press, 1995.

[404] R. Zebulum, M. Pacheco, and M. Vellasco. Evolvable Systems in Hardware Design: Taxonomy, Survey and Applications. In *Evolvable Systems: From Biology to Hardware*, volume 1259 of *LNCS*, pages 344–358. Springer Berlin / Heidelberg, 1997.

[405] R. S. Zebulum, X. Guo, D. Keymeulen, M. I. Ferguson, V. Duong, and A. Stoica. High Ttemperature Experiments using Programmable Transistor Array. In *Proc. IEEE Aerospace Conference*, volume 4, pages 2437–2448 Vol.4. IEEE, 2004.

[406] R. S. Zebulum, A. Stoica, D. Keymeulen, L. Sekanina, R. Ramesham, and X. Guo. Evolvable Hardware System at Extreme Low Temperatures. In *Intl. Conf. on Evolvable Systems (ICES)*, volume 3637 of *LNCS*, pages 37–45. Springer, 2005.

[407] M. Zecca, S. Micera, M. C. Carrozza, and P. Dario. Control of Multifunctional Prosthetic Hands by Processing the Electromyographic Signal. In *Critical Reviews in Biomedical Engineering*, pages 459–485, 2002.

[408] S. Zeng, S. Yao, L. Kang, and Y. Liu. An Efficient Multi-objective Evolutionary Algorithm: OMOEA-II. In *Evolutionary Multi-Criterion Optimization*, pages 108–119, 2005.

[409] Zetex Semiconductors. Zetex Semiconductors, 1996.

[410] B.-T. Zhang and H. Mühlenbein. Evolving Optimal Neural Networks Using Genetic Algorithms with Occam's Razor. *Complex Systems*, 7:199–220, 1993.

[411] C. Zhang, A. Bratt, and I. Macbeth. A New Field Programmable Mixed Signal Array and its Application. In *4th Canadian Workshop on Field-Programmable Devices*, Canada, 1996.

[412] C. Zhang, F. Vahid, and R. Lysecky. A Self-tuning Cache Architecture for Embedded Systems. In *Trans. on Embedded Computing Systems*, volume 3, pages 407–425. ACM, 2004.

[413] Y. Zhang, S. Smith, and A. Tyrrell. Digital circuit design using intrinsic evolvable hardware. In *Evolvable Hardware, 2004. Proceedings. 2004 NASA/DoD Conference on*, pages 55 – 62, 2004.

[414] Y. Zhang, S. L. Smith, and A. M. Tyrrell. Intrinsic Evolvable Hardware in Digital Filter Design. In *EvoWorkshops*, volume 3005 of *LNCS*, pages 389–398. Springer, 2004.

[415] Z.-Y. Zhu and K.-S. Leung. Asynchronous Self-Adjustable Island Genetic Algorithm for Multi-Objective Optimization Problems. In *Congress on Evolutionary Computation (CEC'2002)*, volume 1, pages 837–842, Piscataway, New Jersey, 2002. IEEE Service Center.

[416] E. Zitzler and S. Künzli. Indicator-Based Selection in Multiobjective Search. In *Conference on Parallel Problem Solving from Nature (PPSN)*, pages 832–842. Springer, 2004.

[417] E. Zitzler, M. Laumanns, and L. Thiele. SPEA2: Improving the Strength Pareto Evolutionary Algorithm. Technical Report 103, ETH Zurich, 2001.

[418] E. Zitzler, M. Laumanns, and L. Thiele. SPEA2: Improving the Strength Pareto Evolutionary Algorithm for Multiobjective Optimization. In *Evolutionary Methods for Design, Optimisation and Control with Application to Industrial Problems (EUROGEN 2001)*, pages 95–100. International Center for Numerical Methods in Engineering (CIMNE), 2002.

[419] E. Zitzler, L. Thiele, M. Laumanns, C. Fonseca, and V. da Fonseca. Performance Assessment of Multiobjective Optimizers: An Analysis and Review. *IEEE Trans. Evolutionary Computation*, 7(2):117–132, 2003.

[420] X. Zou, Y. Chen, M. Liu, and L. Kang. A New Evolutionary Algorithm for Solving Many-Objective Optimization Problems. *IEEE Transactions on Systems, Man, and Cybernetics–Part B: Cybernetics*, 38(5):1402–1412, 2008.